PENGUIN  CLAS

DISCOURSES AND SELECTED WRITINGS

EPICTETUS (c.AD 55–135) was a teacher and Graeco-Roman philosopher. Originally a slave from Hierapolis in Anatolia (modern Turkey), he was owned for a time by a prominent freedman at the court of the emperor Nero. After gaining his freedom he moved to Nicopolis on the Adriatic coast of Greece and opened a school of philosophy there. His informal lectures (the *Discourses*) were transcribed and published by his student Arrian, who also composed a digest of Epictetus' teaching known as the *Manual* (or *Enchiridion*). Late in life Epictetus retired from teaching, adopted an orphan child and lived out his remaining years in domestic obscurity. His thought owes most to Stoicism, but also reflects the influence of other philosophers, Plato and Socrates in particular. His influence has been deep and enduring, from Marcus Aurelius in his *Meditations* to the contemporary psychologist Albert Ellis, who has acknowledged his debt to Epictetus in devising the school of Rational-Emotive Behavioural Therapy.

ROBERT DOBBIN was born in New York City in 1958. He received a Ph.D. in Classics from the University of California at Berkeley in 1989, and taught history and classics at the college level for years. He is the author of *Epictetus Discourses: Book One* (Oxford, 1998), as well as articles on Virgil, Plato and Pythagoras. Currently he works as a book editor in northern California.

EPICTETUS

Discourses and Selected Writings

Translated and edited by
ROBERT DOBBIN

PENGUIN BOOKS

PENGUIN CLASSICS

Published by the Penguin Group
Penguin Books Ltd, 80 Strand, London WC2R ORL, England
Penguin Group (USA) Inc., 375 Hudson Street, New York, New York 10014, USA
Penguin Group (Canada), 90 Eglinton Avenue East, Suite 700, Toronto, Ontario, Canada M4P 2Y3
(a division of Pearson Penguin Canada Inc.)
Penguin Ireland, 25 St Stephen's Green, Dublin 2, Ireland (a division of Penguin Books Ltd)
Penguin Group (Australia), 250 Camberwell Road, Camberwell, Victoria 3124, Australia
(a division of Pearson Australia Group Pty Ltd)
Penguin Books India Pvt Ltd, 11 Community Centre, Panchsheel Park, New Delhi – 110 017, India
Penguin Group (NZ), 67 Apollo Drive, Rosedale, North Shore 0632, New Zealand
(a division of Pearson New Zealand Ltd)
Penguin Books (South Africa) (Pty) Ltd, 24 Sturdee Avenue, Rosebank, Johannesburg 2196, South Africa

Penguin Books Ltd, Registered Offices: 80 Strand, London WC2R ORL, England

www.penguin.com

This translation first published in Penguin Classics 2008

049

Translation and editorial material copyright © Robert Dobbin, 2008
All rights reserved

The moral right of the translator and editor has been asserted

Set in 10.25/12.25pt PostScript Adobe Sabon
Typeset by Rowland Phototypesetting Ltd, Bury St Edmunds, Suffolk
Printed and bound in Great Britain by Clays Ltd, Elcograf S.p.A.

ISBN: 978-0-140-44946-4

www.greenpenguin.co.uk

Contents

Introduction   vii
Further Reading   xx
Note on the Translation   xxiii

THE DISCOURSES   1
FRAGMENTS   207
ENCHIRIDION   219

Glossary of Names   246
Notes   251

Introduction

At the beginning of the second century AD, in the reign of the emperor Trajan, a group of young men could be found studying philosophy at a boarding school in Nicopolis, a Roman colony in Epirus (north-west Greece). They were students of Epictetus. In a prefatory letter one such pupil, Arrian by name (c.AD 86–160), takes credit for committing a sizeable number of Epictetus' lessons to print, thereby ensuring their survival. These are the *Discourses*. Arrian is also credited with preparing a digest of his master's thought: the *Manual* or (in Greek) *Enchiridion*. A modest number of fragments attributed to Epictetus have also come down to us (some of them derived from Discourses otherwise lost, as only four books of the eight that Arrian originally published are extant).

Besides being an uncommonly diligent stenographer, Arrian was an author in his own right, best known for his biography of Alexander the Great. He was also a man of the world, a Roman consul and later legate to the Roman province of Cappadocia. Taking into account his own literary aspirations, and the formidable challenge posed by transcribing Epictetus' lectures 'live', i.e. as they were being delivered, some have questioned whether his opening letter is completely trustworthy in characterizing the collection as nothing less than a verbatim record of what the philosopher said, inside and outside the classroom. Most students of the *Discourses* incline to the view that, in the process of effecting the transition of Epictetus' lectures to print, Arrian probably permitted himself a few editorial changes. Establishing the dramatic context of the *Discourses*, in imitation of Plato's Socratic dialogues, may be one of his contributions. But any alterations or 'improvements' he made to the text are unlikely to have been extensive. The books of history and geography that Arrian wrote later are so unlike the *Discourses* in style and content that, even if we did not have his word for it, we would be unlikely to conclude that they were products of the same hand. Arrian published his edition of the *Discourses* soon after Epictetus died, and an unauthorized edition had already been in circulation; so other of Epictetus' students were in a position to judge how faithful Arrian was to the actual words of the master; and we have no record of anyone impugning their essential honesty. On the contrary, Arrian's collection was accepted immediately as an authentic and definitive record of Epictetus' thought, and even though Arrian was responsible for actually writing the book, Epictetus is conventionally, and rightly, treated as their author. Even if we cannot be sure that Epictetus actually said everything attributed to him in the *Discourses*, or in those exact words, we have no reason to doubt that the bulk of the material does derive from what Arrian and others heard while seated at the master's feet.

BIOGRAPHY

Details of Epictetus' life are sketchy; the *Discourses* themselves are our richest source of information. We can only make an educated guess as to the year he was born and the year he died, but are not likely to be far wrong in giving his dates as *c*.AD 55–135. We know that he was born into slavery because he tells us so, and from an ancient inscription we learn that his mother had been a slave. The place of his birth was Hierapolis, a major Graeco-Roman city in what today is south-western Turkey. The native language there was Greek – the Koine or 'common' Greek that derived from the language of classical Athens, but became widely disseminated in a simplified form during the Hellenistic era. The *Discourses* are a principal source for our knowledge of Koine Greek (as is the Greek New Testament, to cite another example).

More than once Epictetus refers to himself as 'a lame old man', but nowhere elaborates on the cause of his disability. Two traditions independent of the *Discourses* give competing accounts. Early Christian authors report that a sadistic master was responsible for rendering him crippled for life. But others interpret 'lame old man' as almost a pleonastic phrase, which is to say that he may have suffered from rheumatism or arthritis as a natural consequence of advancing age. The latter explanation is in fact the more likely. We know who his owner was; his name was Epaphroditus, and Epictetus makes mention of him several times, not exactly in complimentary terms, but not with any hint of bitterness either. Epaphroditus is famous for more than just being Epictetus' master. A former slave himself, after manumission he rose to the position of Nero's secretary in charge of petitions; later he would serve Domitian in the same capacity. Descriptions of life at court frequently appear in the *Discourses*, in terms detailed and vivid enough to suggest that his service to Epaphroditus acquainted Epictetus at first hand with the manners, routines and attitudes of the emperor and his courtiers. We can go further and speculate that in this equivocal position – a slave on the one hand, but also a privileged member of the emperor's inner circle – Epictetus came to appreciate in full the ambiguities of power, and learned to distinguish real freedom from counterfeit. This dialectic of freedom and slavery colours much of his presentation of Stoic thought.

That Epaphroditus allowed Epictetus considerable freedom of movement and association is implied by his attendance at the lectures of Musonius Rufus. Tacitus, a contemporary Roman historian (*c.*AD 56–*c.*117), describes Musonius as the foremost Stoic of his day. We are fortunate that a sample of his lectures was included in an anthology of morally edifying readings, known as the *Suda*, which still survives. Musonius gives lessons in practical ethics, on particular questions such as whether women should be allowed to study philosophy, and what relationship ideally obtains between a husband and wife. While he does not engage the same topics, Epictetus in his *Discourses* displays a similar focus and orientation. Both men concentrate on ethics to the virtual exclusion of physics (cosmological speculation) and logic. Logic and physics feature in the *Discourses*, to be sure, but typically in an ancillary or illustrative role. And neither one gets caught up in ethical theorizing; they always treat ethics with a view to applying it in real life. Reading books and becoming fluent in the doctrines of philosophers are deprecated as ends in themselves. Even more than Musonius, Epictetus has a plain and practical agenda: he wants his students to make a clean break with received patterns of thinking and behaving, to reject popular morality and put conventional notions of good and bad behind them; in short, he aims to inspire in his readers something like a religious conversion, only not by appeal to any articles of faith or the promise of life in the hereafter (Stoics did not believe in the afterlife), but by appeal to reason alone.

Epaphroditus granted Epictetus his freedom – precisely when we don't know – but from then on he devoted his life to the practice and preaching of philosophy. When Domitian, suspecting them of republican sympathies, in AD 95 ordered all the philosophers in Italy to pack up and leave, Epictetus turned this insult to account by moving to Greece and founding his school there (in a spot where he had probably little to fear in the way of competition). Nicopolis, the site he chose, was a Roman colony founded by the emperor Augustus to commemorate his victory over Antony and Cleopatra. It functioned as the *de facto* capital of the province of Epirus. The site had other advantages; it was on the Adriatic coast, making it easy of access for prospective students from Italy. The student body drew mainly from upper-class Roman families who admired Greek culture and were particularly keen to taste of the accumulated wisdom of the Greek philosophers. We have no information as to how long students typically stayed at Nicopolis under Epictetus' tutelage, but it was probably no more than a year or two. The school, in any case, was a success, and when its reputation attracted the attention of the emperor Hadrian (more kindly disposed toward philosophy than his predecessor), he honoured it, and its founder, with a personal visit.

Tradition has it that late in life Epictetus retired from teaching and withdrew to the peace and quiet of family life, under conditions imposed by old age: that is, he became a parent by adopting rather than fathering a child, and took into his home a female servant to serve as a kind of surrogate mother to the child and domestic servant for himself. That he had absented himself from family life for so long shows that he regarded philosophy as a jealous mistress who demanded practically all his time and attention, which family life would not allow. That this renunciation of family life represented a real sacrifice is suggested by the fact that he took to it immediately upon retiring. He evidently thought he had earned the comforts of home after devoting most of his life to improving the lives of others – the successive generations of students who had passed through his school. We have no more news of Epictetus beyond this. After creating this version of a family he was evidently content to settle into it and live out the balance of his years in obscurity.

EPICTETUS AS AN EXPONENT
OF STOICISM

Stoicism was founded in the third century BC by Zeno of Citium; Cleanthes succeeded him as head of the school. But it was Cleanthes' successor, Chrysippus (d. 208 BC), who contributed most to the development of Stoic doctrine and deserves most of the credit for what Stoicism eventually became – the dominant philosophy of the post-classical era. Tacitus furnishes a neat summary of the core principles of Stoic ethics as they were taught in Rome at the time:

> Whether human affairs are directed by Fate's unalterable necessity, or by chance, is a question. The wisest of philosophers disagree on this point. [Epicureans] insist that heaven is unconcerned with our birth and death – is unconcerned, in fact, with human beings generally – with the result that good people often suffer while wicked people thrive. [The Stoics] disagree, maintaining

that although things happen according to fate, this depends not on the movement of the planets but on the principles and logic of natural causality. This school concedes to us the freedom to choose our own lives. Once the choice is made, however, the Stoics warn that the subsequent sequence of events cannot be altered. With regard to practical matters they maintain that popular ideas of good and bad are wrong: many people who appear to be in dire circumstances are actually happy provided they deal with their situation bravely; others, regardless of how many possessions they have, are miserable, because they do not know how to use the gifts of fortune wisely.[1]

'The [Stoic] school leaves us free to choose our own lives.' Confidence in this capacity is a key postulate of the *Discourses*. 'Choice' is one meaning of *prohairesis*, a term that among Stoics is practically unique to Epictetus. According to him the faculty of choice distinguishes humans from irrational animals. We can make considered choices among 'impressions' or 'appearances', meaning anything that comes within range of our senses, together with whatever thoughts and feelings these sensations evoke. While all animals are subject to impressions, those of humans differ by virtue of the fact that we possess the power of language and reason (both faculties expressed by the single word *logos*).

Human impressions have 'propositional content', that is, our minds automatically frame them as a statement, such as 'that is a good thing to have' or 'this is the right thing to do'. They also involve an intermediate step: the impression requires our 'assent' before it generates the impulse to act on it. Drawing on this orthodox Stoic account of human psychology, Epictetus makes two points with an emphasis distinctly his own: (1) that rational animals can hold off acting on impressions until they are scrutinized and assessed; and (2) if they are judged unreasonable – i.e. irrational or merely impractical – we can and should withhold our assent from them. 'The gods have given us the best and most efficacious gift,' he writes, 'the ability to make good use of impressions' (I 1, 7). And: 'Don't let the force of an impression when it first hits you knock you off your feet;

just say to it, "Hold on a moment; let me see who you are and what you represent. Let me put you to the test"' (II 18, 24). These functions of mind define the sphere of 'choice' (*prohairesis*), the upshot being that it is 'up to us' how we act, and that we are responsible for determining the character and content of our lives.

Compared to Epicureanism, which after its founder's death was a closed system whose doctrines were literally engraved in stone (in the form of a lengthy inscription in Lycia composed by one Diogenes of Oenoanda), Stoicism throughout its long history remained a work in progress. It was not considered bad form for one Stoic to criticize another, or grounds for questioning whether one deserved to be considered a Stoic at all. Stoics who parted company with Chrysippus on a fundamental point of doctrine used to be called unorthodox; but this is a judgement of modern scholars, not one we find the Stoics themselves making. Indeed, the Stoics' openness to revision was a particular strength of their school.

In Epictetus you find not only fellow Stoics cited with approval; Plato is praised, Diogenes the Cynic is several times eulogized at length; but Socrates stalks these pages as the philosopher with the greatest moral authority of all. Now, it is true that Socrates was a figure universally admired; not only the Stoics, but Cynics, Sceptics and Epicureans recognized him as their foundational figure and did their best to show that their views were consistent or even identical with those Socrates supposedly held. Everyone, it seems, wanted a piece of him, and to the degree that these rival systems of thought succeeded in presenting themselves as Socratic in inspiration, their reputation with the public was enhanced. In no other Stoic, however – in no other writer from any of the various schools of philosophy – does Socrates figure more prominently than in Epictetus. He features as a philosophical saint and martyr, a model for the Stoic senators named in the first two Discourses who died for their principled opposition to Nero and Domitian; and, so far as his teaching is concerned, he is cited in support of key tenets of Stoic morality: that no one does wrong willingly; that harming another hurts the offender rather than the injured party; that material 'goods' can do as much harm as good, and should therefore be classified as value-neutral; and so forth.

The prominent role allotted to Socrates is part of a broader ecumenical programme, however. The *Discourses* do not just preach to the choir, they are directed as much at sceptics as true believers. By aligning himself with Socrates, and dropping the names of Plato, Diogenes, *et al.* along the way, Epictetus aims to transcend a narrow sectarian appeal and position Stoicism squarely within the philosophical mainstream. References to the Stoic 'paradoxes', those outré views that many found implausible or downright incoherent, are kept to a minimum. Above all Epictetus *argues* for his theses. Socrates *et al.* lend legitimacy to his positions, but are never cited to settle a question out of hand. Stoics emphasized rationality (the *logos*) as man's characteristic quality, and it is by the use of rational argument that Epictetus intends to draw (and over the centuries has managed to gain) a wide and varied audience.

Epictetus' Stoicism is distinctive in other ways too. Because his interest is in ethics primarily, he does not engage with certain theoretical issues that were debated by the original Stoics and their rivals. The controversy over whether there was a place for free will within their deterministic system is nowhere engaged directly. To be sure, he emphasizes repeatedly that our thoughts and actions have immediate and inescapable consequences: 'You have only to doze for a moment, and all is lost. For ruin and salvation both have their source inside you' (IV 9, 16). 'Very little is needed for everything to be upset and ruined, only a slight lapse in reason' (IV 3, 4). Or, to quote Tacitus again, 'Once the choice is made . . . the subsequent sequence of events cannot be altered.' But, as noted above, humans do have freedom to shape mental events – Epictetus is equally adamant about that. And in this area, as he says more than once, 'not even God has the power of coercion over us'.

Other paradoxes, or points of controversy, such as whether there was a moral state intermediate between perfect virtue and utter depravity (the old Stoics denied it), are tacitly deprecated. No one reading deeply in Epictetus can doubt that he believes humans are capable of moral progress, and that it makes sense to distinguish between degrees of virtue and vice. Indeed, nearly every reference to the *Discourses*, from antiquity to the present, assumes that they have no other goal than moral improvement.

The *Discourses* are primarily Stoic documents, but since Stoicism along with the other philosophical sects closed up shop in the sixth century AD, over the centuries many more non-Stoics than Stoics have read them with appreciation. If they continue to speak to the contemporary reader it is because they are grounded in common experience and common sense.

EPICTETUS' INFLUENCE

Epictetus' influence has been enormous. We only have space to pass a few highlights in review. His outreach programme was evidently successful, to judge by the long commentary devoted to the *Enchiridion* by the neo-Platonist philosopher Simplicius (sixth century AD), otherwise known mainly for writing commentaries on Aristotle. In the Preface, Simplicius explains that Epictetus' maxims are beneficial to those who want their bodies and desires to be ruled by rationality.

Marcus Aurelius, in the acknowledgements at the head of his *Meditations*, mentions the discovery of a copy of the *Discourses* as a crucial event in his own intellectual development. The *Meditations* in fact abound in quotations and paraphrases of the *Discourses*. That a Greek slave should be the acknowledged *maître à penser* of a Roman emperor illustrates in a most literal way the famous line of the poet Horace: 'captive Greece captured her uncivilized captor [i.e. Rome]'.

Of decisive importance for his currency during the Middle Ages (and no doubt one reason his writings survived antiquity) is that he was among a handful of pagan authors approved for reading in the early Church. Epictetus himself was esteemed an *anima naturaliter Christiana*, by reason of the supposed consistency between his principles and practice. Besides giving incidental proof of his own reading of Epictetus at many points in his work, the Christian apologist Origen reports that by the third century his fame exceeded even Plato's: 'Plato,' he writes, 'is only found in the hands of those reputed to be philologists. By contrast, Epictetus is admired by ordinary people who have the desire to be benefited and who perceive improvement from his writings' (*Contra Celsum* VI, 2). With a few minor editorial changes (such as the regular replacement of Socrates' name with that of St Paul), the *Enchiridion* was adapted to monastic use and in its Christian habit served the monks of the Eastern Orthodox Church for centuries as an ascetic rulebook.

Through Syriac Christian scholars Epictetus' thought became well known in the Islamic East. The ninth-century philosopher al-Kindi (according to the Muslim historian Ibn al-Nadim (d. 955), 'the best man of his time, called The Philosopher of the Arabs')[2] was appointed by the Abbasid Caliph al-Ma'mun to the House of Wisdom, a centre for the translation of Greek philosophical and scientific texts in Baghdad. His own work of ethics, 'On the Art of Dispelling Sorrows', shows the unmistakable influence of Stoicism in general and Epictetus in particular. There he lays emphasis on the importance of freedom from the world and highlights humans' status as agents, who through their ultimate independence are responsible for their own happiness and independent of others. The weight Epictetus puts on the ephemeral nature of worldly goods is recalled; from chapter 7 of the *Enchiridion* al-Kindi borrows the comparison of earthly life to a ship which has, during the course of its voyage, temporarily anchored at an island and allowed its passengers to disembark; passengers who linger too long on the island risk being left behind when the ship sets sail again. The implicit warning, as in Epictetus, is that we must not become attached to material things (represented by the island and its foodstuffs), because they will invariably be taken away from us when the ship relaunches.

The first printed edition of the *Discourses* appeared in Venice in 1535; within a century they had been translated into all the major European languages; and in one version or another they, and the *Enchiridion*, have remained continuously in print.

Two of the greatest minds of the seventeenth century witness to the fact that Epictetus survived the transition to the modern era with no loss in reputation. Pascal, in his 'Discussion with

Monsieur de Sacy', praises Epictetus for his delineation of human duties and his recommendation that we submit to the will of a providential God. He objects, however, to the assumption, common among ancient philosophers, that human nature was perfectible without the need of God's grace.

> [Epictetus] believes that God gave man the means to fulfill all his obligations; that these means are within his power, that happiness is attained through what we are capable of, this being the reason God gave them to us. Our mind cannot be forced to believe what is false, nor our will compelled to love something that makes it unhappy. These two powers are therefore free, and it is through them that we can become perfect.[3]

That the redemptive message of the Gospels was not available to the ancients makes their morals incomplete. But this Christian caveat aside, Pascal shrewdly identifies and correctly describes a central tenet of Epictetus' teaching. Stoicism purported to be an internally consistent system the doctrines of which were mutually self-entailing across all three branches – logic, physics and ethics. Pascal's contemporary Descartes was deeply affected by his reading of Epictetus, and he seized on one of the philosopher's most original moves, the way he enlists epistemology (specifically humans' use of appearances) in support of his moral principles. In Descartes too we find a close fit between the method of doubt he adopts regarding the truth of our impressions and opinions and his philosophy of life. In the *Rules for the Direction of the Mind*, he states:

> The aim of our studies should be to direct the mind with a view to forming true and sound judgments about whatever comes before it ... [A person should consider] how to increase the natural light of his reason ... in order that his intellect should show his will what decision it ought to make in each of life's contingencies.[4]

Over long stretches Descartes' *Discourse on Method*, the first classic of modern philosophy, reads like nothing so much as a paraphrase of Epictetus. One programmatic passage will have to do by way of illustration:

> I undertook to conquer myself rather than fortune, and to alter my desires rather than change the order of the world, and to accustom myself to believe that nothing is entirely in our power except our own thoughts . . . Here, I think, is the secret of those ancient philosophers who were able to free themselves from the tyranny of fortune, or, despite suffering and poverty, to rival the gods in happiness.[5]

Clearly Epictetus remained one of the ancient sages whom an educated person could be expected to know well, as it was assumed there was still much of truth in him.

We conclude by jumping ahead to the present, noting his surprising importance in the history of psychotherapy. Psychologist Albert Ellis has acknowledged Epictetus as one of the chief inspirations behind the development of Rational-Emotive Behaviour Therapy (REBT), arguably the foremost modality in counselling today. As a college freshman in an informal study group devoted to reading and commenting on major philosophers, Ellis was struck by Epictetus' insistence that 'It is not events that disturb people, it is their judgements concerning them' (*Enchiridion* 5). Ellis openly credits Epictetus for supplying his guiding principle that our emotional responses to upsetting actions – not the actions themselves – are what create anxiety and depression; and that (a point basic to Stoic psychology in general) our emotional responses are products of our judgements – are in fact (irrational) judgements *tout court*: 'Much of what we call emotion is nothing more nor less than a certain kind – a biased, prejudiced, or strongly evaluative kind – of thought. What we call feelings almost always have a pronounced evaluating or appraisal element.'[6] Ellis points out that irrational beliefs often appear in the way people talk to themselves. Compare Epictetus at IV 4, 26–27:

> Someone says, I don't like leisure, it's boring; I don't like crowds, they're a nuisance. But if events ordain that you spend time either

alone or with just a few other people, look upon it as tranquillity and play along with it for the duration. Talk to yourself, train your thoughts and shape your preconceptions.

The more one reads in the literature of self-help, therapy, recovery and so forth, the more apparent it becomes how much is owed to this regularly rediscovered author, whose ideas have proven useful in disciplines such as applied psychology that in his own day had hardly made a start.

NOTES

1. Tacitus, *Annals* VI 22.
2. Al-Kindi, 'Encyclopaedic Scholar of the Baghdad "House of Wisdom"'. http://www.muslimheritage.com/day_life/default.cfm? ArticleID=691&Oldpage=1. Accessed 4 September 2007.
3. Blaise Pascal, 'Discussion with Monsieur de Sacy', in *Pensées and Other Writings*, trans. H. Levi (Oxford, 1995), pp. 182–92, at p. 187.
4. René Descartes, 'Rules for the Direction of the Mind', in *The Philosophical Writings of Descartes*, 2 vols., trans. John Cottingham, Robert Stoothoff and Dugald Murdoch, vol. 3 including Anthony Kenny (Cambridge, 1988), vol. 1, p. 10.
5. René Descartes, 'Discourse on Method', in *The Philosophical Works of Descartes*, ed. E. S. Haldane and G. R. T. Ross (Cambridge, 1931), pp. 80–130, at pp. 96–7.
6. Albert Ellis, 'Early Theories and Practices of Rational-Emotive Behavior Theory and How They Have Been Augmented and Revised During the Last Three Decades', *Journal of Rational-Emotive & Cognitive-Behavior Therapy*, vol. 21, nos. 3–4 (December 2003), pp. 219–43, at p. 232.

Further Reading

Interest in Epictetus is currently experiencing one of its periodic upsurges, and some works of secondary literature deserve notice in this connection. Pride of place belongs to the comprehensive study by A. A. Long, a leading scholar of later ancient philosophy: *Epictetus: A Stoic and Socratic Guide to Life* (Oxford, 2002). Long is also co-editor, with D. Sedley, of the standard sourcebook for Stoicism and the other philosophical schools that post-date Aristotle: *The Hellenistic Philosophers* (Cambridge, 1987).

Readers of the present translation may derive some benefit from my commentary on Book I (Oxford, 1998), though it is intended mainly for academic use. The part logic plays in Epictetus is the subject of an acute study by J. Barnes, *Logic and the Imperial Stoa* (Leiden, 1997).

A personal account of how Epictetus helped a prisoner of war endure extremes of hardship and degradation can be found in J. Stockdale's *Courage under Fire: Testing Epictetus' Doctrines in a Laboratory of Human Behavior* (Stanford, 1993). Stockdale is remembered mainly for being third-party candidate Ross Perot's running mate in the US presidential election of 1992, but during the Vietnam War he spent seven years as a POW, four of them in solitary confinement – solitary, it seems, except for a copy of the *Discourses*. Two lectures, collectively entitled 'Stockdale on Stoicism', are available online: http://www.usna.edu/Ethics/Publications/stoicism1.pdf; http://www.usna.edu/Ethics/Publications/stoicism2.pdf. As testimonials to Epictetus' enduring value they are probably unsurpassed; but by any measure they make very compelling reading.

The ethics of Epictetus feature prominently in the 1998 bestselling novel by Tom Wolfe, *A Man in Full* (New York, 1998), based largely on Wolfe's conversations with Stockdale. Stockdale's essays promoting the wisdom of Epictetus and the values of Stoicism have in recent years been studied by officer candidates in all branches of the American armed forces. Nancy Sherman, a teacher at the US Naval Academy, has published *Stoic Warriors: The Ancient Philosophy behind the Military Mind* (New York and Oxford, 2nd edn 2007).

In two of his final books the French philosopher Michel Foucault singled out Epictetus for his contribution to what he called 'technologies of the self': refined procedures whereby a person learns to control his feelings, thoughts and desires. Epictetus' advice to monitor our thoughts and appearances (or 'representations'), Foucault argues, anticipates Freud: *Technologies of the Self* (Amherst, 1988); *The History of Sexuality: The Care of the Self* (Harmondsworth, 1990).

Epictetus is accorded two chapters in a philosophically rich and wide-ranging study by R. Sorabji: *Self: Ancient and Modern Insights about Individuality, Life, and Death* (Chicago, 2006).

Finally, a new translation of the *Manual* with detailed commentary can be recommended: *Epictetus' Handbook and the Tablet of Cebes: Guides to Stoic Living* (London, 2005) by K. Seddon.

Note on the Translation

My translation is based on the most recent edition of Epictetus' complete works in Greek, that prepared by J. Souilhé (Paris, 1948–65) in the Budé series of classical texts. The footnotes list instances where for various reasons I have chosen not to use Souilhé's text as the basis for my translation.

Epictetus has been called a 'rhetorical wizard', but certain features of his style are less congenial to print than they would have been to oral delivery. An example is his recourse to repetition. This is no sign of a poverty of ideas but, along with his aggressive style, frequent use of metaphor, dialogue, personal example, etc., part of an effort to make his message memorable. Obviously the rationale for returning to the same themes is largely absent when his lectures are available in print, since we can reproduce the same effect for ourselves by reading and rereading them *ad libitum*. Consequently I have omitted from my translation of Books III and IV a number of discourses that I judge to be little more than restatements of ideas developed to better effect elsewhere.

The innumerable editions of the *Enchiridion* attest to the fact that in this form students' acquaintance with Epictetus has for centuries begun and ended. The *Enchiridion* purports to distill his philosophy to essentials, without such stylistic superfluities as the snatches of imaginary dialogue that regularly enliven the exposition of ideas in the *Discourses*. Unfortunately in the process Epictetus is flattened to the point of sententiousness; argument is omitted in favour of bald assertion; and to readers with some background in contemporary (especially analytic) philosophy the book makes a disappointing impression.

Epictetus comes across more as a 'moralizer' than an authentic philosopher. Nonetheless the *Manual* no doubt still has its uses; readers may find it helpful in orienting themselves to Epictetus' thought before exploring the *Discourses* themselves.

The complete set of thirty-odd fragments has been translated from the text of W. A. Oldfather in the Loeb series (London and Cambridge, 1925–8) which is based in turn on H. Schenkl's edition in the Teubner series of classical texts (Leipzig, 1916).

THE DISCOURSES

Arrian to Lucius Gellius, greeting:

I have not composed these words of Epictetus as one might be said to 'compose' books of this kind, nor have I of my own volition published them to the world; indeed, I acknowledge that I have not 'composed' them at all. But whatever I used to hear him say I wrote down, word for word, as best I could, as a record for later use of his thought and frank expression. So they are what you would expect one person to say to another *ex tempore*, not compositions originally intended to be read by posterity. Such being their character, they have somehow, without my knowledge or intention, fallen into the public's hands. Yet I little care whether I shall be judged incompetent in the art of composition; and for his part Epictetus does not care at all if anyone should despise his Discourses, since in uttering them he was clearly aiming at nothing except moving the minds of his audience towards what is best. So if these Discourses achieve that much, they will have exactly the effect that a philosopher's words, in my opinion, ought to have. But if not, the reader should realize that, when Epictetus spoke them, his audience could not help but experience just what he intended them to feel. If the Discourses on their own do not achieve this, then perhaps I am to blame or it simply cannot be helped.

Farewell.

BOOK I

I 1 *Concerning what is in our power and what is not*

[1] In general, you will find no art or faculty that can analyse itself, therefore none that can approve or disapprove of itself. [2] The art of grammar is restricted to analysing and commenting on literature. Music is confined to the analysis of harmony. [3] Consequently neither of them analyses itself. Now, if you are writing to a friend, the art of grammar will help you decide what words to use; but it will not tell you whether it is a good idea to write to your friend in the first place. Music is no different; whether this is a good time to sing and play, or a bad one, the art of music by itself cannot decide.

[4] So what can? The faculty that analyses itself as well as the others, namely, the faculty of reason. Reason is unique among the faculties assigned to us in being able to evaluate itself – what it is, what it is capable of, how valuable it is – in addition to passing judgement on others.

[5] What decides whether a sum of money is good? The money is not going to tell you; it must be the faculty that makes use of such impressions – reason. [6] Reason, in addition, takes the measure of music, grammar and the other arts, judging their benefit and deciding when it's best to use them.

[7] So it's only appropriate that the gods have given us the best and most efficacious gift: the ability to make good use of impressions. Other capacities they did not put in our power. [8] Was it because they did not want to? Personally, I believe that they would have endowed us with those others too, had they been able. But they were not. [9] Since we are on earth,

you see, bound to a material body and material things, we can hardly avoid being limited by these extraneous factors.

[10] Well, what does Zeus say? 'Epictetus, if it were possible, I would have made your little body and possessions both free and unrestricted. [11] As it is, though, make no mistake: this body does not belong to you, it is only cunningly constructed clay. [12] And since I could not make the body yours, I have given you a portion of myself instead, the power of positive and negative impulse, of desire and aversion – the power, in other words, of making good use of impressions. If you take care of it and identify with it, you will never be blocked or frustrated; you won't have to complain, and never will need to blame or flatter anyone. [13] Is that enough to satisfy you?'

'It's more than enough. Thank you.'

[14] And yet, while there is only the one thing we can care for and devote ourselves to, we choose instead to care about and attach ourselves to a score of others: to our bodies, to our property, to our family, friends and slaves. [15] And, being attached to many things, we are weighed down and dragged along with them. [16] If the weather keeps us from travelling, we sit down, fret, and keep asking, 'Which way is the wind blowing?' 'From the north.' 'That's no good. When will it blow from the west?' 'When it wants to, or rather when Aeolus wants it to; because God put Aeolus in charge of the winds, not you.' [17] What should we do then? Make the best use of what is in our power, and treat the rest in accordance with its nature. And what is its nature? However God decides.

[18] 'Must I be beheaded now, and alone?' Well, do you want everyone to be beheaded just because misery loves company? [19] Why not hold out your neck the way Lateranus did at Rome, when condemned by Nero to be beheaded? He held out his neck willingly to take the blow – but the blow was deficient, so he recoiled a bit, but then had enough self-command to offer his neck a second time. [20] And prior to that, when Epaphroditus, Nero's freedman, approached a certain man and asked him about the grounds of his offence, he replied, 'If I want anything, I will tell it to your master.'[1]

[21] What should we have ready at hand in a situation like this? The knowledge of what is mine and what is not mine, what I can and cannot do. [22] I must die. But must I die bawling? I must be put in chains – but moaning and groaning too? I must be exiled; but is there anything to keep me from going with a smile, calm and self-composed?

'Tell us your secrets.'

[23] 'I refuse, as this is up to me.'

'I will put you in chains.'

'What's that you say, friend? It's only my leg you will chain, not even God can conquer my will.'

[24] 'I will throw you into prison.'

'Correction – it is my body you will throw there.'

'I will behead you.'

'Well, when did I ever claim that mine was the only neck that couldn't be severed?'

[25] That's the kind of attitude you need to cultivate if you would be a philosopher, the sort of sentiments you should write down every day and put in practice.

[26] Thrasea used to say, 'I would sooner be killed today than banished tomorrow.'[2] [27] And what did Musonius say to him? 'If you choose death because it is the greater evil, what sense is there in that? Or if you choose it as the lesser evil, remember who gave you the choice. Why not try coming to terms with what you have been given?'

[28] Agrippinus used to say, 'I don't add to my troubles.' To illustrate, someone once said to him, 'You are being tried in the Senate – [29] good luck.' But it was eleven in the morning, and at that hour he was in the habit of taking his bath and exercise. 'Let us be off to exercise.' [30] When he was done, word came that he had been condemned. 'To exile,' he asked, 'or death?' 'Exile.' 'And my estate, what about that?' 'It has not been confiscated.' 'Well then, let us go to my villa in Aricia and have lunch there.' [31] This shows what is possible when we practise what is necessary, and make our desire and aversion safe against any setback or adversity. [32] 'I have to die. If it is now, well then I die now; if later, then now I will take my lunch, since the hour for lunch has arrived – and dying I will tend to later.'

How? As someone who knows that you have to return what belongs to somebody else.

I 2 *How a person can preserve their proper character in any situation*

[1] Man, the rational animal, can put up with anything except what seems to him irrational; whatever is rational is tolerable. [2] Physical hardships are not intolerable by nature. The Spartans, for instance, gladly submit to being whipped because they are taught that it is done for good reason. [3] But what about being hanged – isn't that intolerable? Well, people frequently go and hang themselves, whenever they judge that it is a reasonable course of action.

[4] In short, reflection will show that people are put off by nothing so much as what they think is unreasonable, and attracted to nothing more than what to them seems reasonable.

[5] But standards of reasonableness and unreasonableness vary from one person to the next – just as we consider different things good or bad, harmful or beneficial. [6] Which is why education has no goal more important than bringing our preconception of what is reasonable and unreasonable in alignment with nature.

[7] But this not only involves weighing the value of externals, it also means considering what agrees with our own, individual nature. [8] For one person it is reasonable to be a bathroom attendant, because he only thinks about what punishment and privation lie in wait for him otherwise, and knows that if he accepts the assignment he will be spared that pain and hardship. [9] Someone else not only finds such a job intolerable for him personally, but finds it intolerable that anyone should have to perform it. [10] But ask me, 'Shall I be a bathroom attendant or not?' and I will tell you that earning a living is better than starving to death; so that if you measure your interests by these criteria, go ahead and do it. [11] 'But it would be beneath my dignity.' Well, that is an additional factor that you bring to the

question, not me. You are the one who knows yourself – which is to say, you know how much you are worth in your own estimation, and therefore at what price you will sell yourself; because people sell themselves at different rates.

[12] So, for instance, Agrippinus told Florus to 'Go ahead' when he was debating whether to attend Nero's festival, maybe even participate. [13] But when Florus asked him why he was not going himself, Agrippinus answered, 'I don't even consider the possibility.' [14] Taking account of the value of externals, you see, comes at some cost to the value of one's own character.

[15] So if you want to know if life or death is better, the answer I give is, 'Life.' [16] If you ask about pain versus pleasure, I say, 'Pleasure is preferable.'

'But if I refuse to participate in Nero's festival, he will kill me.'

[17] Go ahead and participate, then – but I still refuse.

'Why?'

Because you think of yourself as no more than a single thread in the robe, whose duty it is to conform to the mass of people – just as a single white thread seemingly has no wish to clash with the remainder of the garment. [18] But I aspire to be the purple stripe, that is, the garment's brilliant hem. However small a part it may be, it can still manage to make the garment as a whole attractive. Don't tell me, then, 'Be like the rest,' because in that case I cannot be the purple stripe.[3]

[19] In his actions Helvidius Priscus showed his awareness of this principle. When Emperor Vespasian sent him word barring him from the Senate, his response was, 'You can disqualify me as a senator. But as long as I do remain a member I must join the assembly.' [20] 'Well join, then, but don't say anything.' 'Don't call on me for my vote and I won't say anything.' 'But I must call on you for your vote.' 'And I have to give whatever answer I think is right.' [21] 'Answer, and I will kill you.' 'Did I ever say I was immortal? You do your part, and I will do mine. It is your part to kill me, mine to die without flinching; your part to exile me, mine to leave without protest.'

[22] And what did Priscus accomplish, who was but a single man? Well, what good does the purple stripe do the robe? Its

lustre is a good example to the rest. [23] If it had been someone else in the same situation whom the emperor barred from entering the Senate, he would have probably said, 'I'm so grateful you can spare me.' [24] In fact, the emperor would not have even bothered to bar him, well aware that the man would either sit there like a blockhead or, if he did speak, would only mouth words he knew that Caesar wanted to hear – and would pile additional inanities on besides.

[25] A certain athlete, at risk of dying unless his genitals were amputated, made a comparable choice. His brother, a philosopher, went and asked him, 'Well, my brother, what's it going to be? Will you have them amputated, and return to life in the gymnasium?' The man refused to submit to the indignity, however, and summoned the will to die. [26] Someone asked, 'Did he choose death as an athlete or as a philosopher?' 'As a man,' Epictetus said, 'one who had competed at the level of the Olympic Games, where he was a familiar figure, and a victor more than once – no occasional visitor to the local gym. [27] Someone else might have even allowed his head to be removed, if his life could have been saved thereby. [28] That's what I mean by having consideration for one's character. And it shows how weighty a factor it can be when it is allowed a regular role in one's deliberations.

[29] 'Come, Epictetus, shave off your beard.'

If I am a philosopher, I will not shave it off.

'But I will cut off your head.'

If that will do you any good, then cut it off.

[30] Someone asked, 'But how do we know what is in keeping with our character?'

Well, how does the bull realize its own strength, rushing out to protect the whole herd when a lion attacks? The possession of a particular talent is instinctively sensed by its owner; [31] so if any of you are so blessed you will be the first to know it. [32] It is true, however, that no bull reaches maturity in an instant, nor do men become heroes overnight. We must endure a winter training, and can't be dashing into situations for which we aren't yet prepared.

[33] Consider at what price you sell your integrity; but please, for God's sake, don't sell it cheap. The grand gesture, the ultimate sacrifice – that, perhaps, belongs to others, to people of Socrates' class. [34] 'But if we are endowed by nature with the potential for greatness, why do only some of us achieve it?' Well, do all horses become stallions? Are all dogs greyhounds? [35] Even if I lack the talent, I will not abandon the effort on that account. [36] Epictetus will not be better than Socrates. But if I am no worse, I am satisfied. [37] I mean, I will never be Milo either; nevertheless, I don't neglect my body. Nor will I be another Croesus – and still, I don't neglect my property. In short, we do not abandon any discipline for despair of ever being the best in it.

I 3 *How to draw the correct consequences from the fact that God is the father of mankind*

[1] If we could completely subscribe, as we should, to the view that we are all primary creatures of God, and that God is father of both gods and men, I don't believe that we would ever think mean or lowly thoughts about ourselves. [2] If the emperor adopts you, no one will be able to put up with your pretension; but knowing that you are the son of God, shouldn't your pride be that much greater?

[3] In fact, though, we react quite differently. Two elements are combined in our creation, the body, which we have in common with the beasts; and reason and good judgement, which we share with the gods. Most of us tend toward the former connection, miserable and mortal though it is, whereas only a few favour this holy and blessed alliance.

[4] Since everyone will necessarily treat things in accordance with their beliefs about them, those few who think that they are born for fidelity, respect and confidence in their use of impressions entertain no mean or ignoble thoughts about themselves, while the majority does the opposite. [5] 'What am I? A

wretched mortal – a feeble piece of flesh.' [6] Feeble indeed – but you have something better than the flesh. So why turn away from this and cling to that?

[7] Because of this connection, some of us sink to the level of wolves – faithless, vicious and treacherous. Others turn into lions – wild, savage and uncivilized. But most of us become like foxes, the sorriest of the lot. [8] For what else is a spiteful, malicious man except a fox, or something even lower and less dignified?

[9] See that you don't turn out like one of *those* unfortunates.

I 4 *On progress*

[1] Whoever is making progress, after learning from philosophers that desire is directed toward good things and avoidance directed toward bad, and having also learned that impassivity and a good flow of life are not attained except through unerring desire and unfailing avoidance – that person will do away with desire altogether, or else defer it to another time, and exercise avoidance only on things within the moral sphere. [2] Because they know that if they try to avoid anything outside the moral sphere they are going to run into something contrary to their aversion and face disaster.

[3] But if virtue holds this promise – to secure happiness, impassivity, and a good flow of life – then progress toward virtue must involve progress toward these other states as well. [4] For wherever the perfection of anything tends, progress is always an approach towards the same thing.

[5] So how is it that, although we are now agreed about the nature of virtue, we still try to demonstrate progress in areas that are unrelated? What is the goal of virtue, after all, except a life that flows smoothly? [6] So who is making progress – the person who has read many of Chrysippus' books? [7] Is virtue no more than this – to become literate in Chrysippus? Because, if that's what it is, then progress cannot amount to anything more than learning as much Chrysippus as we can. [8] We

are agreed, however, that virtue produces one thing, while
maintaining that the approach to it, progress, results in something different. [9] 'This person can read Chrysippus already
by himself. You are making progress, by God,' someone says
sarcastically. 'Some progress that is!' [10] 'Why do you make
fun of him?' 'Well, why do you try to distract him from coming
to an awareness of his faults?' Don't you want to show him the
purpose of virtue, so that he will know what real progress
consists in? [11] Look for it in your volition, friend – that is, in
your desire and avoidance. Make it your goal never to fail in
your desires or experience things you would rather avoid; try
never to err in impulse and repulsion; aim to be perfect also in
the practice of attention and withholding judgement. [12] But
the first subjects are the most essential. If you aim to be perfect
when you are still anxious and apprehensive, how have you
made progress? [13] So let's see some evidence of it. But no, it's
as if I were to say to an athlete, 'Show me your shoulders,' and
he responded with, 'Have a look at my weights.' 'Get out of
here with you and your gigantic weights!' I'd say, 'What I want
to see isn't the weights but how you've profited from using
them.'

[14] 'Take the treatise *On Impulse* and see how well I've
read it.' Idiot. It's not *that* I'm after, I want to know how
you put impulse and repulsion into practice, and desire and
avoidance as well. I want to know how you apply and prepare
yourself, and how you practise attention,* so that I can decide
whether with you these functions operate in harmony with
nature. [15] If you *are*, in fact, acting in accord with nature,
then show me, and I will be the first to say that you are making
progress. But otherwise, be off, and rather than just comment
on books, you might as well go write one yourself. But, in the
end, what good will it do you? [16] You know that a whole
book costs around five denarii.[4] Is the commentator, then,
worth more than that? [17] Don't put your purpose in one
place and expect to see progress made somewhere else.

---

* The alterations of ἐπιβάλλεις to ἐπιβάλλῃ and προστίθεσαι to προτίθεσαι
have been assumed in the translation, the latter ascertained by comparing
πρόθεσις ('attention') in §11 above.

[18] Where is progress, then? If there is anyone who renounces externals and attends instead to their character, cultivating and perfecting it so that it agrees with nature, making it honest and trustworthy, elevated, free, unchecked and undeterred; [19] and if they've learned that whoever desires or avoids things outside their control cannot be free or faithful, but has to shift and fluctuate right along with them, subject to anyone with the power to furnish or deprive them of these externals; [20] and if from the moment they get up in the morning they adhere to their ideals, eating and bathing like a person of integrity, putting their principles into practice in every situation they face – the way a runner does when he applies the principles of running, or a singer those of musicianship [21] – that is where you will see true progress embodied, and find someone who has not wasted their time making the journey here from home.

[22] But anyone whose sole passion is reading books, and who does little else besides, having moved here for this – my advice for them is to go back home immediately and attend to business there, [23] because they left home for nothing. A student should practise how to expunge from his life sighs and sorrow, grief and disappointment, exclamations like 'poor me' and 'alas'; [24] he should learn what death is, as well as exile, jail and hemlock, so at the end of the day he can say, like Socrates in prison, 'Dear Crito, if it pleases the gods, so be it,'[5] – instead of, 'Poor me, an old man – is this what old age held in store for me?' [25] Don't imagine that I am referring to anyone humble or obscure, either; Priam says it, so does Oedipus. In fact, all the kings of legend can be found saying it. [26] For what else are tragedies but the ordeals of people who have come to value externals, tricked out in tragic verse?

[27] If I had to be deceived into believing that externals, which lie outside our power, are not man's proper concern, personally I would consent to such a deception, provided it really could enable me to live an untroubled life, in peace of mind. Which condition you prefer you can determine for yourself.

[28] What does Chrysippus give us? 'To make certain,' he

says, 'that these doctrines promising freedom from passion and serenity are legitimate, [29] take all my books,* and you will find that the knowledge that makes me impassive is faithful to, and in accord with, nature.' How lucky we are! A benefactor – and how great a benefactor! – has shown us the way.[6] [30] Men have erected altars to Triptolemus[7] for giving us the art of farming; [31] but the man who found, disclosed and explained the truth to everyone – not the truth that pertains just to living, but to living well – who among you ever raised an altar, built a temple, erected a statue or venerated God for that? [32] We offer the gods sacrifice because they gave us wheat and wine. But they have produced such wonderful fruit in a human mind, as part of their plan to bestow on humanity the true secret of happiness. Are we going to forget to express our gratitude to them on that account?

I 5 *Against the Sceptics*[8]

[1] If a man objects to truths that are all too evident, it is no easy task finding arguments that will change his mind. [2] This is proof neither of his own strength nor of his teacher's weakness. When someone caught in an argument hardens to stone, there is just no more reasoning with them.

[3] Now, a person can suffer two kinds of petrifaction,[9] that of the intellect, and that of the sense of honour, when somebody assumes a defiant stance, resolved neither to assent to self-evident truths nor leave off fighting. [4] Most of us dread the deadening of the body and will do anything to avoid it. About the deadening of the soul, however, we don't care one iota. [5] Even in the case of the soul, we regard a man as pitiable if he is deficient in thinking or learning. We pity the mentally retarded, and students with learning difficulties. But if somebody's

---

* The translation depends on the emended text printed in von Arnim's *Stoicorum Veterum Fragmenta* III 144: ἀπάθεια, ἅπαντα λάβε μου τὰ βιβλία.

sense of shame and respect are dead, we will actually call this determination.

[6] 'Do you realize that you are awake?'

'No, any more than when I dream and have the impression that I am awake.'

'And is the one impression in no way different from the other?'

'No.'

[7] Can I go on reasoning with such a person? What fire or iron can be applied to him, to make him conscious of his condition? He senses it, but pretends he doesn't; that makes him even worse off than a corpse.

[8] One person does not notice a contradiction in his reasoning; he is unfortunate. Another person notices it, all right, but does not budge and does not back down; he is even more unfortunate. [9] His sense of honour and truthfulness has been excised, and his reason – not excised, but brutalized. Am I to call this strength of character? I can't – any more than I can apply the same name to the 'strength' of degenerates that enables them to say and do in public whatever they please.

I 6 *On providence*

[1] It is easy to praise providence for everything that happens in the world provided you have both the ability to see individual events in the context of the whole and a sense of gratitude. [2] Without these, either you will not see the usefulness of what happens or, even supposing that you do see it, you will not be grateful for it.

[3] If God had created colours, but not the faculty of vision, colours would have been of little use. [4] Or if God had created vision, but not made sure that objects could be seen, vision would have been worthless. [5] And even if he had made them both, but not created light – [6] then neither would have been of any value.

So who contrived this universal accommodation of things to

one another? Who fitted the sword to the scabbard and the scabbard to the sword? No one? [7] In the case of artifacts, it is just this kind of symmetry and structure that regularly persuade us that they must be the work of some artisan, instead of objects created at random. [8] Do sword and scabbard testify to their creator, whereas visible things, vision and light, together, do not? [9] What about the desire of the male for sex with the female, and their ability to use the organs constructed for that purpose – don't they proclaim their creator, too?

[10] All right, then: What about the complex organization of the mind – built so that, when we meet* with sensible objects, we don't just have their forms impressed upon us, we make a selection from among them; and add and subtract impressions to form various kinds of mental combinations; and from certain ideas make inferences to others somehow related[10] – aren't such abilities able to make a big enough impression so that it becomes impossible for us to discount the possibility of a creator? [11] If not, it's left to us to explain who made them, and how such amazing and craftsmanlike abilities came into being by accident, on their own.[11]

[12] Are humans alone in possession of such skills? It's true that there are many skills distinctive to humans, skills that as a rational animal he uniquely needs. But the irrational animals share with man many of the same faculties. [13] Do they also understand what happens? No – because use is one thing, understanding another. God needed animals that use impressions, like us; he had special need of us, though, because we understand their use.[12]

[14] And so for the beasts it is enough to eat, drink, sleep, breed and do whatever else it is that satisfies members of their kind. But for us who have been given the faculty of understanding, [15] this is not enough. Unless we act appropriately, methodically, and in line with our nature and constitution, we will fall short of our proper purpose. [16] Creatures whose constitutions are different have different ends and functions

* The translation assumes the alteration of ἐπιπίπτοντες to ὑποπίπτοντες by comparing Sextus Empiricus *Against the Mathematicians* VIII.60.

accordingly. [17] So, for creatures whose constitution is exclusively designed for use, use on its own suffices; but where the capacity to understand that use is added, the creature will only reach its end by bringing that capacity into play. [18] God created some beasts to be eaten, some to be used in farming, some to supply us with cheese, and so on. To fulfil such functions, they don't need to comprehend impressions or make distinctions among them. [19] Man was brought into the world, however, to look upon God and his works – and not just look, but appreciate. [20] And so it is inexcusable for man to begin and end where the beasts do. He should begin where they do, but only end where nature left off dealing with him; [21] which is to say, in contemplation and understanding, and a manner of life otherwise adapted to his nature. [22] Come to look upon and appreciate God's works at least once before you die.

[23] You eagerly travel to Olympia to see the work of Phidias, and all of you account it a shame to die never having seen the sight.[13] [24] But when there is no need even to travel, when you are already there* because Zeus is present everywhere in his works, don't you want to look at and try to understand them? [25] Will you never come to a realization of who you are, what you have been born for and the purpose for which the gift of vision was made in our case?

[26] 'But difficult and disagreeable things happen in life.' Well, aren't difficulties found at Olympia? Don't you get hot? And crowded? Isn't bathing a problem? Don't you get soaked through in your seats when it rains? Don't you finally get sick of the noise, the shouting and the other irritations? [27] I can only suppose that you weigh all those negatives against the worth of the show, and choose, in the end, to be patient and put up with it all. [28] Furthermore, you have inner strengths that enable you to bear up with difficulties of every kind. You have been given fortitude, courage and patience. [29] Why should I worry about what happens if I am armed with the virtue of fortitude? Nothing can trouble or upset me, or even seem annoying. Instead of meeting misfortune with groans and

---

* Reading ἔστε for ἔστιν.

tears, I will call upon the faculty especially provided to deal with it.

[30] 'But my nose is running!' What do you have hands for, idiot, if not to wipe it? [31] 'But how is it right that there be running noses in the first place?' [32] Instead of thinking up protests, wouldn't it be easier just to wipe your nose?

What would have become of Hercules, do you think, if there had been no lion, hydra, stag or boar – and no savage criminals to rid the world of? [33] What would he have done in the absence of such challenges? Obviously he would have just rolled over in bed and gone back to sleep. So by snoring his life away in luxury and comfort he never would have developed into the mighty Hercules. And even if he had, what good would it have done him? [34] What would have been the use of those arms, that physique, and that noble soul, without crises or conditions to stir him into action?

[35] 'In that case, perhaps he should have created them himself, by searching for a lion to bring into his land, and a boar and a hydra.' [36] That would have been the act of a fool and a fanatic. Still, by showing up and being discovered, they proved useful as tests of Hercules' manhood.

[37] Now that you know all this, come and appreciate the resources you have, and when that is done, say, 'Bring on whatever difficulties you like, Zeus; I have resources and a constitution that you gave me by means of which I can do myself credit whatever happens.'

[38] But no. There you sit, worrying that certain events might happen, already upset and in a state about your present circumstances. So then you reproach the gods. [39] What else can come of such weakness except impiety? [40] And yet God has not merely given us strength to tolerate troubles without being humiliated or undone, but, as befitted a king and true father, he has given them to us free from constraint, compulsion and impediment. He has put the whole matter in our control, not even reserving to himself any power to hinder us or stand in our way. [41] And even though you have these powers free and entirely your own, you don't use them, because you still don't realize what you have or where it came from. [42] Instead

you sit crying and complaining – some of you blind to your
benefactor, and unable to acknowledge his existence; others
assailing God with complaints and accusations from sheer
meanness of spirit.

[43] I am prepared to show you that you have resources and
a character naturally strong and resilient; show me in return
what grounds you have for being peevish and malcontent.

I 7 On the utility of changing arguments, hypothetical arguments and the rest

[1] Most people do not realize that practice in changing arguments, hypothetical arguments, arguments that conclude with
a question and so forth, has a bearing on morals. [2] For we
are interested in how the good man will act and acquit himself
in any situation. [3] So let someone say that the virtuous man
will spurn question and answer, or that, if he does engage in it,
will be indifferent as to whether he behaves carelessly or at
random. [4] And* if we accept neither alternative, then we have
to concede that some study must be made of the areas with
which questioning and answering are especially concerned.

[5] For what does reason purport to do?

'Establish what is true, eliminate what is false and suspend
judgement in doubtful cases.'

[6] And is that all one has to learn?

'Yes.'

Well, is it enough if you don't want to be conned in the use
of money, just to be told to accept real coins and reject counterfeit ones?

[7] 'No, it is not enough.'

What else is necessary?

'Obviously the art of testing and distinguishing genuine coins
from fake ones.'

[8] And so too in the case of reason, in addition to what we

* The translation assumes the change of μὴ to ἤ.

named, we also have to learn how to test and distinguish what
is true, false and unclear.

'Necessarily.'

[9] What else does reason prescribe?

'To accept the consequence of what has been admitted to be
correct.'

[10] And is this all you need to know?

'No, you also need to learn the rules of consequence, and how
a conclusion sometimes follows from one premise, sometimes
from several premises in combination.'

[11] Then surely this too must be acquired by the man intent
on acquitting himself intelligently in logical matters – both
when he offers his own proofs and demonstrations and when
he is following the demonstrations of others, so that he isn't
fooled when they produce sophisms as if the proofs were really
sound. [12] And so there has developed among us study and
training in conclusive arguments and logical figures – both of
which have proven indispensable.

[13] Now, there are cases where we have rightly granted the
premises, and yet they yield a conclusion which, though false,
nevertheless logically follows from the premises. [14] What am
I to do then? Accept the false conclusion? [15] How can I?
Say I erred in granting the premises? That has been ruled out
too. Say it did not follow from the premises? But this is not an
option either.

[16] So what should I do in such cases? Well, just as it is not
enough to have borrowed money to establish that you're still
in debt, you still must stand by the loan and not have repaid it
already; so in this case it is not enough to have granted the
premises to establish that we must admit the conclusion: we
must still be committed to the same premises. [17] Now, if the
premises remain what they were when we granted them, then
we are under every obligation to stand by what was granted
and accept what follows. [18] But if they do not remain as they
were, we don't have to accept it,* [19] because the conclusion

---

* §18 is added to the text *exempli gratia* to eke out the argument and emend
an evident lacuna.

no longer holds for us. Nor is it fitting that we accept it, since we have retracted our admission of the premises.[14]

[20] That's why we need to study premises of this kind, and in particular ones that involve changes and alterations such that, in the very process of questioning, answering, drawing conclusions and so forth, they undergo changes and cause the untutored to become confused when confronted with the conclusions. Why? [21] To avoid acting in these matters in a confused, awkward or inappropriate way.

[22] It is no different with hypotheses and hypothetical arguments. It is sometimes necessary to posit an hypothesis as a basis for the succeeding argument. [23] Then should we grant every hypothesis that is proposed, or not? And if not every one, then which? [24] And once we have admitted an hypothesis, should we abide by the admission come what may, or should we sometimes repudiate it? Should we accept what is consistent with it and reject what is in conflict?

'Yes.'

[25] But someone says, 'I will make you accept the hypothesis of something possible and lead you on to something impossible.'[15] Will the wise man refuse to engage with such a person, and avoid all dialogue and examination? [26] But of all people he is supposed to be most adept in argument, expert in question and answer, and proof against sophisms and deceit. [27] Or will he engage with him but without caring whether he argues in a confused or careless manner? In that case how then will he be the sort of man we imagine him to be? [28] But in default of such training and preparation how can he follow the progress of an argument? [29] If someone can show us that he can, then all our logical exercises were a waste of time; they were otiose all along, not entailed by our preconception of a philosopher.

[30] Why are we still lazy, indifferent and dull? Why do we look for excuses to avoid training and exercising our powers of reason? [31] 'Look, if I err in such matters I haven't killed my father, have I?' No, fool – for there was no father there for you to kill! What did you do instead? You made the only mistake you had the opportunity to make.

[32] You know, I once said the same thing to Musonius when he reproached me for not discovering the omission in a certain syllogism. I said, 'It's not like I burned down the Capitol.' And he said, 'Idiot, the omission here *is* the Capitol.' [33] I mean, are these the only crimes, killing your father and burning down the Capitol? But to use one's impressions recklessly, carelessly and at random, to fail to analyse an argument as either valid proof or fallacy, and, in a word, to fail to see in the act of question and answer what agrees with your position and what conflicts – is nothing wrong in all of that?

I 8 *That talents are treacherous for the uneducated*

[1] It is possible to vary the forms of rhetorical proofs and enthymemes in as many ways as it is possible to vary terms that are equivalent to each other. [2] Take, for example, the following argument: 'If you borrowed money from me and did not repay it, you owe me the money.' This is equivalent to: 'It is not the case that you borrowed and did not repay and do not owe me the money.' [3] And no one is better equipped to argue skilfully than the philosopher. Because if the enthymeme is an incomplete syllogism, someone trained in the complete syllogism will *a fortiori* be no less proficient handling the incomplete syllogism.

[4] 'So why aren't we training ourselves and each other in this sort of argumentation?'

[5] Because at the moment, even though we aren't being trained in these topics – aren't, in fact, being distracted at all, so far as *I* have any say in the matter, from the business of improving our character – we still aren't making progress toward the goal of virtue. [6] So what can we expect if we take on this additional project, especially since it won't just distract us from weightier matters, but will be no small cause of pride and egotism? [7] Proof and persuasion are great talents, when they are trained, and especially when they're complemented by a certain amount of verbal elegance. [8] In general every talent

when it gets into the hands of the morally weak comes with the risk of making them conceited and full of themselves. [9] I mean, what's to stop a promising young student from becoming a slave to – rather than a master of – these topics? [10] Won't he brush these cautions aside and parade his learning in front of us, proud, elated and deaf to anyone who would forcefully remind him of the studies he has given up, and the areas where he stills falls short?

[11] 'But wasn't Plato a philosopher?'[16]

Yes, and Hippocrates was a physician.

'And look at how well Hippocrates expresses himself.'

[12] Yes, but is it in his capacity as a physician that Hippocrates expresses himself so well? Don't confuse qualities that are found in the same writer only incidentally. [13] If Plato had been strong and handsome, should I also try to become strong and handsome, as if this were essential to philosophy, since there was one particular philosopher who combined philosophy with good looks? [14] Can't you tell the difference between what makes people philosophers and the qualities that are only found in them by chance?

I mean, if I were a philosopher, would you be required to become lame as well?[17]

So am I slighting these talents? [15] Not at all – any more than I would disparage the gift of sight. [16] But ask me what the real good in man's case is, and I can only say that it is the right kind of moral character.

I 9 *What are the consequences for us of being related to God?*

[1] If what philosophers say about the kinship of God and man is true, then the only logical step is to do as Socrates did, never replying to the question of where he was from with, 'I am Athenian,' or 'I am from Corinth,' but always, 'I am a citizen of the world.' [2] After all, why say, 'I am Athenian'? Why not just identify yourself with the exact spot your sorry body was

dropped at birth? [3] Clearly, you prefer the higher designation because it not only includes that insignificant spot, it also includes your parents and all your ancestors before you; and it's on these grounds that you characterize yourself as Athenian or Corinthian.

[4] But anyone who knows how the whole universe is administered knows that the first, all-inclusive state is the government composed of God and man. He appreciates it as the source of the seeds of being, descending upon his father, his father's father – to every creature born and bred on earth, in fact, but to rational beings in particular, [5] since they alone are entitled by nature to govern alongside God, by virtue of being connected with him through reason. [6] So why not call ourselves citizens of the world and children of God? And why should we fear any human contingency? [7] If being related to the emperor or any of the other great ones at Rome is enough to live without fear, in privilege and security, shouldn't having God as our creator, father and defender protect us even more from trouble and anxiety?

[8] 'But how am I supposed to eat, if I am destitute?' someone says.

Well, what about slaves, what about runaways – what do they depend on when they flee their masters? On their lands, their servants and their silver plate? Hardly; they rely on themselves, and still manage to survive. [9] So is our philosopher citizen-of-the-world going to rest his confidence in others wherever he lives or travels, rather than depend on himself? Is he going to be even lower and more servile than irrational wild beasts, all of whom are self-sufficient, provided with food and a mode of survival adapted to and in harmony with their nature?

[10] Personally I think that, as I am older than you, I shouldn't have to sit here trying my best to keep you from thinking small, or having mean and humble thoughts about you. [11] On the contrary, if there are young men among you who know of their kinship with the gods, and know that we have these chains fastened upon us – the body, possessions and whatever is required for our biological support and sustenance

– I should be discouraging them from the wish to shed all these
things as so many chains and return to their kind.

[12] That's the effort that should absorb your teacher and
mentor, if he really were one. And you for your part would
come to him saying, 'Epictetus, we can no longer stand being
tied to this hateful body, giving it food and drink, resting it
and cleaning it, and having to associate with all manner of
uncongenial people for its sake. [13] Such things are indifferent,
are they not, and as nothing to us; and death no evil thing?
Aren't we akin to God, having come from him? [14] Let us go
home, then, to be free, finally, from the shackles that restrain
us and weigh us down. [15] Here we find robbers and thieves,
and law-courts, and so-called despots who imagine that they
wield some power over us precisely because of our body and
its possessions. Allow us to show them that they have power
over precisely no one.'

[16] Then it would be my turn to say, 'Friends, wait upon
God. Whenever he gives the sign and releases you from service,
then you are free to return. But for now agree to remain in the
place where you've been stationed. [17] Your time here is short
enough, and easy to endure for people of your convictions. No
despot, thief or court of law can intimidate people who set little
store by the body and its appurtenances. So stay, don't depart
without good reason.'

[18] That is the kind of advice that should pass between a
teacher and an idealistic youth. [19] But what's the reality? You
– and your teacher – are no better than carcasses. No sooner
have you eaten your fill today than you sit and start worrying
about where tomorrow's food will come from. [20] Look, if
you get it, then you will have it; if not, you will depart this life:
the door is open. Why complain? What place is there left for
tears? What occasion for flattery? Why should one man envy
another? Why should he admire those who have many possessions, or those who are strong in power and quick to anger?
[21] What can they do to us, or for us, after all? The things
they have power to do are of no interest to us; and as for the
things we do care about, these they are powerless to affect. No

one with convictions of this kind can be made to act against their will.

[22] So how did Socrates stand in this regard? Exactly how one would expect of someone who perceived keenly his kinship with the gods. [23] 'If you were to say to me now, "We will release you on these conditions, that you no longer engage in these dialogues that you have been engaging in up to now, and won't give any more trouble to anyone young or old," [24] I will answer that it is absurd to suppose that, if a general of yours stationed me at a post, I would have to maintain and defend it, choosing to die a thousand times rather than quit, but if God has assigned us a post with a set of duties, we might decide to abandon *that*.'

[25] There you have a man who was a genuine kinsman of the gods. [26] But we, on the other hand, identify with our stomachs, guts and genitals. Because we are still vulnerable to fear and desire, we flatter and creep before anyone with the power to hurt us where any of those things are concerned.

[27] A man once asked me to write to Rome for him because he had met with what most people consider misfortune. He had once been rich and famous but later lost everything, and was living here in Nicopolis. So I wrote a letter on his behalf in a deferential tone.

[28] When he had read the letter he handed it back to me, saying, 'I wanted your help, not your pity; nothing really bad has happened to me.'

[29] Similarly, Musonius used to test me by saying, 'Your master is going to afflict you with some hardship or other.' [30] And when I would answer, 'Such is life,' he would say, 'Should I still intercede with him when I can get the same things from you?' [31] For in fact it is silly and pointless to try to get from another person what one can get for oneself. [32] Since I can get greatness of soul and nobility from myself, why should I look to get a farm, or money, or some office, from you? I will not be so insensible of what I already own.

[33] For men who are meek and cowardly, though, there is no option but to write letters for them as if they were already

dead. 'Please grant us the body of so-and-so together with his meagre ration of blood.' [34] For, really, such a person amounts to no more than a carcass and a little blood. If he were anything more, he would realize that no one is ever unhappy because of someone else.

I 10 *To those who have applied themselves to advancement at Rome*

[1] If we philosophers had applied ourselves to our job as seriously as those old men in Rome pursue their interests, we, too, might be getting somewhere. [2] I have a friend even older than I who is now in charge of the grain supply in Rome. When he passed through here on his return from exile, what things he said in disparagement of his former life, swearing when he returned that from then on he would devote himself exclusively to a life of peace and tranquillity. 'How much time have I got left, after all?'

[3] And I said to him, 'I don't believe you. As soon as you get a whiff of Rome you will forget everything you've said' – and I added that if the least access to court became available to him, he would rush in, singing hymns of praise to the Almighty. [4] 'Listen, Epictetus,' he said, 'if you find me even putting a foot inside the court, feel free to think as little of me as you like.' [5] So what did he do? Before he even reached the limits of the capital he received letters from Caesar, immediately forgot all he'd said, and doesn't seem to have given it a thought since. [6] I'd like to be there with him now to repeat to him the words he said when passing through here, and add, 'How much more shrewd a prophet I proved than you!'

[7] Well, am I implying that man is an animal unfit for action? Not at all. So why aren't we more active? [8] I mean, look at me. When day begins, I remind myself of the author we are supposed to be reading; but then I think to myself, 'Who cares how this or that student reads the author; first let me get my sleep!'

[9] And yet how can their business compare in importance to ours? If you could see them at Rome, you would find that they do nothing all day but vote on a resolution, then huddle together a while to deliberate about grain, land or some other means to make a living. [10] Is it the same thing to receive a petition that reads, 'Please allow me to export a bit of grain,' and 'Please learn from Chrysippus how the universe is governed, and what place the rational creature has in it; find out, too, who you are, and what constitutes your good and your evil'? [11] Is one to be compared with the other? Do they deserve the same degree of application? [12] Is it equally wrong to neglect this one as that?

Well, am I and the other teachers the only ones who are lazy and indifferent? [13] You young people are even worse. Old men like us, you know, when we see children at play, like nothing better than to join them in their game. Likewise, I would be a lot more excited about joining you in serious study if I were once to see you bright-eyed and enthusiastic.

I 11 *Concerning family affection*

[1] During a visit from a magistrate Epictetus, in the course of conversing, asked the man whether he had a wife and children. [2] He replied that he did. Epictetus then asked, 'And how do you like it?'

'I'm miserable,' he said.

So Epictetus asked, 'How so? [3] Men don't marry and have children in order to be miserable, but to be happy.'

[4] 'I'm so anxious about my poor children,' the man said, 'that the other day, when my little daughter was sick and appeared in danger of her life, I could not bear even to remain with her. I had to leave her side and go off until word was brought me that her condition had improved.'

'Well,' said Epictetus, 'do you think you acted correctly in this case?'

[5] 'I acted naturally,' he answered.

'If you can convince me that you acted naturally, I am ready on my side to show that anything done in accord with nature is done correctly.'

[6] 'It's what nearly all we fathers go through.'

'I don't dispute that reactions like yours occur,' Epictetus said. 'The point at issue between us is whether they ought to. [7] For by your reasoning we must allow that tumours happen for the good of the body, because they happen, and that doing wrong is in accord with nature, because all, or at least most of us, do wrong. [8] So show me how, exactly, you acted in accordance with nature.'

'I don't think I can,' the man said. 'Why don't you show me instead how it is *not* in accordance with nature, and shouldn't happen?'

So Epictetus said, [9] 'Well, if we were in any uncertainty about white and black things, what criterion would we adduce to choose between them?'

'Sight,' the man said.

'And what about things hot and cold, or hard and soft – what would decide in those cases?'

'Touch.'

[10] 'Now, since we have a difference of opinion about what is in agreement with nature and what is right and wrong, what standard should we apply here, do you think?'

'I don't know,' the man said.

[11] 'Well, ignorance in discriminating between colours, smells or flavours probably does no great harm. But not to know about right and wrong, about what is natural in man's case and what is not – is that a minor shortcoming, do you think?'

'No, a very great one, I admit.'

[12] 'Consider now – is everything that people judge to be good and appropriate rightly judged so? Can Jews, Syrians, Egyptians and Romans all be right in the opinions they have about food, for example?'[18]

'How could they?'

[13] 'Instead, if the opinions of the Egyptians are right, I suppose that the others are wrong. Or if the Jews are right, then the others can't be.'

'No, they cannot.'

[14] 'And where there is ignorance, there is also want of learning and instruction in essentials.'

The man agreed.

[15] 'Once you've realized this, you will occupy your mind and devote all your attention toward finding that standard that discriminates between what is natural and what is not; and then apply it to particular cases as they arise.

[16] 'For the present, I can only offer the following by way of assistance toward solving our problem. [17] Tell me, then, do you think family affection is good and agrees with nature's norms?'

'I do.'

'Can family affection be good and natural,* while what agrees with reason is not good?'

'Of course not.'

[18] 'So whatever is rational will not be in conflict with family affection.'

'I suppose not.'

'Because, if they were, one would be in agreement with nature while the other would have to conflict.'

'Correct.'

[19] 'So if there's anything out there that's both affectionate and rational, this we can safely say is also both right and good.'

'Agreed.'

[20] 'Now, to leave your child's side when she is sick, and go away, is not a rational act, and I don't suppose that even you will argue otherwise. But we still have to consider whether it is consistent with family affection.'

'Then let's do so.'

[21] 'Was it right for you, being affectionately disposed toward your child, to go off and leave her? Let's take her mother instead. Doesn't she feel affection for her daughter?'

[22] 'Of course she does.'

'Then should she, too, have left her?'

---

* The translation assumes that the phrase 'good and natural' is repeated, which the argument seems to require.

'No.'

'And the nurse – does she have affectionate feelings toward the girl?'

'She does.'

'So should she, also, have left her?'

'Certainly not.'

'And her personal slave and teacher, doesn't he have feelings for her?'

'Yes.'

[23] 'I suppose that means that he, too, should have gone off and left her – the result being that, owing to this very great affection on the part of parents as well as guardians, the girl would have been completely forsaken by those who love and protect her, to die in the company of people who had no part in bringing her up, and therefore no special feelings for her.'

'I can hardly suppose so.'

[24] 'In fact, it is unfair and illogical to say that people whose affection is the equal of yours should not be permitted to do what you claim was justified in your case owing to this very great affection you profess.'

'True enough.'

[25] 'I mean, if you were sick, would you want your family, your wife, children and the rest, to be so caring as to walk away from you and leave you to yourself?'

'No.'

[26] 'And would you want to be so loved by them that, because of their love, you would always suffer sickness in isolation? Isn't that more like the affection you pray your enemies would show you, that they should go away and leave you be? And if so, the inescapable conclusion is that what you did was no act of affection at all.

[27] 'Well, it had to have been something that affected you so much that you walked out on your child. It might be related to the impulse that made a man at Rome cover his head while his favourite horse was running, and who later required sponges to be revived when his horse unexpectedly won. [28] The precise explanation for such behaviour might be out of place here. For now, assuming that philosophy contains at least a grain of

truth, it's enough to be convinced that you will not find it by looking for any cause outside yourself. The same thing is always the reason for our doing or not doing something, for saying or not saying something, for being elated or depressed, for going after something or avoiding it. [29] It's the same reason that you're here now listening to me, and I'm saying the things that I'm now saying – [30] our opinion that all these things are right.'

'Of course.'

'If we saw things differently we would act differently, in line with our different idea of what is right and wrong. [31] This, then, was the cause of Achilles' lamentations – not the fact that Patroclus died, since other people don't carry on so when a friend or companion dies – but the fact that he *chose* to lament. [32] The same cause lies behind your desertion of your daughter – you thought it was a good idea at the time. Conversely, if you stay with her, it would be for the same reason. Now you are about to return to Rome; that is your decision – but if it changes, you won't go. [33] In other words, it isn't death, pain, exile or anything else you care to mention that accounts for the way we act, only our opinion about death, pain and the rest.

[34] 'Well, have I convinced you of this, or not?'

'You have,' the man said.

'As the cause is, so is the result. [35] Whenever we do something wrong, then, from now on we will not blame anything except the opinion on which it's based; and we will try to root out wrong opinions with more determination than we remove tumours or infections from the body. [36] By the same token, we will acknowledge opinion as the source of our good behaviour too. [37] But wife, child, slave or neighbour – in the future we won't name any of them as authors of the evil in our lives, in the knowledge that, unless we judge things in a particular light, we won't act in the corresponding manner. And we, not externals, are the masters of our judgements.'

'Agreed.'

[38] 'So, starting today, we won't trouble to assess or analyse land, slaves, horses or dogs as to their quality or condition – only our opinions.'

'Well, I hope so,' the man said.

[39] 'You see, you are going to have to become a student again – that universal figure of fun – if you really mean to subject your opinions to honest examination. And you know as well as I do that this assignment can't be completed overnight.'

I 12 *On satisfaction*

[1] On the subject of the gods, there are those who deny the existence of divinity outright. Others say that God exists, but is idle and indifferent and does not pay attention to anything. [2] A third group says that God exists and is attentive, but only to the workings of the heavens, never affairs on earth. A fourth group says that he does attend to earthly affairs, including the welfare of humanity, but only in a general way, without worrying about individuals. [3] And then there is a fifth group, Odysseus and Socrates among them, who say that 'I cannot make a move without God's notice.'[19]

[4] Before doing anything else we need to examine these views separately to decide which are true and false. [5] Because if the gods do not exist, what sense can be made of the command to 'follow the gods'?[20] And how can it be a sensible goal if they exist, but do not have any cares? [6] Even supposing that they exist and care, if that care does not extend to people, and, in point of fact, to me personally, it is still no worthwhile goal.

[7] The intelligent person, after due consideration of the question, will decide to submit his will to the ruler of the universe, as good citizens submit to the laws of the state.

[8] Education should be approached with this goal in mind: 'How can I personally follow the gods always, and how can I adapt to God's government, and so be free?' [9] Freedom, you see, is having events go in accordance with our will, never contrary to it.

[10] Well – is freedom the same as madness? Of course not. Madness and freedom are poles apart. [11] 'But I want my wishes realized, never mind the reason behind them.' [12] Now,

that's madness, that's insanity. Freedom is something good and valuable; to arbitrarily wish for things to happen that arbitrarily seem to you best* is not good, it's disgraceful.

How do we approach the practice of writing? [13] Do I want to write the name 'Dion' whatever way I please? No, I learn to want to write it the way it is supposed to be written. The case is the same with music, [14] the same with every art and science; it would not be worth the trouble to learn them, otherwise, if they accommodated everyone's wishes. [15] And freedom, the greatest possession of all, is the last thing you would expect to be different, where wishes are given carte blanche. Getting an education means learning to bring our will in line with the way things happen – which is to say, as the ruler of the universe arranged. [16] He arranged for there to be summer and winter, abundance and lack, virtue and vice – all such opposites meant for the harmony of the whole; and he gave us each a body and bodily parts, material belongings, family and friends.[21]

[17] It is with this arrangement in mind that we should approach instruction, not to alter the facts – since this is neither allowed, nor is it better that it should be – but in order to learn the nature of what concerns us, and keep our will in line with events. [18] Can we avoid people? How is that possible? And if we associate with them, can we change them? Who gives us that power? [19] What is the alternative – what means can be found for dealing with them? One that ensures that we remain true to our nature, however other people see fit to behave. [20] That's not what you do, though. No, you gripe and protest against circumstance. If you're alone, you call it desolation, if you're in company you describe them all as swindlers and backstabbers; you curse your own parents, your children, your siblings and neighbours. [21] When you are by yourself you should call it peace and liberty, and consider yourself the gods' equal. When you're with a large group you shouldn't say you're in a mob or crowd, but a guest at a feast or festival – and in that spirit learn to enjoy it.

What is the downside for those who refuse to accept it? To

* The translation assumes the deletion of δ' after τὰ.

be just as they are. [22] Is someone unhappy being alone? Leave him to his isolation. Is someone unhappy with his parents? Let him be a bad son, and grumble. Is someone unhappy with his children? Let him be a bad father. [23] 'Throw him in jail.' What jail? The one he is in already, since he is there against his will; and if he is there against his will then he is imprisoned. Conversely, Socrates was *not* in prison because he chose to be there.[22]

[24] 'But my leg is crippled.'

Slave, are you going to be at odds with the world because of one lame leg? Shouldn't you rather make the world a gift of it, and gladly return it to the one who gave it to you originally? [25] Are you going to make Zeus your enemy, and set your face against the Fates, with whom Zeus spun the thread of your destiny at the moment you were born, laying out his plans for you?

[26] You ought to realize, you take up very little space in the world as a whole – your body, that is; in reason, however, you yield to no one, not even to the gods, because reason is not measured in size but sense. [27] So why not care for that side of you, where you and the gods are equals?

[28] 'It's my bad luck to have awful parents.'

Well, you couldn't very well choose them beforehand, saying, 'Let this man have intercourse with this woman, at this particular, so that I can be conceived.' [29] Your parents had to come first, then you had to be born the way you are, of parents the way *they* are.

[30] Does that mean you have to be miserable? Let's suppose you didn't understand what you had the power of vision for; it would be your bad luck if you decided to close your eyes just at the moment a beautiful painting passed before you. You are even unluckier for being oblivious to the fact that you have the power of patience to deal with your difficulties. [31] You forget the virtues of character you have in reserve, just when problems that they can control present themselves, and you could use their help.

[32] You should thank the gods for making you strong enough to survive what you cannot control, and only respon-

sible for what you can. [33] The gods have released you from
accountability for your parents, your siblings, your body, your
possessions – for death and for life itself. [34] They made you
responsible only for what is in your power – the proper use of
impressions. [35] So why take on the burden of matters which
you cannot answer for? You are only making unnecessary
problems for yourself.

I 13 *On the treatment of slaves*

[1] When someone asked how it was possible to eat in a manner
pleasing to the gods, Epictetus said, 'If is done justly and equit-
ably, in moderation, with restraint and self-control – isn't that
pleasing to the gods?

[2] 'When you ask for hot water and the slave ignores you;
or if he hears you but brings in water that is barely lukewarm;
or if he is not even to be found in the house – to refrain from
anger and not explode in that situation, won't that find favour
with the gods?'

[3] 'But how are we to bear with such slaves?'

'My friend, it's a matter of bearing with your own brother,
who has Zeus as his ancestor and is a son born of the same
seed as yourself, with the same high lineage.

[4] 'If you have been placed in a position above others, are
you automatically going to behave like a despot? Remember
who you are and whom you govern – that they are kinsmen,
brothers by nature, fellow descendants of Zeus.'

[5] 'But I have a bill of sale for them, while they have none
for me.'

'Don't you see that, instead of the laws of the gods, you only
have regard for the earth, the pit and the contemptible laws of
the dead?'

I 14 *That God supervises everyone*

[1] Someone asked Epictetus how a person could be convinced that everything he did was supervised by God.

'Don't you believe,' he answered, 'that all things are united as one?'

'I do,' the other said.

[2] 'Well, don't you think that there is interaction between things on earth and the things in heaven?'

'Yes.'

[3] 'How else, after all, could things take place with such regularity, as if God were issuing orders? When he tells plants to bloom, they bloom, when he tells them to bear fruit, they bear fruit, when he tells them to ripen, they ripen. Similarly, when he tells them to drop their fruit, shed their leaves, draw in and lie dormant for the winter, all that they do too. [4] How else explain that the waxing and the waning of the moon, and the coming and going of the sun, coincide with such obvious changes and fluctuations here on earth?

[5] 'Well, if plants* and our bodies are so intimately linked to the world and its rhythms, won't the same be true of our minds – only more so? [6] And if our minds are so intimately connected with God as to be divine sparks of his being, is he not going to perceive their every movement, since the parts in motion participate in his nature?

[7] Now you, for your part, are capable of reflecting in detail on God and his government, while also tending to human affairs. You can process in your intellect and senses a wealth of thoughts and impressions simultaneously. There are impressions that you assent to, others that you reject; sometimes you suspend judgement altogether. [8] Your mind can store so many of these impressions and from a wide range of sources too. Under their influence, the mind proceeds to form ideas that correspond with particular impressions. That's how we form

---

* The translation assumes the reading 'plants' (φύτα) transmitted in the text of Stobaeus to 'leaves' (φύλλα) in the MSS.

memories, and how the many varieties of art and science are created.

[9] 'And now God – are we going to deny him the ability to oversee everything that happens, even when we know that he is present everywhere and enjoys a kind of communion with the world?

[10] 'The sun is capable of illuminating a large part of the universe, just leaving unlit the small shadow that the earth casts.[23] Well, here is God, who created the sun (which is minuscule in relation to the whole universe), and who still causes the sun to turn – wouldn't you say he is in a good position to see everything that goes on?'

[11] 'And yet,' someone objects, 'I cannot understand all these things at one and the same time.'

'Is anyone saying that your capacities are the equal of God's? [12] Nevertheless, he has provided each of us with an individual guardian deity, which stays by our side and is in charge of looking after us – a guardian who never sleeps and is impossible to distract. [13] Is there any guardian to whose care he could have committed us that is better or more vigilant? Whenever you close your doors and turn out your lights, remember, never say to yourself that you are alone; [14] you're not. God is inside, and so is your private deity; and neither of them requires light to watch you by.

[15] 'This is the deity who deserves your pledge of allegiance, as soldiers swear before Caesar. If they want to be paid, they must swear to put the emperor's safety first. You, however, who have been chosen to receive an abundance of blessings – and for free – why won't you swear a similar oath, and, if you have done so already, why not reaffirm the commitment?

[16] 'What is that oath? You swear that under no circumstances will you disobey, press charges, or find fault with God and his gifts. You won't shrink from life's essential tasks or trials. [17] Can anyone seriously compare the soldier's oath with ours? They swear to honour no one more than Caesar; we swear to honour no one more than ourselves.'

I 15 *What philosophy professes*

[1] Someone asked Epictetus' advice on how to get his brother to stop being on bad terms with him. Epictetus said, [2] 'Philosophy does not claim to secure for us anything outside our control. Otherwise it would be taking on* matters that do not concern it. For as wood is the material of the carpenter, and marble that of the sculptor, so the subject matter of the art of life is the life of the self.'

[3] 'Well, what about my brother's life?'

'That, in turn, belongs to his own art of living. With respect to yours, it is one of the externals – no different from land, health or reputation; and philosophy makes no promises concerning those. [4] In every situation I will keep the soul's governing principle in agreement with nature.'

'Whose governing principle?'

'Only the one inside *me*.'

[5] 'How, then, do I stop my brother from being angry with me?'

'Bring him to me and I will speak with him; but about his anger I have nothing to say to *you*.'

[6] The man consulting with Epictetus then asked, 'What I want to know is this, then: how can I stay true to nature even if my brother won't reconcile with me?'

[7] 'Nothing important comes into being overnight; even grapes or figs need time to ripen. If you say that you want a fig now, I will tell you to be patient. First, you must allow the tree to flower, then put forth fruit; then you have to wait until the fruit is ripe. [8] So if the fruit of a fig tree is not brought to maturity instantly or in an hour, how do you expect the human mind to come to fruition, so quickly and easily? Don't expect it, even if I were personally to tell you it was possible.'

* The translation assumes the emendation of ἀνέξεται to ἀναδέξεται.

I 16 *On providence*

[1] Do not be surprised if other animals have their biological necessities provided for them – not just food and drink, but a place to sleep – and have no need of shoes, bedding or clothes, while humans, on the other hand, need all these things. [2] It was not expedient in the case of creatures born to serve others, not themselves, to have made them in any way deficient in these respects. [3] After all, think what it would be like if we had to worry about finding clothes and shoes, or food and drink, for our sheep and asses, in addition to having to provide these essentials for ourselves.

[4] Just as soldiers report to their commander at the ready, clothed, armed, and shod – and it would be too much to expect the commander to have to equip them out of his own time and pocket – so nature has created the animals that are born for service ready for our use and in no need of further attention. [5] The result is that a single small child, armed with no more than a stick, can control an entire flock of sheep.

[6] As it is, though, we neglect to give thanks for not having to bestow on beasts the same care as we do on ourselves, then complain to God concerning our own condition. [7] Yet, I swear, if we had an ounce of gratitude or respect, the least aspect of creation would be enough to get us to admit the existence of providence. [8] And I'm not talking about great things, now; take the mere fact that milk is produced from grass, and that cheese comes from milk, and wool can grow out of skin. Who is it that has created or conceived these things? 'No one,' people say. What ignorance and gall!

[9] Let's leave the chief features of nature aside, and just consider its secondary effects. [10] Is there anything of less utility than a beard? But nature has found a most becoming use even for that, enabling us to discriminate between the man and woman. [11] Nature identifies itself even at a distance: 'I am a man: come and deal with me on these terms. Nothing else is needed; just take note of nature's signs.'

[12] In the case of woman, in addition to mingling a softer

note in her voice, nature has removed the hair from her chin. But you say, 'The creature could have done very well without this distinguishing mark; we could announce of ourselves that we are man or woman.' [13] But you miss the point: look how proud, handsome and becoming the sign is, much more attractive than the cock's comb, prouder even than the lion's mane. [14] That is why we should safeguard the signs that God gave us and by virtue of which the genders were intended to be distinguished.

[15] Are these the only works of providence relevant in our case? Hardly. In fact, there are no words adequate to praise them or do them justice. If we had sense, there is nothing better we could do with our time than praise God and proclaim his good works, whether in public or private. [16] We should praise him even while we're busy digging, ploughing or eating. 'God is great – he has given us these instruments to work the earth. [17] God is great – he has given us hands, a mouth and a stomach, the ability to grow unconsciously, and to breathe while we're asleep.' [18] This is what we ought to sing on every occasion – more especially the greatest and holiest hymn, celebrating the ability he bestowed on us to understand his works, and use them systematically.

[19] Well, since most of you are blind, I suppose there has to be someone who fills this role, and will praise God on others' behalf. [20] And what is a lame old man like myself good for, anyway, except singing God's praises? If I were a nightingale or a swan, I would sing the song either of them was born to sing. But I am a rational being, so my song must take the form of a hymn. [21] That is my job, which I will keep to as long as I am permitted; and I invite any and all of you to join me.

I 17 *Concerning the necessity of logic*

[1] Since reason is what analyses and coordinates everything, it should not go itself unanalysed. Then what will it be analysed by? [2] Obviously by itself or something different. Now, this

something different must either be reason or something superior to reason – which is impossible, since there is nothing superior to reason. [3] But if it is analysed by reason, what, in turn, will analyse *that* reason? Itself? If that's the case, however, the first occurrence of reason could have done the same; whereas if another form of reason is required, the process will continue for ever.

[4] 'Yes, but in any case it is more important that we tend to our passions, and our opinions, and the like.'

So it is lectures about these subjects that you'd rather hear? Fine. [5] But if you say to me, 'I don't know whether your arguments are sound or not,' or if I use a word in an ambiguous sense and you ask me to 'Please distinguish' – well, I'm not going to be in a mood to oblige you, I'm more liable to say, 'It's more important that we tend to our passions and our opinions, and the like.'

[6] Which, I suppose, is why Stoics put logic at the head of our curriculum – for the same reason that, before a quantity of grain can be measured, we must settle on a standard of measurement. [7] If we don't begin by establishing standards of weight and volume, how are we going to measure or weigh anything? [8] And similarly in the present case – if we haven't fully grasped and refined the instrument by which we analyse and understand other things, how can we hope to understand them with any precision?

[9] 'But a measuring bowl is a mere thing of wood, and doesn't put forth fruit.'

It measures grain, however.

[10] 'Matters of logic are unproductive as well.'

Well, we will see about that. But even if you are right, because it analyses and distinguishes them logic functions, in a way, as the weight and measure for abstract matters, and that is reason enough, the experts say, to study it. [11] Who says so? Besides Chrysippus, Zeno and Cleanthes, I mean?[24] [12] How about Antisthenes? It was he who wrote, 'The beginning of education is the examination of terms.' And as we know from Xenophon, Socrates routinely began his talks by analysing terms, in order to forestall any uncertainty as to their meaning.

[13] Is this the ultimate achievement, then – getting to where we can understand and interpret Chrysippus? Nobody is saying that. [14] Well, what is, then? Understanding the will of nature. Yes, but can you understand it alone and unaided? Evidently you could still use help; because if it is true that we always err unwillingly,[25] and if you were already in possession of the truth, it would be reflected in your flawless behaviour.

[15] But *I* don't understand the will of nature. Who will explain it to me? I'm told Chrysippus can. [16] So off I go to find out what this interpreter of nature has to say. But then there's a passage I have trouble with, so I cast about for someone to explain the explanation. 'Here,' I say, 'have a look and tell me what this means' – as if the thing were in Latin.*
[17] What right has the commentator to feel superior? Even Chrysippus has no right to be proud if he only explains the will of nature and does not follow it; how much less entitled to pride is his interpreter!

[18] It's not Chrysippus *per se* we need, but only insofar as he helps us understand nature. We don't need the prophet for his own sake, but *through* him we think we can divine the future and better understand the signs that the gods send. [19] We don't need the victim's entrails for their own sake, only for the sake of the signs they convey. And we don't worship the crow or the raven – we worship God, who communicates by means of them. [20] Now imagine me before a priest or prophet, to whom I say, 'Please examine this victim's entrails; what are they telling me?' [21] After carefully spreading them out, he announces, 'It's written here that you have a will incapable of being coerced or compelled. [22] Start with assent: can anyone prevent you from agreeing with what is true?'

'No.'

'Or force you into believing what is false?'

'No.'

[23] 'Plainly, then, in this area your will cannot be hindered,

---

* The translation assumes that καθάπερ εἰ ʽΡωμαϊστί is not part of the quotation but a remark on it. In Epictetus' milieu it was probably not uncommon for someone to ask another for help in understanding a bit of Latin, whether as part of an inscription, for example, or letter.

forced or obstructed. [24] Let's look at desire and impulse: you see it's just the same. One impulse can only be overruled by another.'

[25] 'What about if someone threatens me with death, though; surely he compels me then?'

'It isn't what you're threatened with – it's the fact that you prefer to do anything rather than die. [26] It's your set of values that compelled you: will acting on will. [27] If God had made it possible for the fragment of his own being that he gave us to be hindered or coerced by anyone – himself included – then he wouldn't be God, and wouldn't be looking after us the way a god ought to. [28] "That," the priest says, "is what I find inscribed in the sacrifice. This is God's signal to you: if you want, you are free; if you want, you will blame no one, you will accuse no one – if you want, everything will happen according to plan, yours as well as God's."

[29] 'That's the kind of prophecy I go to this priest for, and to the philosopher; out of reverence, not for him, but for his powers of interpretation.'

I 18 *Don't be angry with wrongdoers*

[1] Philosophers say that people are all guided by a single standard. When they assent to a thing, it is because they feel it must be true, when they dissent, it is because they feel something isn't true, and when they suspend judgement, it is because they feel that the thing is unclear. [2] Similarly, they say that in the case of impulse people feel that its object must be to their advantage, and that it is impossible to consider any one thing advantageous and desire something different, or consider one thing right and have an impulse to do something else.

If all this is true, then what grounds do we have for being angry with anyone? [3] We use labels like 'thief' and 'robber' in connection with them, but what do these words mean? They merely signify that people are confused about what is good and what is bad. So should we be angry with them, or should we

pity them instead? [4] Show them where they go wrong and
you will find that they'll reform. But unless they see it, they are
stuck with nothing better than their usual opinion as their
practical guide.

[5] 'Well, shouldn't we do away with thieves and degenerates?'

Try putting the question this way: [6] 'Shouldn't we rid
ourselves of people deceived about what's most important,
people who are blind – not in their faculty of vision, their ability
to distinguish white from black – but in the moral capacity to
distinguish good from bad?' [7] Put it that way, and you'll
realize how inhumane your position is. It is as if you were to
say, 'Shouldn't this blind man, and this deaf man, be executed?'
[8] Because if loss of the greatest asset involves the greatest
harm, and someone is deprived of their moral bearings, which
is the most important capacity* they have – well, why add
anger to their loss? [9] If you must be affected by other people's
misfortunes, show them pity instead of contempt. Drop this
readiness to hate and take offence. [10] Who are you to use
those common curses, like 'These damned fools,' etc.? [11] Let
them be. Since when are you so intelligent as to go around
correcting other people's mistakes?† We get angry because we
put too high a premium on things that they can steal. Don't
attach such value to your clothes, and you won't get angry with
the thief who takes them. Don't make your wife's external
beauty her chief attraction, and you won't be angry with the
adulterer. [12] Realize that the thief and the adulterer cannot
touch what's yours, only what is common property everywhere
and not under your control. If you make light of those things
and ignore them, who is left to be angry with? As long as you
honour material things, direct your anger at yourself rather
than the thief or adulterer.

* The translation of §8 assumes Schenkl's supplement to the text: ἡ τῶν
μεγίστων ἀπώλειά ἐστιν μέγιστον δ' ἐν ἑκάστῳ . . .
† The following reading is assumed in the translation of §§10–11 (conjectural
supplements in brackets): μὴ [εἰσενέγκ]ῃς τὰς φωνὰς ταύτας ἃς οἱ πολλοὶ τῶν
φ[ιλοψογούν]των 'τούτους οὖν τοὺς καταράτους καὶ μιαροὺς [μωρούς].'
Ἔστω· σὺ πῶς ποτ' ἀπεσοφώθης ἄφνω [οὕτως ἵν' ἄλλοις] χαλεπὸς εἶ;.

[13] Look at it this way. You have beautiful clothes and your neighbour does not. You have a window and want to give them an airing. The neighbour does not know what man's good consists in, but imagines it means having beautiful clothes – the opinion you happen to share. [14] It's a foregone conclusion that he's going to try and steal them. I mean, when starving people see you gobbling down food all by yourself, you know one of them will make a grab at it. So don't provoke them – don't air your clothes at the window!

[15] Something similar happened to me the other day. I keep an iron lamp by my household shrine. Hearing a noise from my window, I ran down and found the lamp had been lifted. I reasoned that the thief who took it must have felt an impulse he couldn't resist. So I said to myself, 'Tomorrow you'll get a cheaper, less attractive one made of clay.' [16] A man only loses what he has. 'I lost clothes.' Yes, because you had clothes. 'I have a pain in the head.' Well, at least you don't have a pain in the horns, right? Loss and sorrow are only possible with respect to things we own.

[17] 'But the tyrant will chain –' What will he chain? Your leg. 'He will chop off –' What? Your head. What he will never chain or chop off is your integrity. That's the reason behind the ancient advice to 'know yourself'.

[18] We should discipline ourselves in small things, and from there progress to things of greater value. [19] If you have a headache, practise not cursing. Don't curse every time you have an earache. And I'm not saying that you can't complain, only don't complain with your whole being. If your servant is slow to bring you a bandage, don't roll around and yell, 'Everybody hates me!' Who wouldn't hate such a person? [20] Walk upright and free, trusting in the strength of your moral convictions, not the strength of your body, like an athlete. You weren't meant to be invincible by brute force, like a pack animal. [21] You are invincible if nothing outside the will can disconcert you.

So I run through every scenario and consider them as an athlete might: 'He lasted the first round; how will he do in the second? [22] What if it's hot? What if it's the Olympics?' Similarly: 'If you entice him with money, he will turn up his nose. But what if it's a pretty girl – whom he meets in the dark? What if you tempt him with fame? Or test him with censure – or applause? Or death?' All these he can handle. [23] But what if it's really sweltering – that is, what if he's drunk? Or delirious? Or dreaming?[26] If he can come through safely under all these conditions – well, that's the invincible 'athlete' so far as I am concerned.

I 19 *How we should act towards the powerful*

[1] A person who enjoys some advantage, or just believes they do, will invariably grow to be arrogant, especially if they are uneducated. [2] The tyrant, for example, will say to you, 'My power is supreme.'

'Will you do something for me then? I want uncurbed desire. Do you even have it to give? I want my aversion error-free. Do you have that? How about a faculty of impulse that is faultless? [3] No, you have no connection to that. Look, you entrust yourself to the pilot's expertise when on board ship, and to the superior skill of the driver when you are in a carriage. [4] It's no different with other skills. So what does *your* advantage amount to?'

'Everybody gives me their attention and respect.'

'Right, and I pay attention to my blackboard, wiping it, and washing it; and for my oil flask I'll even drive a nail in the wall. Does that make these things better than me? No – it just means that they are useful to me somehow. I look after my horse too, [5] I wash its feet and brush its coat. The fact is, everyone looks after themselves; if they curry favour with you it's as if they're currying their horse. Who is there who respects you as a human being? [6] Who wants to be like you, to emulate you the way people emulated Socrates?'

'But I can cut off your head.'

'Good point; I had forgotten that I should look out for you as I would look out for some virus or infection, and erect an altar to you on the model of the Altar of Fever at Rome.[27]

[7] 'What frightens most people and keeps them subdued? It can't be the tyrant and his bodyguards; what nature has made free can only be disturbed or hampered by itself. [8] A person's own thoughts unnerve them. If a tyrant threatens to chain our leg, whoever holds his leg in high regard will beg for mercy, whereas the person who cares more for his character will answer back, "Go ahead and chain it, if that's what you want."'

'And you don't care?'

'I don't care.'

'Just wait, I'll show you who's in charge!'

[9] 'How do you propose to do that? Zeus himself has given me my freedom; he was not going to allow any son of his to be enslaved. You are master of my corpse, come help yourself to *that*.'

[10] 'What about when you petition me for a favour, isn't that proof of your regard?'

'No, it's me looking after myself. If you press the point, I will concede that in the process I give you the same attention I give my dishes.

[11] 'Look, this is not selfishness, it's the nature of the beast; everything we do is done for our own ends. The sun moves across the sky for its own ends.[28] Even Zeus acts for his own aims. [12] But when Zeus wants to be "Rain-Bringer", or "Grain-Giver", or "Father of Gods and Men", it's obvious that he can only gain his goals and earn his epithets by doing some benefit for the world at large. [13] In the same way he made the rational animal, man, incapable of attaining any of his private ends without at the same time providing for the community.

[14] 'The upshot is that it is not anti-social to be constantly acting in one own's self-interest. [15] We do not expect someone, after all, to be indifferent regarding himself and his welfare. It's the basis of our principle of appropriation,[29] the instinct that drives everyone's behaviour. [16] Consequently when people are mistaken in the views they hold about things outside the will – thinking that they are good or evil – they naturally are going to grovel before tyrants. [17] And if only it ended there! But they grovel before the tyrant's lackies too. Tell me,

how do underlings suddenly become sages when the emperor elevates them to the post of bathroom attendant? Why are we suddenly saying "Felicio's[30] advice to me was very astute." [18] I hope he gets kicked out of the toilet, so I can see you change your mind again and declare publicly that he's a fool.

[19] 'Epaphroditus once owned a slave, a shoemaker, whom he sold because he was no good. As chance would have it, he was bought by one of the imperial household and became shoemaker to Caesar. You should have seen Epaphroditus flatter him then! [20] "And how is my friend Felicio today?" [21] Whenever one of us asked, "Where is the master?" he would be told, "He is in conference with Felicio." [22] Hadn't he sold him off because he was useless? [23] How did he become so knowledgeable all of a sudden? Well, that's what comes of valuing anything not under control of the will. [24] Someone is raised to the office of tribune and accepts congratulations on every hand. One person kisses his eyes, another his cheek, his slaves even kiss his hands. When he gets home, he finds lamps being lit in his honour. [25] He mounts the Capitol, where he offers a sacrifice of thanks. Now who, I ask you, has ever offered sacrifice for right desires, or for impulses in agreement with nature? We only thank the gods, it seems, for what we popularly suppose are the good things in life.

[26] 'A man spoke with me today about accepting a priest-hood of Augustus.[31] I told him not to touch it. "You will lay out a lot of money for little in return."'

[27] 'But the clerk will add my name to public contracts.'

'Are you planning to be there every time a contract is signed, so you can announce to the assembled, "That's my name he's writing down there"? [28] Even if you can attend these signing ceremonies now, what will you do when you die?'

'But my name will survive me.'

'Carve it in stone and it will survive you just as well. Outside Nicopolis, though, no one is going to remember you.'

[29] 'But I get to wear a crown of gold.'

'If you have your heart set on wearing crowns, why not make one out of roses – you will look even more elegant in that.'

I 20 *Concerning reason, and how it studies itself*

[1] Every craft or faculty has a field with which it is primarily concerned. [2] When the faculty happens to be like what it studies, it naturally comes to study itself. When it is different, however, then it cannot. [3] To give an example: shoemaking works on leather, but the craft itself is quite distinct from leather; therefore, it does not study itself. [4] The art of grammar has to do with written speech, but *is* it written speech? No. Therefore, it cannot study itself.

[5] Now, for what purpose did nature arm us with reason? To make the correct use of impressions. And what is reason if not a collection of individual impressions? Hence, it naturally comes to turn its analysis on itself. [6] And what does the virtue of wisdom profess to investigate? Things good, bad and indifferent. And what is wisdom itself? Good. And ignorance? Bad. It is natural for wisdom too, then, to investigate itself, as well as its opposite.

[7] Therefore, the first and most important duty of the philosopher is to test impressions, choosing between them and only deploying those that have passed the test. [8] You know how, with money – an area where we believe our interest to be much at stake – we have developed the art of assaying, and considerable ingenuity has gone into developing a way to test if coins are counterfeit, involving our senses of sight, smell, hearing and touch. [9] The assayer will let the denarius drop and listen intently to its ring; and he is not satisfied to listen just once: after repeated listenings he practically acquires a musician's subtle ear. [10] It is a measure of the effort we are prepared to expend to guard against deception when accuracy is at a premium.

[11] When it comes to our poor mind, however, we can't be bothered; we are satisfied accepting any and all impressions, because here the loss we suffer is not obvious. [12] If you want to know just how little concerned you are about things good and bad, and how serious about things indifferent, compare your attitude to going blind with your attitude about being

mentally in the dark. You will realize, I think, how inappropriate your values really are.

[13] 'But this calls for a lot of preparation, and hard study.'

So what? Do you think the greatest art can be acquired easily, and overnight? [14] It's true that the principal doctrine of the philosophers is briefly stated; you have only to read Zeno to see my meaning. [15] How long does it take to say, 'The goal is to follow the gods,' and 'The essence of the good is the proper use of impressions'? [16] But, just because it is so brief, the formula prompts other questions: 'What is God, and what is an impression? How does individual nature compare with the nature of the whole?' Now the inquiry is beginning to drag out.

[17] Here we have Epicurus saying that goodness is none other than the flesh. But then there are lectures to sit through about man's dominant principle – that is to say, about what his substance and essence are – and the explanation begins to grow long again. It's not likely that the good of a snail lies in its shell, so is it likely that Epicurus is correct in identifying man's good with his body?

[18] Take yourself, Epicurus. Even *you* have a faculty that is greater than the flesh – the faculty which, having examined and thought through the evidence, concluded that flesh was the principal thing. [19] And why are you so fond of burning the midnight oil, working hard to produce so many books on our behalf? Obviously, it must matter to you that we be put in possession of the truth. But who are we, and, more to the point, who are we to you?

Well, now the explanation of Epicurus' views is growing lengthy too . . .

I 21 *To people who want to be admired*

[1] When someone is properly grounded in life, they shouldn't have to look outside themselves for approval.

[2] 'My friend, what is it you want?'

'I am satisfied if my desires and aversions agree with nature, if I exercise impulse and refusal as I was born to do, and if I practise purpose, design and assent the same way.'

'So why are you acting so stuck up?'

[3] 'I want everyone I meet to admire me, to follow me around shouting, "What a great philosopher!"'

[4] And who exactly are these people that you want to be admired by? Aren't they the same people you are in the habit of calling crazy? And is this your life ambition, then – to win the approval of lunatics?

I 22 *On preconceptions*

[1] Everyone has preconceptions. And one preconception does not contradict another. I mean, who of us does not assume that what is good is beneficial and choice, in all cases to be desired and pursued? Who of us does not assume that justice is fair and appropriate? So where does conflict come in? [2] In the application of preconceptions to particular cases. [3] One person, for instance, will say, 'Well done, there's a brave man,' while another says, 'He isn't brave, he's just deranged.'

This is how conflict originates, [4] and it is the source of difference among Jews, Syrians, Egyptians and Romans. They don't dispute that what is holy should be preferred above everything else and in every case pursued; but they argue, for example, over whether it is holy or unholy to eat pork. [5] This is also the basis of the conflict between Agamemnon and Achilles. Call them up before us.

'What do you say, Agamemnon? Shouldn't we do what is right and proper?'

'Naturally.'

[6] 'What about you, Achilles? Wouldn't you, of all people, say that we ought to do what is appropriate?'

'Of course.'

'All right, then, apply your preconceptions.'

[7] It is just here that conflict starts. Because one says, 'I shouldn't have to return Chryseis to her father,' and the other

says, 'Indeed you'd better.' It's obvious that one of them is misapplying his preconception of what is appropriate. [8] Then Agamemnon says, 'Fine, if I have to give Chryseis back, then I should get one of the other men's prizes in return.' Achilles says, 'It's not mine you intend to take, I hope.' 'Yours, that's right.' 'Why should *I* be penalized?' 'Because it's not right that I be the only one to go without.' And this is how conflicts originate.

[9] What does it mean to be getting an education? It means learning to apply natural preconceptions to particular cases as nature prescribes, and distinguishing what is in our power from what is not. [10] The operations of the will are in our power; not in our power are the body, the body's parts, property, parents, siblings, children, country or friends.

[11] Where should we put the good, then – to which of the two classes of things are we going to assign it? To the class of things in our power. [12] It follows that neither health nor fitness are good, nor are our children, parents or country.

'That view is not going to win you many friends or converts.'

[13] Well, let's transfer the designation 'good' to health and other externals and see what happens. Suppose someone meets with misfortune and loses these 'goods'; can they still be happy? 'Impossible.' You might ask, too, how they will remain on good terms with their neighbours, since we naturally incline to self-interest. [14] And if it is in my interest to own land, it is in my interest to rob them of it. If it is in my interest to own a coat, it is in my interest to pinch one from the baths. There you have the genesis of wars, factions and seditions.

[15] And how will I be able to stay right with God? Because if I'm harmed and meet with misfortune, I begin to doubt whether he is looking after me. And if he won't help me, why should I give him my regard? I want nothing to do with a god who allows me to be in my present state. So I begin to hate him, [16] and wonder if the temples and statues we dedicate to him are not intended to placate a malignant force, like Fever. Honorary titles like 'Saviour', 'Rain-bringer' and 'Fruit-bringer' are no longer applicable to him – and all this comes of identifying 'the good' with externals.

[17] What should we do? That's the topic of inquiry for the person who is truly out to philosophize and think deep. Now, if I am in the dark as to what is good and bad, I'm crazy. [18] But if I locate 'the good' in the realm of the will I risk being ridiculed. Some grey old man rattling his gold rings and shaking his head at me will come along and say, 'Listen, my boy, philosophy's all right up to a point, but don't get carried away. This question is ridiculous. [19] Philosophers can teach you logic, but you know better than they do the right way to behave.' [20] 'Well, if I know what to do, as you say, don't make an objection if what I choose to do is philosophize.' I'm not going to try to engage this fatuous old fool in logic. But if I ignore him altogether, he'll explode in indignation. [21] So I have no choice but to say to him, 'Humour me as you would someone in love. I can't help myself, you see, I'm mad.'

I 23 *Against Epicurus*

[1] Even Epicurus realizes that we are social creatures by nature, but once he has identified our good with the shell,[32] he cannot say anything inconsistent with that. [2] For he further insists – rightly – that we must not respect or approve anything that does not share in the nature of what is good.

[3] So how is it that we are suspicious – we who supposedly have no natural affection for our children?[33] Why is it, Epicurus, that you dissuade the wise man from bringing up children? Are you afraid that he may become emotionally involved and unhappy? [4] And is that because you have been anxious on behalf of your house-slave Mouse?[34]

Well, what's it to Epicurus, anyway, if his little Mouse comes crying to him?*

[5] No, he realizes that, once a child is born, it is no longer in our power not to love or care for it. [6] Which is why he

---

* The translation assumes that αὐτοῦ, the last word in §4, should be emended to the dative αὐτῷ ('comes crying *to him*').

says that a man of sense will not take part in politics either*;
he knows the kinds of personal connections that politics
involves. So what's to keep us from living as if we were as
unsocial as flies?

[7] But as if he didn't know this, he has the gall to suggest
that we should abandon our children. Even a sheep does not
desert its own offspring, or a wolf; should a human desert his?
[8] Would you have us be as foolish as sheep or as savage as
wolves – neither of which abandons its young? [9] Come on,
whoever remembers your advice when they see their little child
fallen and crying on the ground?

[10] Personally, I imagine that your own mother and father,
even had they predicted that you were going to say such things,
would not have exposed[35] you.

I 24 *How we should struggle with circumstance*

[1] The true man is revealed in difficult times. So when trouble
comes, think of yourself as a wrestler whom God, like a trainer,
has paired with a tough young buck. [2] For what purpose?
To turn you into Olympic-class material. But this is going to
take some sweat to accomplish. From my perspective, no one's
difficulties ever gave him a better test than yours, if you are
prepared to make use of them the way a wrestler makes use of
an opponent in peak condition.

[3] Now we are sending you to Rome as a spy. And we don't
want one who is easily frightened, or one who will turn back
at the first sound of noise, or glimpse of shadow, announcing
hysterically that the enemy is practically at the gates. [4] If
you tell us on your return, 'Conditions are terrible in Rome,
everywhere death, exile, poverty, informants – everything a
shambles. Fly, the enemy is upon us!' [5] – we will respond by

* The change of the aorist πολιτεύσασθαι to the future πολιτεύσεσθαι has
been assumed in the translation, based on comparison with the discussion of
Epicurus' ethical views transmitted in Diogenes Laertius, *The Lives of the
Philosophers* X 119.

telling you in future to keep your forecasts to yourself. Our only mistake was in sending a spy like you in the first place.

[6] Diogenes[36] went scouting before you did and came back with a very different report. Death, he said, was not evil because it was not dishonourable. Reputation was the empty noise of fools. [7] And he said other things that helped remove the element of fear from pain and poverty. In his manner of life he preferred the minimum of clothing to a purple gown, and the bare ground to a bed, however soft. [8] And as proof of such claims, he produced his assurance, his serenity, his freedom – as well as his tough, radiant physique.

[9] 'There is no enemy near by,' he said. 'All is peace and tranquillity.'

'Explain, Diogenes.'

'Look for yourself: am I wounded, disabled or in flight from any enemy force?'

[10] That's the kind of spy we honour. *You* bring us back a report full of a lot of random noise. Go off and make a better search, this time without the trepidation.

[11] 'What should I do then?'

What do you do when you leave a ship? Do you walk off with the rudder and oars? No; you leave with your own gear, your oil-flask and wallet. So just remember what belongs to you, and you won't lay claim to what doesn't.

[12] The emperor says to you, 'Remove your broad hem.'

'Very well, I'll wear the narrow hem.'

'Remove that too.'

'All right, I'll wear the ordinary toga now.'[37]

'Take your toga off.'

'Fine, I'll go naked.'

[13] 'Now your very composure provokes me.'

'Take my whole body, then.'

Is there any reason to fear someone to whom I stand ready to surrender my miserable corpse?

[14] But so-and-so will not leave his estate to me. Well? I forgot that none of it was mine. How then do we call it mine? As we call the bed in an inn mine. If the innkeeper dies and leaves you his bed, fine; but if he leaves it to someone else, then

he will have it, and you will find a replacement. [15] And if you
don't, then you will have to sleep on the ground. Only rest easy
there and snore away, because, remember, tragedies take place
among the rich – among kings, and potentates. No poor man
swells a tragedy except as a member of the chorus. [16] Kings
start off well enough: 'Deck the palace halls.' But then around
the third or fourth act, we get, 'O Cithaeron, why did you
receive me?'[38] [17] Fool, where are your crowns, your diadem?
Even your guards can't help you now.

[18] So when you stand before one of those tyrants, just bear
in mind that you are in the presence of a tragic figure – and not
the actor, either, but Oedipus himself.

[19] 'But he's so lucky to be able to walk around with an
entourage.'

Well, I too mingle with the masses and so am attended by an
entourage. [20] The chief thing to remember is that the door is
open.[39] Don't be a greater coward than children, who are ready
to announce, 'I won't play any more.' Say, 'I won't play any
more,' when you grow weary of the game, and be done with it.
But if you stay, don't carp.

I 25 *More on the same theme*

[1] If what we've been saying is true and we aren't being ridiculous, or merely pretending to believe that what is good or bad
for us lies in the will and that we are indifferent to everything
else – then why do we continue to experience fear and anxiety?
[2] No one has power over our principles, and what other
people do control we don't care about. So what is your problem,
still?

[3] 'My problem is that I want specific instructions on how
to act in line with these principles.'

What other orders do you need than those Zeus has given
you already? He has given you what is your own unrestricted
and unrestrained; what is not yours he has made restricted and
restrained. [4] What commandment, then, did you arrive with

when he sent you here? 'Protect what belongs to you at all costs; don't desire what belongs to another.' Trustworthiness is your own, decency and a sense of shame;* no one can take them from you or prevent you from using these qualities except yourself – which you do the moment you begin to care about what isn't yours, surrendering what *is* yours in the process.

[5] With such directions and commands from Zeus, what additional ones do you hope to get from me? Am I greater or more to be trusted? [6] Keep his commandments and you won't need others. And as proof that he has delivered them to you, bring your preconceptions to bear. Bring the arguments of philosophers. Bring what you've often heard, and often said yourself; what you've read, and what you've practised.

[7] Just how long should we apply these precepts that we have from God, before breaking up the game? [8] Just so long as the game remains a pleasure. At the Saturnalia a king of the revels is chosen by chance, because this is the convention.⁴⁰ Then our 'king' hands out orders: 'Drink up! You there, mix the wine! You, sir, give us a song! You, join the party; while you there – get lost!' And we play along with him, so that the game will not be spoiled on our account. [9] But if the 'king' says, 'Imagine that you are unhappy,' and I demur, who is going to force me? [10] If, on the other hand, the programme calls for the re-enactment of Achilles' quarrel with Agamemnon, and the actor in the role of king says to me, 'Go and get Briseis away from Achilles,' [11] I'll go. When he says, 'Return,' I'll return.

The way we handle hypothetical arguments can also serve as a model for our behaviour.⁴¹ 'Let's assume that it is night.'

'Fine.'

'Then is it day?'

'No, because I've accepted the hypothesis that it is night.'

[12] 'Let's assume, in the manner of a game or play, that you pretend to believe that it is night.'

'OK.'

---

* The addition of 'decency and a sense of shame' to the text has been adopted on the basis of many parallel passages in the *Discourses*.

'Now, believe that it really *is* night.'

[13] 'That does not follow from the hypothesis.'

The same rules apply in life: 'Let's assume you've come upon hard times.'

'Granted.'

'Then you are unfortunate.'

'Yes.'

'And suffering.'

'Yes.'

'Now believe that what has happened to you is bad.'

'That does not follow from the hypothesis. Besides, there is another who won't let me.'[42]

[14] How long should we submit to the rules of the game? As long as it serves my turn, and I find the part congenial. [15] Some dour, inflexible types will say, 'I can't eat at this man's table if it means listening to his war stories again: "I told you, friend, how I scrambled up the hill; now we came under renewed bombardment…"' [16] But another person in the same situation might say, 'The meal is what matters; let him rattle on to his heart's content.' [17] It is for you to arrange your priorities; but whatever you decide to do, don't do it resentfully, as if you were being imposed on. And don't believe your situation is genuinely bad – no one can make you do that. [18] Is there smoke in the house? If it's not suffocating, I will stay indoors; if it proves too much, I'll leave. Always remember – the door is open.

[19] 'Do not remain in Nicopolis,' they say to me; so I don't remain there.

'Don't stay in Athens either.'

So I quit Athens.

'Not Rome either.'

So I abandon Rome.

[20] 'Live on Gyara.'[43]

But for me living on Gyara amounts to more smoke in my house than I can stand. So I depart to the one place no one can stop me from going, where everyone is made welcome. [21] And when I remove my last piece of clothing – my skin – then no one can lay a hold of me any longer. [22] Which is why

Demetrius was emboldened to say to Nero, 'You threaten me with death, but nature threatens *you*.'

[23] If I cherish my body, I make a slave of myself, if I cherish my property, I make a slave of myself; [24] because I've disclosed the means to make me captive. When a snake pulls back its head, right away I think, 'Hit it just there, on the part that it's protecting.' In the same way you may be sure that whatever you are seen to protect, that will become your enemy's focus of attack. [25] Keep this in mind, then there will be no one you will need to fear or flatter.

[26] 'But I want to sit in the senators' gallery.'

Look, the crowd is of your own creation, you're treading on your own toes.

[27] 'But how else am I to get a clear view of the stage?'

If you don't want to be crowded, don't attend the theatre. What's the difficulty? Or wait until the show is over, then seat and sun yourself at leisure in the senators' seats. [28] In general, remember that it is we who torment, we who make difficulties for ourselves – that is, our opinions do. What, for instance, does it mean to be insulted? [29] Stand by a rock and insult it, and what have you accomplished? If someone responds to insult like a rock, what has the abuser gained with his invective? If, however, he has his victim's weakness to exploit, then his efforts are worth his while.

[30] 'Strip him.' What do you mean, 'him'? Take his garment, you mean, and remove that. 'I have insulted you.' 'A lot of good may it do you.' [31] That is what Socrates practised, maintaining always the same even temper. But it seems that we would practise and study anything rather than how to remain free and unenslaved.

[32] 'Philosophers speak in paradoxes.'

And what of the other arts – are they different? What is more paradoxical than cutting into a person's eye to restore their vision? If someone suggested this procedure to a person ignorant of medicine, they would laugh in the practitioner's face. [33] Little wonder, then, if many of the truths of philosophy also impress the masses as paradoxical.

I 26 *What is the law of life?*

[1] When a person was reading the hypothetical arguments, Epictetus said, 'This is a law concerning hypotheses, that we must accept what follows by way of conclusion. Even more cogent is the law of life that obliges us to act in accordance with nature. [2] If we mean to obey it in every area, on every occasion, clearly we must never allow what nature prescribes to escape us, and allow into our lives what runs contrary to nature.

[3] 'So philosophers start us out with logic, since it's easier, reserving more problematic subjects for later. In the study of logic, there is nothing to distract us; whereas in practical matters our attention is constantly pulled in other directions. [4] Whoever insists on jumping right into practical matters risks making a fool of himself, since it's not easy tackling harder subjects first. [5] And this is the right defence to use with parents upset with their children because they study philosophy: "Have it your way, father: my judgement is poor and I don't know what I really should be doing. But if this can neither be learned nor taught, then don't blame me for it. If it can, however, then either teach it to me yourself, or let me learn it from someone who professes to know; [6] since I hope you don't suppose that if I'm doing the wrong thing it's by choice. So what else could explain my error but ignorance? [7] And wouldn't you rather I be cured of that? When did anger, however, ever teach someone to play music or pilot a ship? Do you imagine that your anger is going to help teach me the far more complex business of life?"

[8] 'But that line of argument assumes that such actually is your motive for studying philosophy; [9] anyone learning logic and attending philosophy lectures to make a show of erudition at a dinner party is satisfied just to win the respect of some senator seated beside him. [10] For that is where the important matters are, and treasures there are accounted trifles here. Consequently, it is hard to be master of one's impressions in

matters of ethics, where things that muddle the judgement are so many.

[11] 'I know of one man who cried, clinging to Epaphroditus' knees, saying how miserable he was now that he was down to his last million. [12] And what did Epaphroditus do – laugh at him as you are laughing now? No, he was appalled, and said, "Dear man, how did you keep silent up till now? How have you endured it?"'

[13] When Epictetus corrected the person reading the hypothetical arguments and the person who had set him the reading began ridiculing him, Epictetus said, 'You are laughing at yourself. You did not prepare the student properly or make sure he could understand these arguments. And still you use him as a reader. [14] Well then,' he said, 'if a mind doesn't have the aptitude to follow and judge a conjunctive argument, why do we assume it's capable of awarding praise, assigning blame or forming a judgement about things good and bad? If that person thinks ill of a person, will the other person care? Or if he admires someone, will that someone jump for joy – when in such minor matters of logic he can't make an inference or draw a correct conclusion?

[15] 'This, then, is the beginning of philosophy – an awareness of one's own mental fitness. Consciousness of its weakness will keep you from tackling difficult subjects. [16] As it is, though, some people strain at a pamphlet and still want to devour an entire treatise. Naturally they can't digest it, and get heartily sick of the whole business. [17] They need to first figure out what their capacity is. In the realm of logic it is easy to refute someone ignorant of the subject. But in the affairs of life, no one offers himself to be examined, and whoever presumes to examine us we resent. [18] And yet Socrates used to say that the unexamined life was not worth living.'

I 27 *In how many ways impressions arise, and what
aids we should provide against them.*

[1] Impressions come to us in four ways: things are and appear
to be; or they are not, and do not appear to be; or they are, but
do not appear to be; or they are not, and yet appear to be. [2]
The duty of an educated man in all these cases is to judge
correctly. And whatever disturbs our judgement, for that we
need to find a solution. If the sophisms of the Pyrrhonists and
the Academics[44] are what trouble us, we must look for the
antidote. [3] If it is the plausibility of things, causing some
things to seem good that are not, let us seek a remedy there.
If it is habit that troubles us, we must try to find a corrective
for *that*.

[4] What aid can we find to combat habit? The opposed
habit. [5] You hear people commonly saying things like, 'He
died, the poor man'; 'His father perished, his mother too'; 'He
was cut down in his prime, and in a foreign land.' [6] Lend
your ear to different descriptions, distance yourself from statements such as these, check one habit with its opposite. Against
sophistry one should have the practice and exercise of rational
argument. Against specious impressions one should have clear
preconceptions polished and ready to hand.

[7] When death appears an evil, we should have ready the
fact that it is a duty to avoid evil things, whereas death is
necessary and cannot be avoided. [8] I mean, where am I going
to go to get away from it? Maybe I am not Sarpedon, the son
of Zeus, so that I can say in the same grand manner, 'I will go,
and either win the prize for valour myself, or give another the
opportunity to gain it.'[45] The former may be beyond us, but at
least the latter is within our reach. [9] And where can I go to
escape death in any case? Tell me the country, give me the name
of the people who are safe from death, where I can get asylum;
provide me with the magic charm. No, I cannot escape death,
[10] but at least I can escape the fear of it – or do I have to die
moaning and groaning too?

Passions stem from frustrated desire; [11] so if I am able to shape conditions to suit my wishes, I will do so, but if not, I am ready to maul anyone who stands in my way. [12] People by nature cannot endure being deprived of the good or meeting up with evil. [13] And if, in the end, I can't alter circumstances, or tear to pieces the person who prevents me, then I sit and bawl, abusing everyone I can think of, including Zeus and the other gods. For if they do not look after me, why should I care about *them*? [14] 'But you will be blasphemous.' Well, what punishment could they devise in that case that would make my situation worse? Remember that, as a rule, unless piety and self-interest can be reconciled, piety cannot be preserved. Don't you find that convincing?

[15] Let the Pyrrhonist and Academic philosophers step forward to face us.

'For my part, I have no leisure for these controversies, nor can I simply side with convention.'[46]

[16] Now, if I had a dispute about property I would have called in a lawyer to help with my case. What will meet my needs in this instance? [17] The process of perception – whether it involves the entire body or only a part – this I may not be able to explain, because either alternative seems problematic to me. But that you and I are not the same person – of that I'm quite certain. [18] I mean, when I want to swallow something, I never carry it to *your* mouth, but my own. And when I want bread, I don't grab a broom, I head straight for the bread like an arrow to its target.* [19] And you Sceptics, who dismiss the evidence of the senses – do you act any differently? Which one of you ever went to the mill when you were in need of a bath?

[20] 'Well, shouldn't we be diligent defenders of convention, then, and watchful for any attack on it?' [21] Certainly – provided we have the leisure for controversies of this kind. The person who is trembling, upset and inwardly broken in spirit needs to spend his time differently, though.

---

* The translation in §18 assumes the change of προκόπτων to πρὸς σκοπόν.

I 28 *That we should not be angry with people; and what people account great and small*

[1] The cause of our assenting to the truth of something is that it appears to be fact. [2] And it is impossible to assent to anything that does *not* appear to be fact. Why? It is the mind's nature: it will assent to the truth, reject what is false and suspend judgement in doubtful cases.

[3] Here, I will prove it to you: feel, if you can, that it is night now. 'Impossible.' *Don't* feel that it is now day. 'Impossible.' Feel, or don't feel, that the number of stars is even. 'Impossible.' [4] So when someone assents to a false proposition, be sure that they did not want to give their assent, since, as Plato says, 'Every soul is deprived of the truth against its will.'[47] [5] They simply mistook for true something false.

Now, with respect to our actions, the case is analogous, only instead of true and false we react to impressions of right and wrong, good and bad, honest and dishonest. [6] And it is impossible to think that an action will do us good and not choose to do it.

[7] What about Medea, though – she who says:
I know that the acts I intend are wrong
But anger is the master of my intentions.
That only amounts to saying that she thinks gratifying her anger by exacting revenge on her husband is preferable to keeping her children safe.[48] [8] 'Yes, but she is in error.' Well, demonstrate to her clearly that she is in error and she will not act on her idea. As long as you don't lay it out for her, though, she has nothing besides her own idea of right and wrong to guide her. [9] So don't get angry at the poor woman for being confused about what's most important, and accordingly mutating from human being to snake. Pity her instead. We take pity on the blind and lame, why don't we pity people who are blind and lame in respect of what matters most? [10] Whoever keeps in mind that our actions are all determined by our impressions, which can either be right or wrong – now, if the impression is correct, we are innocent, but if it is incorrect we pay for it

ourselves, since it is impossible that someone else should be penalized for our error – whoever keeps this in mind will not be angry or upset with anyone, won't curse, blame, resent or malign anyone either.

[11] 'So in your view great tragedies are merely the result of this – somebody's "impression"?'

The result of that and that alone. [12] You take the *Iliad*: it's nothing but people's impressions and how they dealt with them. An impression made Paris rob Menelaus of his wife, and an impression got Helen to run away with him. [13] Now, if an impression had come to Menelaus that perhaps he was better off losing such a wife – well, that would have meant the loss to us not just of the *Iliad* but of the *Odyssey* as well.

[14] 'So you're saying that matters so great owe their origin to something so trivial?'

But what do you mean by 'matters so great'? Wars, factions, the loss of many men, the razing of cities – tell me what's so 'great' about all that? [15] What's so great about slaughtering many sheep or cattle, or burning a lot of storks' or swallows' nests? [16]

'Can you really compare the two?' Why not? In the one case human bodies are lost, in the other case the dead happen to be farm animals. People's houses burn, so do storks' nests. [17] What's so earth-shaking or awful in that? Show me how a house, considered merely as shelter, is better than a stork's nest.

[18] 'How can a stork be compared with a human being?' Where the body is concerned, there is lots of similarity, only in man's case his body inhabits houses composed of bricks and timber, while storks' nests are made of sticks and mud.

[19] 'So is there no distinction between a person and a stork?'

Of course there is, but not in regard to these externals. [20] Reflect and you'll realize that man excels in other respects: in taking cognisance of his own behaviour; in being sociable, trustworthy and honourable; in learning from his own mistakes; in brains. [21] What counts as good and bad for man can be found precisely in those respects in which he differs from the beasts. If his special qualities are kept safe behind stout walls, and he does not lose his honour, trustworthiness or intelligence, then the man is saved. But lose or take away any of these qualities and the man himself is lost.

[22] Everything significant depends on this. Did Paris' tragedy lie in the Greeks' attack on Troy, when his brothers began to be slaughtered? [23] No; no one is undone by the actions of others. That was the destruction of storks' nests. His tragedy lay in the loss of the man who was honest, trustworthy, decent and respectful of the laws of hospitality. [24] Wherein did Achilles' tragedy lie? The death of Patroclus? Not at all. It was that he gave in to anger, that he whined about losing a mere woman and lost sight of the fact that he was there not for romance but for war. [25] Those are the genuine human tragedies, the city's siege and capture – when right judgements are subverted; when *thoughts* are undermined.

[26] 'Women are driven into captivity, children are enslaved, and men are put to the sword. Is none of this bad?'

[27] What's the basis for adding that description? Let me in on it too.

'Why don't you explain instead how they are *not* evils?'

[28] Let's turn to our standards, produce our preconceptions. I mean, this is what flabbergasts me. If there's a question about weight, we don't formulate a judgement at random; if it's a matter of judging straight and crooked, we don't make our decision based on whim. [29] If the truth of the case makes any difference to us at all, then none of us operates in the dark. [30] Yet when it comes to the first and foremost cause of good and bad conduct; when it's a matter of doing well or ill, of failure or success – only then do we proceed blindly and erratically, only then are we found to lack anything like a scale or measure. A sense impression appears and right away I react. [31] Am I better than Agamemnon and Achilles, insofar as they do and suffer such wrongs by following their impressions, while the impression does not satisfy me? [32] Is there any tragedy with a different source? What is the *Atreus* of Euripides? An impression. The *Oedipus* of Sophocles? An impression. The *Phoenix*? An impression. *Hippolytus*?[49] An impression. [33] What kind of person, then, pays no attention to the matter of impressions,

do you think? Well, what do we call people who accept every one indiscriminately?

'Madmen.'

And do we act any differently?

I 29 *On steadfastness*

[1] The essence of good and evil consists in the condition of our character. [2] And externals are the means by which our character finds its particular good and evil. [3] It finds its good by not attaching value to the means. Correct judgements about externals make our character good, as perverse or distorted ones make it bad.

[4] God has fixed this law, and says, 'If you want something good, get it from yourself.' But you say, 'No, I'll get it from another.' I say, 'No – get it from yourself.' [5] If a tyrant threatens me at court, I say, 'What is he threatening?' If he says, 'I will put you in chains,' I say, 'He is threatening my hands and feet.' [6] If he says, 'I will behead you,' I say, 'He is threatening my neck.' If he says, 'I will throw you into prison,' I say, 'He is threatening my entire body'; if he threatens exile, I say the same. [7] 'Well, then, aren't *you* threatened, even a little?' If I feel that these things are nothing to me, then no. [8] But if I fear for any of them, then, yes, it is I who am threatened.

Who is there left for me to fear, and over what has he control? Not what is in my power, because no one controls that except myself. As for what is not in my power, in that I take no interest.

[9] 'So do you philosophers teach contempt for rulers?'

Not at all. You don't find any of us preaching defiance of them within their range of competence. [10] My body, my property, my standing in society, my friends – they can have them all. And I challenge anyone to say that I encourage others to lay claim to those things.

[11] 'Yes,' the king says, 'but I want control over your judgements too.' Who gave you that power? You cannot add the

judgements of others to your conquests. [12] 'I will win by way of fear.' You do not seem to realize that the mind is subject only to itself. It alone can control it, [13] which shows the force and justice of God's edict: the strong shall always prevail over the weak. [14] 'Ten are stronger than one.' Yes, for what, though? For taking people captive, for killing or dragging them off, for taking away their property. For main force, yes, ten are better than one. [15] But one person with right judgements is superior to ten without. Numbers here are irrelevant. Put them in the balance, the person with correct ideas will outweigh all the others.

[16] 'To think of the indignities Socrates suffered at the hands of the Athenians!' Not 'Socrates,' stupid, express yourself more carefully: 'To think that Socrates' poor body should have been seized and hauled off to prison by men stronger than it, that somebody gave his poor body hemlock, that it grew progressively colder until it was dead.' [17] What seems unjust, or outrageous, in this, or worth blaming the gods for? Didn't Socrates have resources to compensate? [18] Where was the essence of the good for him – and who is more to be heeded in that regard, him or you? 'Anytus and Meletus can kill me, but they cannot harm me,'[50] he says, and: 'If it pleases the gods, so be it.'

[19] Produce a person who can get the better of someone whose judgements are superior. You can't, though, try as you might. This is God's law and nature's: 'Let the best man win.' But 'best' in his area of expertise. [20] One body is stronger than another body, many bodies are stronger than one; a thief has the advantage here over one who is not a thief. [21] This is how I came to lose my lamp:[51] the thief was better than I am in staying awake. But he acquired the lamp at a price: he became a thief for its sake, for its sake, he lost his ability to be trusted, for a lamp he became a brute. And he imagined he came out ahead!

[22] Fine words, you may say – but now I have been seized by the cloak and am being dragged downtown. Bystanders shout, 'Hey, philosopher, what good did your views do you after all? Look, you're being hauled off to prison and soon will

be beheaded.' [23] Tell me, what *Introduction to Philosophy* could I have read that would have saved me from being dragged away if a stronger man grabs me by the cloak; or could have kept me out of prison if I am assaulted by a gang of ten? [24] What philosophy has taught me, though, is to be indifferent to events beyond the will's control. [25] Haven't you profited in this respect too? So don't look for help from philosophy except in areas where you have learned that help from it can be found. [26] As I sit in prison I can say, 'Whoever laughs at me is deaf to the real meaning of words, can't understand what they hear, and doesn't even care to know what it is philosophers say or do. Let them be.'

[27] But the answer comes: 'Come out of prison.' If you have no further need of me in prison, I'll come out; if you need me, I'll go back in again. [28] 'How long will you keep this up?' For as long as the mind chooses to be with the body. But when the mind no longer consents, then you can take my body, and farewell to it. [29] Only, we must not part with it rashly or irrationally, or on trivial pretext. Because, again, God does not wish it. He needs us, he needs the world that we help populate. If he sounds the signal for retreat, though, as he did for Socrates, we must obey the signal as if it came from our commander-in-chief.

[30] Well, should we try telling this to the ignorant mob? [31] What would be the point? It's enough if we are convinced of it ourselves. When children come up to us clapping their hands and shouting, 'Today is good Saturnalia,' do we say, 'The Saturnalia is not "good"?' Of course not, we clap our hands right along with them. [32] As for you, if you can't change a person's mind, realize that he is no more than a child – and clap hands with him. And if you can't bring yourself to do that, then just keep quiet.

[33] It is essential that we remember this, so that, when troubles arise, we will know that it's time to exhibit what we've learned. [34] A student fresh out of school who gets into difficulty is like someone practised in the solving of syllogisms; if anyone gives him an easy one, he says, 'Give me a knotty one instead, I want a bit of practice.' In the same way, athletes don't

like to be paired with pushovers. [35] '*He* can't lift me,' one says, 'this other guy is better built.' No, when the crisis comes, we groan and say, 'I wanted to keep on learning.' Keep learning what? If you didn't learn these things in order to demonstrate them in practice, what *did* you learn them for?

[36] I suppose there might be some who are sitting here losing patience and thinking, 'Why don't I get to face the kind of challenge he did? I am growing old in a corner, when I could be winning a crown at Olympia! When will I be nominated for a similar trial?'

That is the attitude that all of you should adopt. [37] There are gladiators at Rome who get frustrated if they are not called out and matched with an opponent, all the while begging God and their own supervisors to be allowed to do battle one-on-one. None of you here shows anything like the same mettle. [38] Which is why I would like to escape to Rome to see my favourite wrestler in action, how *he*, at least, puts policy into practice.

[39] 'These are not the circumstances that I want.' Is it up to you to choose them? You have been given that particular body, these particular parents and brothers, this particular social position and place to live. You come to me hoping that I can somehow change these circumstances for you, not even conscious of the assets that are already yours that make it possible to cope with any situation you face. [40] 'It is yours to choose the exercise, mine to manage it well.' Right, but instead you say, 'Don't set me that kind of hypothetical argument, give me that one instead; don't give me that compound proposition, give me that other one.' [41] The time is coming when actors of tragedy will identify with their masks, their high-heeled boots, and their long robe. Wake up, those are props representing your circumstances and situation. [42] Say something so that we'll know whether you are a tragic actor or the comic relief – because of the costume you two have in common. [43] Does the tragic actor disappear, if you take away his boots and mask and bring him onstage a mere shadow of his former self – or is he there still? If he has the right voice, he remains.

[44] So it is in life: take a governorship. 'I take it and, when

I take it, I show how a real philosopher acts.' [45] Take off
your senator's robe and put on beggar's rags – and let's have a
look at you then. 'Well, so what? I still have the gift of a fine
voice to show off.' [46] What role do you appear in now? As a
witness called by God. [47] 'Step forward, you, and bear witness
for me; you earned the right to represent me as a witness. Is
anything good or bad that is independent of your will? Do I do
any man harm? Have I put each man's advantage under the
control of anyone except himself?' What witness do you bear
God? [48] 'I'm in difficulty, lord, and pitiable: no one cares
about me, no one helps me; I'm the object of universal scorn.'
[49] Is that the witness you are going to bear, making a mockery
of God's summons, when he honoured you and judged you
worthy to be his public spokesman?

   [50] But what if someone in authority pronounces you godless and atheistic?[52] How are you affected? 'I have been judged
godless and atheistic.' [51] Nothing more? 'Nothing.' If he had
passed judgement on a conditional argument, and said, 'The
proposition that "If it is day, it is light" I declare to be false,
what has happened to the conditional? Who is judged in this
case? Who has been condemned – the conditional, or the person
who got it wrong?'

   [52] Well, then, who is this man who is empowered to pass
judgement on you? Does he know anything about what is
religious or irreligious? Has he studied and learned about it?
Where, and from whom? [53] You know, a musician has no
consideration for anyone who mistakes the highest string on
the lyre for the lowest; and anyone who affirms that, in a circle,
lines that extend from the centre to the circumference can be
unequal is not going to win the respect of mathematicians. [54]
So – a true philosopher is under no obligation to respect vulgar
opinion as to what is religious or irreligious, what is just or
unjust. What dishonour he brings on philosophers in general if
he did! That's not what you learned here.

   [55] Wouldn't you rather leave petty arguments about these
subjects to do-nothings who sit in a corner and receive their
little stipend, or get nothing and whine about it? Step forward
and make use of what you've learned. [56] It isn't more logic

chopping that is needed – our Stoic texts are full of that. What we need now are people to apply their learning and bear witness to their learning in their actions. [57] Please, be the one to take on this character, I am tired in my teaching of invoking examples from the past, I want to be able to hold up an example from my own time.

[58] Consideration of these factors belongs to people who have the leisure for it; because man is an animal made for abstract thought. [59] But, for our honour's sake, let's not be seen studying them as if we were slaves who have run away. We should sit composed, without distraction, listening now to the tragic actor, now to the musician – not act like escapees who are moved to praise the performers while continually glancing nervously around, and who come apart completely if their master's name is dropped. [60] It is beneath the dignity of philosophers to study nature in this spirit. For what does 'master' mean? Man is not the master of another man, only death and life are, pleasure and pain.

So bring Caesar and not these other things before me and I am resolute. [61] But when he comes in thunder and lightning brandishing these things, and I show fear in response, in effect I have been brought face to face with my master, just like a runaway slave. [62] Even while I have a reprieve from these factors, my attention to the performance is no better than the slave's. I wash, drink, sing, but all in a spirit of gloom and foreboding. [63] If, however, I liberate myself from my master – which is to say, from the emotions that make my master frightening – what troubles can I have? No man is my master any longer.

[64] Well, is it our duty to announce these truths to everyone? No, instead we need to make allowances for people without the benefit of education, and say to ourselves, 'He is telling me to do this because he imagines it's good for himself as well; so I can't blame him.' [65] Socrates himself forgave his jailer when he began to drink the hemlock, and the man broke down in tears, saying, 'It shows great generosity of spirit for him to grieve for us.' [66] Does he say to the jailer, 'That's why we wouldn't let the women in!' No, he only says that to his close

friends – to those who can assimilate it. The jailer, though, he indulges as he would a child.

I 30 *How to prepare for trouble*

[1] In the event that you are haled before someone wielding the reigns of power, remember that there is somebody else looking down from above, and you have to answer first to *him*. [2] So he examines you: 'How did you categorize exile, imprisonment, chains, death and disgrace, when you were in school?'

'I said they were indifferent.'

[3] 'And what do you call them now? They haven't changed, I presume?'

'No.'

'Well, have *you* changed?'

'No.'

'Then define for me now what the "indifferents" are.'

'Whatever things we cannot control.'*

'Tell me the upshot.'

'They are nothing to me.'

[4] 'Remind me what you thought was good.'

'The will and the right use of impressions.'†

'And the goal of life is what?'

'To follow God.'

[5] 'And do you stand by that now?'

'I say it even now.'

'Go, then, in confidence, holding fast to these convictions. You'll see what it's like to be a young person with an education, alongside people who have none. [6] I promise that you will feel somewhat like this: "Why do we serve such a long and difficult apprenticeship – in preparation to face nonentities? [7] Is this what 'authority' meant? Are the courtyards, the palace

---

* The translation assumes the addition of τὰ ἀπροαίρετα after ἀδιάφορα.
† Emending the text to read: προαίρεσις καὶ χρῆσις οἵα δεῖ φαντασιῶν.

staff, the guards no more than this? Was this why I sat through so many lectures? It all amounts to nothing – and I was expecting to be overwhelmed."'

BOOK II

II 1 *That confidence does not conflict with caution*

[1] To some people, perhaps, what we philosophers say will appear impossible. But let us investigate, all the same, whether it's true that in our daily lives we can act with both caution and confidence. [2] It seems impossible because the two are evidently opposites – and opposites (supposedly) cannot co-exist. But what most people consider strange I think can be explained on the following hypothesis: [3] if we are talking about using confidence and caution on the same objects, we might fairly be accused of trying to reconcile irreconcilables. But our claim does not involve anything so strange.

[4] We have often said, and shown, that the use of impressions represents for us the essence of good and evil, and that good and evil have to do with the will alone. And if that is true, [5] then nothing is impractical in the philosophers' advice to 'Be confident in everything outside the will, and cautious in everything under the will's control.' [6] For if evil is a matter of the will, then caution is needed there; and if everything beyond the will and not in our control is immaterial to us, then those things can be approached with confidence. [7] And so, you see, that's how we can be cautious and confident at the same time – and, in fact, confident owing to our caution. For, being on our guard against evils, we approach things whose nature is *not* evil in a spirit of assurance.

[8] Instead, however, we act like deer. When deer are frightened by the feathers, they seek safety in the hunters' nets.[1] Confusing ruin with refuge, they come to an ill-timed death.

[9] Similarly, fear afflicts us in matters outside the will's control, while we act confidently and casually in matters dependent on the will as if they were of no importance. [10] To be deceived or rash, to act shamelessly or with unbridled lust – none of this matters to us as long as we have success in affairs outside the will. Death, exile, pain and ill repute – there you will find the impulse to tremble and run away.

[11] So, you would expect when error involves the things of greatest importance, our natural confidence is perverted into rashness, thoughtlessness, recklessness and shamelessness. At the same time, all fear and agitation, we exchange our natural caution and reserve for meekness and timidity. [12] Transfer caution to the will and the functions of the will, and the mere wish will bring with it the power of avoidance. But if we direct it at what is outside us and is none of our responsibility, wanting instead to avoid what's in the control of others, we are necessarily going to meet with fear, upset and confusion. [13] Death and pain are not frightening, it's the fear of pain and death we need to fear. Which is why we praise the poet who wrote, 'Death is not fearful, but dying like a coward is.'

[14] So be confident about death, and caution yourself against the fear of it – just the opposite, in other words, of what we are doing now. Now we shrink from death, whereas our views about death hardly concern us, we hardly give them a thought, and are completely apathetic. [15] Socrates used to call such fears 'hobgoblins',[2] and rightly so; just as masks scare and frighten children since they haven't seen them before, we react to events in much the same way and for much the same reason. [16]

What is a child? Ignorance and inexperience. But with respect to what it knows, a child is every bit our equal. [17] What is death? A scary mask. Take it off – see, it doesn't bite. Eventually, body and soul will have to separate, just as they existed separately before we were born. So why be upset if it happens now? If it isn't now, it's later. [18] And why now, if that happens to be the case? To accommodate the world's cycle; because the world needs things to come into being now, things to come into being later – and it needs things whose time is now complete.

[19] Pain too is just a scary mask: look under it and you will see. The body sometimes suffers, but relief is never far behind. And if that isn't good enough for you, the door stands open; otherwise put up with it. [20] The door needs to stay open whatever the circumstances, with the result that our problems disappear.[3] [21] The fruit of these doctrines is the best and most beautiful, as it ought to be for individuals who are truly educated: freedom from trouble, freedom from fear – freedom in general. [22] The masses are wrong to say that only freeborn men are entitled to an education; believe the philosophers instead, who say that only educated people are entitled to be called free. [23] I will explain. What else is freedom but the power to live our life the way we want?

'Nothing.'

Do you want to live life doing wrong?

'No.'

Therefore, no one doing wrong is free. [24] Do you want to live your life in fear, grief and anxiety?

'Of course not.'

So no one in a state of constant fear is free either. By the same token, whoever has gained relief from grief, fear and anxiety has gained freedom. [25] What confidence, then, can we have in our own dear legislators when they say that only freeborn people are entitled to an education, when the philosophers contend that only people already educated can be considered free? God will not allow it, you see.

[26] 'What about a master who performs the ceremony of manumitting a slave? Is nothing accomplished by that?'

Certainly it is – the master has performed the ceremony; and, on top of that, he has paid a five per cent tax to the state.

[27] 'But his slave – hasn't he come by his freedom in the process?'

No more than he has instantly come by peace of mind. I mean, consider your own case: you have slaves, and the power to free them. [28] But what master, I wonder, do you yourself serve? Money? Women? Boys? The emperor or one of his subordinates? It has to be one of them, or you wouldn't fret about such things.

[29] This is why I so often repeat to you the need to think about them and have these thoughts ready to hand, namely, the knowledge of what you should treat with confidence, and what you should treat with caution – that you can treat with confidence whatever lies outside the will, but must treat with caution what lies within.

[30] But you say, 'Didn't I read to you, and didn't you take note of my performance?'

[31] I noticed your clever phrases, yes – and you can have them. Show me instead how you practise desire and aversion to get what you want and avoid what you do not want. As for those treatises of yours, if you have any sense, you will go and burn them.

[32] 'But wasn't Socrates a writer, and a prolific one at that?'[4] Yes, but for what purpose? Since there wasn't always someone available whose ideas he could examine or who could examine Socrates' own in turn, sometimes he would test and examine himself, forever subjecting to scrutiny one assumption or another. [33] That's the writing of a real philosopher; whereas pretty phrases in dialogue form he leaves to others – aesthetes* and idlers who lie about and have no patience with logical reasoning because they're too stupid.

[34] Even now, if the opportunity presents itself, I know you will go off to read and make public those compositions, and you'll pride yourself on being fluent in the dialogue form. [35] Don't do it, man. What I would rather hear from you is, 'Look how I don't fail in my desires, or have experiences I don't want. I'll prove it to you in the case of death, I'll prove it to you in the case of physical pain, in the case of prison, of condemnation, and ill repute.' That's the real test of a youth fit to finish school. [36] Forget about that other stuff, don't let people hear you giving public recitations; and even if someone praises you, restrain yourself, be content to look like a nobody or know-nothing.

[37] Show them this, though, that you know how not to fail in your desires or experience what you don't desire. [38] Let

---

* Reading αἰσθήτοις for ἀναισθήτοις.

others practise lawsuits, solve logical puzzles or syllogisms. Your duty is to prepare for death and imprisonment, torture and exile – [39] and all such evils – with confidence, because you have faith in the one who has called on you to face them, having judged you worthy of the role. When you take on the role, you will show the superiority of reason and the mind over forces unconnected with the will. [40] Then that paradox will no longer seem so paradoxical or absurd – that we should be confident and cautious at the same time: confident in relation to things outside the will, cautious about things within.

II 2 *On tranquillity*

[1] If you are headed to court, consider carefully what it is you want to keep and in what area you want to win. [2] If you want to keep your character in line with nature, you have every hope of success, all the means you need, and not a worry in the world. [3] Because if you want to keep what is yours by right and is by nature free – and these are the only things you want – you have nothing to worry about. No one else controls them or can take them away from you. [4] If you want to be a man of honour and a man of your word, who is going to stop you? You say you don't want to be obstructed or forced to do something against your will – well, who is going to force you to desire things that you don't approve, or dislike something against your better judgement?

[5] Ah, but they will threaten you with punishments that overawe you. But how can they make you think of those sufferings as something you are obligated to avoid? [6] As long as desire and aversion are under your control, there is nothing more to worry about. [7] There is your opening statement, your exposition, your proof – and there lies success, the last word, and acquittal. [8] Which is why Socrates, when he was told to prepare himself for trial, said, 'Haven't I been preparing for it my whole life?' [9] Preparing for it how? 'I've tended to my

own affairs, and never done anything in violation of the law, either publicly or privately.'

[10] If, however, you want to keep hold of externals – your body, belongings and reputation – then my advice to you is that your preparations better begin early and will have to be long. You will need to research the character of the judge, of course, and make a study of your opponent too. [11] If grovelling is called for, then be prepared to grovel – to weep and holler too. [12] Whenever externals are more important to you than your own integrity, then be prepared to serve them the remainder of your life. Don't hedge and agree to be their slave, then change your mind later; [13] commit to one or the other position at once and without reserve. Choose to be either free or a slave, enlightened or a fool, a thoroughbred or a nag. Either resign yourself to a life of abuse till you die, or escape it immediately. For God's sake, don't put up with years of abuse, and *then* change your mind! [14] This humiliation can be avoided before it begins: just decide now what you think is truly good and bad.*

[15] I mean, do you think that, if Socrates had any concern for what others could do to him, he would have stood before the court and said, 'Anytus and Meletus can kill me, but cannot harm me'? [16] Do you think he was fool enough not to see that this approach was going to lead to a very different result?[5] So why not make remarks that are more provocative?†

[17] It's like my friend Heraclitus,[6] who had a lawsuit about a piece of property on Rhodes. After proving to the jury that he had right on his side, he came to his concluding remarks and said, 'But I am not going to plead with you, and I don't care what you decide. You are more on trial here than I am.' With the result that he sabotaged his case. [18] And why was it necessary? Don't plead – but don't go on to *say*, 'I won't plead' – not unless there is a point in provoking the jurors deliberately,

---

* The remainder of §14 is probably an intrusion and has been omitted from the translation; it does not suit the context, and does not even make sense on its own: 'Where truth is also. Where truth and nature are, there is caution. Where truth is, there is confidence, where nature is.'

† Reading προσερεθίζειν for προσερεθίζει.

as in Socrates' case. [19] As for you, if you're planning some such parting shot, why bother to speak at all, why even show up at court? [20] Because if you want to be crucified, just wait, and the cross will come. But if reason demands that you appear and do your best to be persuasive, you must do what is entailed – while safeguarding what is yours.

[21] Thus, it is stupid to say, 'Tell me what to do!'[7] What should I tell you? It would be better to say, 'Make my mind adaptable to any circumstance.' [22] Saying 'Tell me what to do' is like an illiterate saying, 'Tell me what to write whenever I'm presented with a name.' [23] If I say 'John' and then someone else comes along and gives him 'Jane' instead of 'John' to write, what is going to happen? How is he going to write it? [24] If you have learned your letters, though, you are ready for anything anyone dictates. If you are not prepared, I don't know what I should tell you to do. Because there may be events that call for you to act differently – and what will you do or say then? [25] So hold on to this general principle[8] and you won't need specific advice. If you hanker after externals you are going to be twirled round and round at the will of your master. [26] 'Who's my "master"?' Whoever controls what you desire or dislike.

II 3   *Addressed to people who recommend others to philosophers*

[1] It was a shrewd reply that Diogenes[9] gave the person who asked him for a letter of reference: 'The person whose favour you seek will know that you're human as soon as he sees you; as to whether you're a good or a bad one – well, either he's a competent judge of character or he isn't. If he is, he can decide that on his own too, and if he's not, a thousand letters from me aren't going to make him one. [2] A coin might as well ask for a recommendation to get someone to declare it genuine. If that someone is trained in distinguishing authentic coins from counterfeit, it will speak for itself.'

[3] And so it is in life. We need standards such as exist in the case of silver, so that we can make a similar claim as the assayer's: 'Bring me any coin at all, I will tell you whether or not it's genuine.' [4] Instead, it is in analysing syllogisms that we like to be able to say, 'Bring me any you like, and I can judge whether it is or is not analytic.'[10] Why? Because we know how to analyse arguments, and have the skill a person needs to evaluate competent logicians. [5] But in life what do I do? What today I say is good tomorrow I will swear is bad. And the reason is that, compared to what I know about syllogisms, my knowledge and experience of life fall far behind.

II 4 Addressed to someone who had been caught cheating on his wife

[1] Epictetus was saying that, as human beings, we are born to be faithful to one another, and that whoever denies this denies their humanity. Just then, a well-known scholar entered the room – one who had been caught in adultery while in Rome. [2] So Epictetus continued, 'But what are we really doing when we throw away our innate faithfulness, to intrigue with our neighbour's wife? We are ruining and destroying – well, what? How about the man of trust, principle and piety that once was? [3] And is that all? Aren't we also ruining the idea of neighbourliness, friendship and community? What position are we putting ourselves in? How am I supposed to deal with you now? As a neighbour? A friend? Some friend! A fellow citizen? But how can a fellow citizen like you be trusted?

[4] 'Look, if you were a bowl so leaky that you were good for nothing any more, you would be tossed in the rubbish dump, and no one would take the trouble to pick you out. [5] What are we going to do with a human who can't fill the most basic human role? Fine, you can't function as a friend; how would you do as a slave? Who would have any confidence in you, though, even in that capacity? So how would you like to be tossed in the rubbish too, like a leaky bowl – like dung?

[6] 'Then you are heard to say, "No one gives me any respect as a man of letters." That's because you're a vile and worthless human being! It's as if wasps were to protest that they get no respect; everyone runs away from them, some people will even swat them, given the chance. [7] Your prick is such as to infect everyone you sting with heartache and aggravation. What would you have us do with you? There isn't any place you will fit.

[8] 'Hold it, though – doesn't nature intend women to be shared?[11] I grant it – but in the way a roast is shared among dinner guests. Very well, after each guest has received his share, if you feel like it, why not grab your neighbour's portion too? Steal it when he's not looking, or just stretch out your hand and grab all you can manage to put away. If you can't actually snatch the meat, at least wipe your hands on it, and lick the grease off your fingers. What fine company you will make – just like Socrates' fellow diners in the *Symposium*.'[12]

[9] 'Well, what about the theatre – it's open to all citizens, is it not?'

'Sure, so when everyone has taken their seats, just come along and throw somebody out of theirs. [10] That, you may say, is how women are common property too.

'Look, try this instead: when the judge, like the host at a private party, has assigned them, be satisfied to claim your own share, don't be a glutton and steal someone else's. "But I'm a scholar who understands Archedemus!" [11] You can understand Archedemus and still be an adulterer and a cheater, a wolf or an ape rather than a human being; what's to stop you?'

II 5 *How confidence and carefulness are compatible*

[1] Material things *per se* are indifferent, but the use we make of them is not indifferent. [2] The question, then, is how to strike a balance between a calm and composed attitude on the one hand, and a conscientious outlook that is neither slack nor careless on the other.[13] Model yourself on card players. [3] The

chips don't matter, and the cards don't matter; how can I know what the deal will be? But making careful and skilful use of the deal – that's where my responsibility begins.[14] [4] So in life our first job is this, to divide and distinguish things into two categories: externals I cannot control, but the choices I make with regard to them I do control. Where will I find good and bad? [5] In me, in my choices. Don't ever speak of 'good' or 'bad', 'advantage' or 'harm', and so on, of anything that is not your responsibility.

[6] 'Well, does that mean that we shouldn't care how we use them?'

Not at all. In fact, it is morally wrong not to care, and contrary to our nature. [7] Be careful how you use them, because it's not unimportant – but at the same time be calm and composed, because things in themselves don't matter. [8] Where it *does* matter, no one can compel me or stand in my way. And where I can be stopped or compelled, well, getting those things is not in my control – and not good or bad in any case. But the way I use them *is* good or bad, and depends on me.

[9] It isn't easy to combine and reconcile the two – the carefulness of a person devoted to externals and the dignity of one who's detached – but it's not impossible. Otherwise happiness would be impossible.[15] [10] It's something like going on an ocean voyage. What can I do? Pick the captain, the boat, the date, and the best time to sail. [11] But then a storm hits. Well, it's no longer my business; I have done everything I could. It's somebody else's problem now – namely the captain's. [12] But then the boat actually begins to sink. What are my options? I do the only thing I am in a position to do, drown – but fearlessly, without bawling or crying out to God, because I know that what is born must also die. [13] I am not Father Time; I'm a human being, a part of the whole, like an hour in a day. Like the hour I must abide my time, and like the hour, pass. [14] What difference does it make whether I go by drowning or disease? I have to go somehow.

[15] You will find that skilled ballplayers do the same thing. It's not the ball they value, it's how well they throw and catch

it that counts as good or bad. [16] That is where the grace and skill lie, the speed and expertise – speed such that I can't catch one of their throws even if I spread out my coat to do it, and skill such that, if I throw the ball, however badly, one of them is bound to catch it. [17] If we are afraid to throw the ball, or nervous about catching it, then the fun is lost; and how can we preserve our composure when we are uncertain about what next to do? 'Throw it,' someone says, 'Don't throw it,' another says, 'Throw it already!' says someone else. It turns into a shouting instead of a sporting match.[16]

[18] Socrates, you might say, knew how to play ball. In his case, the arena was the courtroom. 'Tell me, Anytus,' he said, 'how can you say I don't believe in God? We are agreed, are we not, that there are minor gods and heroes – the children of gods or the mixed issue of gods and men?' [19] Anytus conceded the point. 'Well, if someone acknowledged that there were animals of mixed parentage – half breeds such as mules – don't you think they would also have to believe in the existence of horses or asses – the creatures that produced them?'[17] [20] It's just as if the man were playing ball. Only the ball in his case was life, imprisonment, exile or execution – with the prospect of losing his wife, and having his children reduced to the status of orphans. Those were the stakes of the game, and still he played, and handled the ball with aplomb.

[21] That's what we need: the star athlete's concentration, together with his coolness, as if it were just another ball we were playing with too. To be sure, external things of whatever kind require skill in their use, but we must not grow attached to them; whatever they are, they should only serve for us to show how skilled we are in our handling of them.

It's like weaving: the weaver does not make the wool, he makes the best use of whatever wool he's given. [22] God gives you food and property, and can take them back – your body too. Work with the material you are given. [23] If you come through all right, most people you meet will congratulate you on surviving. A shrewd judge, however, will praise you and share in your pleasure only if he sees that you acted honourably in the case; not, however, if he sees that your success was owed to anything dishonest. When happiness is come by fairly, others are happy for us too.

[24] 'Then how are some externals said to be in accordance with nature, others contrary to nature?'[18] That only applies to us considered separately. I agree that for my foot it is in accordance with its nature to be clean; but considered as a foot and not separately, it is right and proper for it to tramp through mud, step on needles – there may even be a time when it will have to be amputated for the sake of the body as a whole. It wouldn't be a foot otherwise.

We have to assume that a similar distinction applies to us personally. [25] What are you? A human being. If you think of yourself as a unit apart, then it is in accordance with your nature to live to old age, to be rich, and be healthy. But if your view of yourself involves being part of a whole, then, for the sake of the whole, circumstances may make it right for you to be sick, go on a dangerous journey, endure poverty, even die before your time. Don't complain; [26] just as it would not be a foot, don't you realize that in isolation you would not be a human being? Because what is a human being? Part of a community – the community of gods and men, primarily, and secondarily that of the city we happen to inhabit, which is only a microcosm of the universe *in toto*.

[27] 'And that's why now I'm being put on trial?' And why someone else falls sick, why another undertakes a voyage, why someone else dies, and still another is convicted. In this body, this universe, this community, it is inevitable that each of us faces some such event. [28] Your job, then, is to appear before the court, say what you have to say and make the best of the situation. [29] Then the judge declares you guilty. 'I wish you well, judge. I did my part, you can decide if you did yours.' Because the judge runs a risk too, don't forget.

II 6 On 'indifference'[19]

[1] The conjunctive argument[20] is indifferent, but how you handle it is not indifferent; it is tantamount to knowledge, opinion, or ignorance. In the same way, life is indifferent, but the use we make of it is not indifferent. [2] So when you hear that even life and the like[21] are indifferent, don't become apathetic; and by the same token, when you're advised to care about them, don't become superficial and conceive a passion for externals.

[3] It is good to be clear about the level of your talent and training. That way, when unfamiliar topics arise, you will know enough to keep still, and not be put out if there are students more advanced than you. [4] You will show your own superiority in logic; and if others are disconcerted over that, mollify them by saying, 'Well, I had a good teacher.' [5] The same applies to subjects that require some practical training; don't pretend you have a particular skill if you don't yet; yield to whoever has the requisite experience; and for your own part take satisfaction in an awareness that your persistence is helping you become expert in the subject yourself.

[6] 'Go pay so-and-so your respects.'

'I call on him – but not on my knees.'

'And you were not let in.'

'Well, you see, I don't know how to break through windows. When I find the door shut, either I have to go through the window or leave.'

[7] 'So, talk to him.'

'OK, I talk to him.'

'How?'

'As an equal.'

[8] But you did not get what you wanted – because of course that was up to him, not you. So don't take responsibility for it. Always remember what is yours, and what belongs to other people, and you won't have trouble. [9] Apropos, Chrysippus said: 'As long as the future is uncertain to me I always hold to those things which are better adapted to

obtaining the things in accordance with nature; for God himself
has made me disposed to select them. [10] But if I knew that
my destiny at present was to fall ill, I would even wish for it.
My foot, too, if it had intelligence, would volunteer to get
muddy.'

[11] Look, isn't wheat grown for the express purpose of
turning brown, and doesn't it turn brown in preparation for
being harvested? It is not grown for its own sake. [12] If it
could talk, I suppose it would beg never to be harvested? Come,
that's actually a curse we put on people's crop, that it not be
brought to harvest. [13] Know that for humans, too, it's no less
of a curse not to die – the same as 'Please, God, don't let their
wheat ripen, don't let it be brought in.' [14] But because we're
the only animals who not only die but are conscious of it even
while it happens, we are beset by anxiety. The reason can only
be that we do not know who we are, and have not studied what
it means to be a human being – the way horse trainers, for
instance, learn the ways of horses.

[15] Look at Chrysantas, though: just as he was poised to
stab an enemy combatant he heard the trumpet sound retreat
and froze; that's how much he set the captain's will above his
personal welfare.[22] [16] Yet even when fate calls, not one of us
is prepared to obey. We suffer what we suffer not willingly, but
with sobs of protest, and call it all 'circumstances'. [17] What
are circumstances? If by that you mean your situation, everything is 'circumstances'. But if you mean 'problems', where's
the problem in something that was born, dying? [18] Death
could come by way of a knife, torture, the sea, a piece of
masonry, a despot – why do you care? 'All roads to Hades are
of equal length.'[23] [19] Well, to tell you the truth, death by
despot is less protracted. No despot ever took six months to
cut a throat, whereas a fatal illness often lasts a year. 'Circumstances', 'troubles' – this is all a lot of noise and a clamour of
meaningless names.

[20] You say, 'I risk execution by the emperor.'

I face no less a danger here in Nicopolis, where earthquakes
are a common occurrence. As to you, aren't you risking your
life every time you cross the Adriatic?

[21] 'But even one's opinions can get one into trouble here in Rome.'

Do you mean your own? No one can force you to hold an opinion against your will. And if you are referring to other people's, how can *their* wrong opinions pose any danger to you?

[22] 'I also face the danger of exile.'

What is exile? Being somewhere other than Rome?

'Exactly. My God, what if I'm sent to Gyara?' Well, if that's tolerable for you, you will go; if not, you have the choice of another destination, the place even the person who sent you to Gyara is headed, whether they like it or not.

[23] So why make such a big deal of going to trial? It isn't worth all the preparation. A young man with any talent might well say, 'I wasted my time listening to so many lectures, writing so many compositions, and sitting for so long next to an old man who didn't amount to much himself.'

[24] There is only one thing you need to remember, the rule that distinguishes what is yours from what isn't. Don't ever lay claim to anything belonging to others. [25] Court and prison are two places, one high, the other low. Your character, however, can be kept the same in either place – if you decide it should. [26] We will rival Socrates when we can spend our time in prison composing hymns. [27] But considering our attitude up to now, I wonder if in prison we could even stand someone else offering to read us his own compositions.

'Don't bother me; don't you realize the problems I've got?* You think I can listen to poetry in my position?'

'Why, what is it?'

'I'm sentenced to death!'

'And the rest of us aren't?'

* reading ἄττα for τὰ.

II 8 *What is the substance of the good?*

[1] God is helpful. Whatever is good is also helpful. It is reasonable to suppose, then, that the divine nature and the nature of the good will correspond. [2] So what is the divine nature? Is it flesh? Be serious. Do we associate it with real estate and status? Hardly. It is mind, intelligence and correct reason.

[3] So look no further than there for the substance of the good. Of course, you won't find it in plants and animals. In man, however, it consists in just those qualities that distinguish him from other animals. [4] Since plants do not even have the power of perception, 'good' and 'evil' are not applicable to them. Evidently, 'good' and 'bad' presume the power of using impressions. [5] But is that enough? If it is, then you must speak of 'good' in connection with animals besides man, as well as 'happy' and 'unhappy' – [6] but there is a very good reason that you don't. Because, however well they may use impressions, animals lack the ability to reflect on them. Nor should they have it, since they were born to serve, not command. [7] Is the donkey in a position of command? It was created because man needed an animal with a strong back able to carry big loads; the creature had to be able to walk, as well. Which is why it was endowed with the power of using impressions – otherwise it couldn't walk. And that is about the extent of its endowments. [8] After all, if the donkey had also acquired the ability to reflect on its use of impressions, it would quite rightly refuse to obey us and serve our needs. It would, in fact, be mankind's equal and peer.

[9] So if it is absent from plants and animals, it's only logical that you should look for the nature of the good where you ordinarily apply the word. [10] True, they are God's creatures too, but not creatures placed in a position of authority, not parts of God. [11] You, on the other hand, *are* a creature placed in charge, and a particle of God himself; there is a bit of God within you.

[12] Why don't you know of this relation, and of your origins? When you eat, bear in mind who it is exactly you are feeding. When you have sex, reflect who you are during the act.

In conversation, exercise, discourse – do you remember that it is God you are feeding, God you are exercising? You carry God around with you and don't know it, poor fool. [13] Don't imagine I am talking about some external deity made of silver or gold. You carry the living God inside you and are blind to the fact that you desecrate him with your dirty words and dirty thoughts – [14] none of which you would dare repeat if there were even a mere statue of a god near by. God himself is there within, seeing and overhearing everything you do and say – and do you care? You pariah, you have no sense of your own heritage.

[15] What are we anxious about when we graduate a young man from school and out into the real world? That he will make mistakes, eat poorly, have sexual affairs, humiliate himself and go around in rags, or else affect the latest fashions. And why? [16] Because he is ignorant of his personal god and does not realize who goes with him when he leaves school and his former friends. Yet we indulge him when he writes to us to say, 'I wish you here with me.' [17] You have God there with you – who else do you need? Whoever you invite to come and visit – would they tell you any different?

[18] Suppose you were one of Phidias' statues – his Zeus or his Athena.[24] You would certainly have a sense of who you were then, and of who brought you into being. And if you had a brain, you would make an effort to avoid doing anything that would bring shame on either your creator or yourself, such as being caught in an embarrassing position by the spectators come to see you. [19] But Zeus has created you; shouldn't that make you even more careful about the impression you make? What is Phidias compared to Zeus? How, for that matter, can their creations be compared? [20] What other work of art comes ready equipped with the very powers the artist displayed in making it? Do marble statues? No, nor do bronze, gold or ivory ones. The Athena of Phidias, once its arm was raised to support the statue of Victory, has maintained that pose for the duration of its long existence. Zeus' works, on the other hand, are living, breathing creatures, with the power of perception and judgement.

[21] He made you, and you mock him. Why? He not only made you; of all his creatures, you alone were given the power of self-determination. [22] You not only ignore that, you bring shame on the faith he placed in you. You would not have been so negligent in caring for an orphan if God had put one in your way. [23] He has entrusted you to yourself, saying, 'I had no one more dependable than you; just see that he keeps the qualities he was born with: integrity, honour, dignity, patience, calmness and poise.' But you can't even do that.

[24] However, there will be people who say, 'Why is this person so serious and self-important?' If it seems like pretension, it's only because I don't have complete confidence in the principles that I've learned and espouse. I still fear for my own frailty. [25] But grant me the confidence, and I will show you the right look and bearing; then you will see the finished statue all bright and gleaming. [26] And don't expect a study in smugness. After all, the Zeus at Olympia does not project an air of hauteur. He looks at us right in the eye – just the way one ought to look when on the point of saying: *'My word is true and irrevocable.'*[25]

[27] That is the sort of person you'll find I am: trustworthy, honourable, noble and poised. [28] Not, to be sure, immune to death, age or disease, like God, but still prepared to die and face illness with a godlike dignity. [29] That much is mine to do, even if I cannot accomplish the rest.

In short, I will show you that I have the strength – of a philosopher. 'And what strength would that be?' A will that never fails to get what it wants, a faculty of aversion that always avoids what it dislikes, proper impulse, careful purpose and disciplined assent. That's the human specimen you should prepare yourselves to see.

II 10 *Social roles as a guide to conduct*

[1] Who are you? In the first place, a human being, which is to say, a being possessed of no greater faculty than free choice, with all your other faculties subordinate to it, choice itself being unconfined and independent. [2] Next, consider the gift of reason: it sets you apart from wild animals; it sets you apart from sheep. [3] By virtue of these two faculties you are a member of the universe with full citizen rights; you were born not to serve but to govern, because you understand the divine order and its pattern.

[4] Now, what does the title 'citizen' mean? In this role, a person never acts in his own interest or thinks of himself alone, but, like a hand or foot that had sense and realized its place in the natural order, all its actions and desires aim at nothing except contributing to the common good. [5] Therefore, philosophers rightly say, 'If a good person knew that sickness, death or disability lay in his future, he would actually invite them, because he realizes that this is part of the universal plan and that the universe has precedence over a constituent, and the city over any one citizen. [6] But since we don't know the future, we're justified in sticking to things that are preferable by nature, because this, after all, is our instinct from birth.'

[7] Next, remember that you are somebody's son. What does this social role mean? It means regarding everything of yours as belonging to your father as well, always letting him have his way, never trying to hurt him with your words or actions, or griping about him behind his back. Defer to him at every opportunity, and in the same spirit cooperate with him as best you can.

[8] Next, know that you are a brother. This role also calls for deference, respect and civility. Never get into family fights over material things; give them up willingly, and your moral standing will increase in proportion. [9] Make a gift of your box seat in the theatre, or a bit of food, if that's at stake, and see the gratitude you get in return – how much greater it is than the sacrifice.

[10] Finally, reflect on the other social roles you play. If you are a council member, consider what a council member should do. If you are young, what does being young mean, if you are old, what does age imply, [11] if you are a father, what does fatherhood entail? Each of our titles, when reflected upon, suggests the acts appropriate to it.

[12] If you go off and yell at your brother, my reaction is to say, 'You've forgotten who you are and what you stand for.' [13] I mean, if you were a metalworker who fumbled with his tools, you would have lost touch with the metalworker you once were. If you forget what it means to be a brother and become your brother's enemy, don't think you've made a trivial exchange. [14] If you are transformed from a decent, social human being into some mean, snarling, dangerous beast, is there no loss involved? Or do you have to lose money before you feel penalized? Is losing money the only loss that counts with us?

[15] If you lost the capacity to read, or play music, you would think it was a disaster, but you think nothing of losing the capacity to be honest, decent and civilized. [16] Yet those other misfortunes come from some outside cause, while these are your own fault. Moreover, it is neither honourable to have those other abilities nor dishonourable to lose them, whereas it *is* dishonourable to lose these capacities and a misfortune for which we have only ourselves to blame. [17] A catamite is deprived of his manhood, his seducer is no longer the man he was either, and is compromised in a hundred other ways besides. [18] An adulterer does away with a just, decent and honourable human being – the good neighbour and citizen he might have been. A sorehead incurs one kind of loss, a coward another – [19] but no one is bad without loss or penalty of some kind.

Now, if you look for their penalty in terms of money, you might find them all safe and scot-free; they could even be helped and rewarded for their offence if they gain by it financially. [20] But, if money is your only standard, then consider that, by your lights, someone who loses their nose does not suffer any harm.

'Yes they do, they're maimed physically.'

[21] But what if they are deprived just of the sense of smell – in other words, isn't there an associated psychic faculty, which is good to have and a misfortune to lose?

[22] 'What do you mean by "psychic faculty"?'

Aren't we born with a sense of fairness?

'We are.'

If you destroy it, is there no harm, is nothing sacrificed, don't we lose something dear? [23] Don't we have an innate sense of honour, a sense of benevolence, a sense of kindness and compassion? Well, if someone willingly parts with *these* sensibilities, do you suppose they go unpunished and unhurt?

[24] 'Well, does that mean that if someone wrongs me I shouldn't hurt them in return?' First of all, look at what wrongdoing is and remember what you have heard about it from philosophers.[26] [25] Because if 'good' as well as 'bad' really relate to our choices, then consider whether your position does not amount to saying something like, [26] 'Well, since that guy hurt himself with the injustice he did me, shouldn't I wrong him in order to hurt myself in retaliation?'

[27] So why don't we actually picture it to ourselves this way? Instead, we see injury only where physical or financial loss is incurred, whereas if the loss stems from our own choices, then we don't suspect any harm has been done. [28] After all, we don't get a headache after an error in judgement or an act of injustice; we don't get eye trouble or stomach ache, we don't lose property. [29] And for us those are the only things that matter. As to whether our character will remain loyal and honest, or become false and depraved, we don't care about that in the least – except insofar as it comes up for examination in school; [30] the result being that our debating skills improve at the cost of our character.

II 11 *Starting philosophy*

[1] People who come to philosophy the right way – by the front door, as it were – begin by acknowledging their own faults and limitations in areas of most urgency. [2] The isosceles triangle and the half-tone or quarter-tone scale – we have no knowledge pertaining to these subjects when we come into the world. We have to learn about them later through specialized training; with the result that no one untrained in these subjects pretends to know about them.

[3] The situation is otherwise in the case of our ideas about good and bad, right and wrong, appropriate and inappropriate, happiness, duty, and obligation. We are born with an innate understanding of what these words mean. [4] So everyone uses them, which is to say, everyone tries to apply the related preconceptions to specific things. [5] 'Her action was good, it was her duty, it was not her duty, she was fortunate, she was not fortunate, she is honest, she is dishonest . . .' You hear such phrases all the time, because no one is in any doubt about how to use the words. No one feels they have to wait to be told their meaning, the way we once had to learn our letters or be taught how words are pronounced. [6] The reason is that we come into the world knowing some things that nature, you might say, has taught us already; and, building on this knowledge, we come to form our opinions.

[7] 'Well, whatever you may say, I know good from bad, and have an idea of the good.'

You have one, I allow.

'And I put it into practice.'

You use it in specific instances, yes.

'And I use it correctly.'

[8] Well, that's the crux, because this is where opinions become an issue. Starting with the ideas we take for granted, we get into arguments whenever we apply them incorrectly. [9] If, along with the innate ideas, we came into the world with knowledge of how they should be applied, we would be perfect wise men from the moment we were born.

[10] Now, you think that you do possess this extra knowledge of how to apply preconceptions in particular instances. How did you come by it?

'It's my opinion.'

But someone else has a different opinion, and also believes that he is the one applying his preconceptions correctly. Am I right?

'I guess so.'

[11] And if you clash over the application of preconceptions, you can't both be using them correctly.

'Agreed.'

[12] Well, can you come up with a better aid to their application than your opinion? I mean, a lunatic acts in accordance with his own opinion of what is good; but in his case can it function as an adequate guide?

'No.'

So let's move beyond opinion; is there nothing better?

[13] Here you have philosophy's starting point: we find that people cannot agree among themselves, and we go in search of the source of their disagreement. In time, we come to scorn and dismiss simple opinion, and look for a way to determine if an opinion is right or wrong. At last, we focus on finding a standard that we can invoke, just as the scale was invented to measure weights, and the carpenter's rule devised to distinguish straight from crooked. [14] That is the beginning of philosophy.

Are everyone's opinions correct? How can they be, when some conflict?

[15] 'All right, not all are correct. But ours are.'

Well, why ours instead of the Syrians' or Egyptians' – why mine rather than those of any person picked at random?

'No reason.'

Therefore, the fact that someone holds this or that opinion will not suffice to make it true, any more than we are inclined to trust a person's word in dealing with weights and measures. In both cases, we have developed an objective standard instead. [16] So is there no standard for our case beyond opinion? Is it only humanity's most important values that are going to remain vague and subjective? [17] There must be one. So let's hunt for it; and once we've found it, let's commit to never making a single move without reference to it. [18] I conceive this discovery as the antidote to the madness that results from exclusive reliance on opinion as the criterion of truth. And from then on, starting with the familiar preconceptions, clearly defined, we will proceed to apply them to particular objects and events in a methodical manner.

[19] Name me a subject for discussion now.

'Pleasure.'

[20] All right, put it to the test, lay it on the scales. For something to be good, it must be something we can rely on and trust.

'I agree.'

Well, can we trust anything that comes and goes?

'No.'

[21] And is pleasure constant?

'No.'

Then take it out of the scale and banish it from the realm of goods.

[22] But if you're none too sharp and missed it the first time, let's try a different test. Something good should be a source of pride, correct?

'Yes.'

And can one really take pride in a momentary pleasure? Please don't say yes, or I will think you barely deserve to be regarded on the same level as draft animals.

[23] That is the way things are weighed and disagreements settled – when standards are established. [24] Philosophy aims to test and set such standards. [25] And the wise man is advised to make use of their findings right away.

II 12 *On the art of argumentation*

[1] The philosophers of our school have told us precisely what we need to learn in order to know how to practise logical argument. But when it comes to practising it correctly in a

particular situation – there we have no experience at all. [2] Just give us a random person to engage in dialogue and we won't know what to do with him. After asking the person a few questions, if we don't get the kinds of answer we expect, we throw up our hands and resort to ridicule or verbal abuse, saying, 'He's not a philosopher, it just isn't possible to engage him in dialogue.'

[3] Well, when a guide meets up with someone who is lost, ordinarily his reaction is to direct him on the right path, not mock or malign him, then turn on his heel and walk away. [4] As for you, lead someone to the truth and you will find that he can follow.[27] But as long as you don't point it out to him, don't make fun of him; be aware of what *you* need to work on instead.

[5] Consider how Socrates behaved. He would compel whomever he spoke with to voice their views, and one interlocutor was enough. Which is why he could say, 'Everyone else can go hang, I am only interested in what the person I'm talking to has to say. No one's vote counts with me except that of my partner in dialogue.'[28] [6] Socrates would lay out the implications of their views so incisively that, regardless of who they were, they would all admit an inconsistency and back off from it:

[7] 'Is a man racked by envy happy?'

'Not at all, they're miserable.'*

'Miserable over something bad? But whoever heard of envy for something bad?'

[8] Thus he made him say that envy is pain provoked by something good.

'I mean, would someone be envious over something he cared nothing for?'

'Obviously not.'[29]

[9] That is what Socrates would do: he would quit only after he had fleshed out an idea and explored its implications. He wouldn't just say, 'Define envy for me,' then, when his

---

* The following sentence has been omitted as an intrusive gloss: 'He made his interlocutor switch his position.'

interlocutor had ventured on a definition, say, 'Wrong: your definiens is not extensionally equivalent to the definiendum' – [10] technical terms which are incomprehensible and off-putting for the layman, and which we can't resist using for that very reason. [11] As for using language that would enable even a non-philosopher, depending on his view, to answer with a simple yes or no – well, we don't know how to engage anyone on that level. [12] And what happens is that we realize that we can't do it and give up the attempt – those of us with any discretion, anyway. [13] Most people are impulsive, however, and, having committed to the thing, they persist, just making more confusion for themselves and others until it all ends in mutual recrimination.

[14] Now that is the first thing Socrates was known for – never turning dialogue into dispute, never introducing rudeness or invective, although he would put up with the insults of others in order to avoid a fight. [15] And if you want to know how effective he was, read Xenophon's *Symposium*; you will see how many fights he is credited there with resolving. [16] Among the poets, too, one of the highest forms of compliment is conveyed in the line:

He could cut short a quarrel, however great, with his diplomacy.[30]

[17] But nowadays engaging in logical dialogue is just not a very safe business, in Rome especially. Because of course you can't do it off in a corner somewhere. You may find yourself approaching a senator, someone with money, and asking him: 'Do you know, sir, to whom you have entrusted the care of your horses?'

[18] 'I do.'

'Is it some random person with no knowledge of horses?'

'Of course not.'

'What about your money and clothes?'

'I don't hand them over to just anyone either.'

[19] 'And as to your body, you've already found someone to entrust with its care?'

'Naturally.'

'An expert, obviously, in either exercise or medicine?'

'Yes.'

[20] 'Are these the things you value most, or have you got something better than them all?'

'And what would that be?'

'The faculty that uses all of them, and assigns each their place and value.'

'You mean the soul?'

[21] 'Good guess; that's precisely what I mean.'

'Absolutely, I think that is far and away a more precious possession than the others you mentioned.'

[22] 'So, then, tell me the steps you've taken to care for the soul. As intelligent as you are, and as politically prominent, surely you would not casually look on and allow the most prized of your possessions to be neglected and go to ruin.'

'No, of course not.'

[23] 'Well, if you have looked after it personally, did you learn how from another person, or discover the means yourself?'

[24] At this point you run the risk of him saying, 'What business is that of yours, sir? What are you to me?' Pester him further, and he is liable to punch you in the nose. [25] I myself was once keen for this sort of discourse, until I met with just such a reception.

II 13 *On nerves*

[1] Whenever I see a person suffering from nervousness, I think, well, what can he expect? If he had not set his sights on things outside man's control, his nervousness would end at once. [2] Take a lyre player: he's relaxed when he performs alone, but put him in front of an audience, and it's a different story, no matter how beautiful his voice or how well he plays the instrument. Why? Because he not only wants to perform well, he wants to be well received – and the latter lies outside his control.

[3] He is confident as far as his knowledge of music is

concerned – the views of the public carry no weight with him there. His anxiety stems from lack of knowledge and lack of practice in other areas. Which are what? [4] He doesn't know what an audience is, or what approval from an audience amounts to. Although he knows well enough how to play every note on the guitar, from the lowest to the highest, the approval of the public – what it means and what real significance it has – this he does not know and has made no effort to learn. [5] Necessarily, then, he is going to get nervous and grow pale. Now, I won't go so far as to say that he's not a true musician if I see that he suffers from stage fright. But I can say one thing – several things, in fact.

[6] I can start by calling him a stranger and say, 'This person has no idea where he's living, and for all his time in residence here still doesn't know the laws of the country or its customs. He does not know what is permitted and what is not. Furthermore, he has never taken the trouble to call on a lawyer who will tell him, and explain how things operate here. [7] He won't sign a contract without knowing how to draft one properly, or hiring somebody who does. He isn't casual about signing for loans or offering guarantees. But when it comes to desire, aversion, impulse, plans and projects, he applies himself to all of these without benefit of legal counsel. [8] How do I know? He wants what he cannot have, and does not want what he can't refuse – and isn't even aware of it. He doesn't know the difference between his own possessions and others'. Because, if he did, he would never be thwarted or disappointed.

Or nervous.

Just think: [9] we aren't filled with fear except by things that are bad; and not by them, either, as long as it is in our power to avoid them. [10] So, if externals are neither good nor bad, while everything within the sphere of choice is in our power and cannot be taken away by anyone, or imposed on us without our compliance – then what's left to be nervous about? [11] We agonize over our body, our money, or what the emperor is going to decree – never about anything inside us.

I mean, do we worry whether we are going to make an error in judgement? No, because it is under our control. Or having

an unnatural urge? No again. [12] So if you see someone pale
with nerves, be like a doctor who diagnoses liver trouble based
on a patient's yellow skin. Say, 'This man's desire and aversion
are unhealthy, they aren't functioning properly, they're
infected. [13] Because nothing else can account for his change
in colour, his shivering, his chattering teeth, and "this constant
fretting and shifting from foot to foot".'[31]

[14] All of which explains why Zeno was not nervous about
his meeting with Antigonus.[32] What Zeno valued Antigonus
had no power over, and as a philosopher he cared nothing for
the things that the king did command. [15] It was Antigonus
who was anxious before their meeting. Naturally – he wanted
to make a good impression, which was beyond his control.
Zeno, for his part, had no wish to please the king; no expert
needs validation from an amateur. [16] So what do I need *your*
approval for? You don't know the measure of a man, you
haven't studied to learn what a good or a bad person is, and
how each one gets that way. No wonder you're not a good
person yourself.

[17] 'How do you make that out?'

It is not in a good person's nature to grieve, complain or
whine; they don't go pale, tremble and say, 'What kind of
hearing or reception will he give me?' [18] Idiot, that's his
concern – don't concern yourself with other people's business.
It's his problem if he receives you badly.

'True.'

And you cannot suffer for another person's fault. So don't
worry about the behaviour of others.

[19] 'All right, but I worry about how I will talk to him.'

Can't you talk to him any way you like?

'I'm afraid that I may say something gauche.'

[20] Look, when you are about to spell the name 'Dion', are
you afraid that you will slip up?

'No.'

And why not? It's because you have practice in writing the
name.

'True.'

And you would have the same confidence reading it.

'Yes.'

The reason is that any discipline brings with it a measure of strength and confidence in the corresponding arts. [21] Now, you have practice speaking. What else did they teach you at school?

'Syllogisms and changing arguments.'[33]

But why, if not to be accomplished in conversation? And by accomplished I mean refined, assured, intelligent, not easily flustered or refuted – and fearless, on top of all that.

'Agreed.'

[22] Well, then, you are in the position of a soldier on horse-back who is about to face a mere foot soldier, on ground that you have gone over and he has not. And still you're nervous?

'But he can literally kill me!'

[23] Well, then, speak the truth, you sorry specimen, don't put on airs and call yourself a philosopher. Face up to who your betters are. As long as you have this attachment to the body, be ready to submit to anyone or anything of superior physical force.

[24] As for speaking, Socrates must have practised the art, look at his answer to the Thirty Tyrants, his defence before the jury, his conversations in jail.[34] Diogenes too had practised how to speak, witness the free and easy way he talked to Alexander, Philip, the pirates and the person to whom the pirates sold him as a slave.[35]* [26] As for you, go back to your work and don't ever leave it. Settle back in your alcove, think up new syllogisms, and share them with your friends. [27] You are plainly not cut out for the role of public leader.

---

* There is a lacuna in the text at this point; a sentence fragment (§25) has been omitted from the translation.

II 14 *To Naso*[36]

[1] A visitor from Rome, together with his son, was present at one of his lectures when Epictetus said, 'This is the way I teach' – then abruptly stopped talking. [2] The man pleaded with him to go on, but Epictetus said: The learning process is boring to anyone completely new to, and unfamiliar with, a skill. [3] Now, the skill's finished product leaves no doubt as to its utility, most are even pleasing or attractive. [4] It is not exciting, for instance, to follow the progress of a shoemaker in his art, but shoes are not only useful, they are usually aesthetically pleasing to a degree. [5] Or the training of a carpenter – it is very tedious for people who are not carpenters to watch, but the finished cabinetry justifies the effort. [6] Music makes my point most obviously: attend a music lesson, and you will think it involves the most monotonous training of all. But the results please and entertain everyone.

[7] In our school, we picture the philosopher's goal more or less as follows: bring the will in line with events, so that nothing happens contrary to our wishes and, conversely, nothing fails to happen that we want to happen. [8] Pursue it, and the reward is that neither desire nor aversion will fail in their aims; and we will fill all our roles in society – as son, father, brother, citizen, man, woman, neighbour, fellow voyager, ruler or ruled – without conflict, fear or rancour.

[9] That is how we picture the philosopher's goal. The next step is finding how to make it reality. [10] Becoming a carpenter or pilot, we realize, requires some formal training. Is it unreasonable to suppose that it will take more than just the desire to be good or bad – that the student of philosophy will also have to learn a few things of his own? So we look for some guidance. [11] Philosophers say that the first thing to learn is that God exists, that he governs the world, and that we cannot keep our actions secret, that even our thoughts and inclinations are known to him. [12] The next thing to learn about is the divine nature, because we will have to imitate the gods if we intend to obey them and win their favour. [13] If the divine

nature is trustworthy, then we should be trustworthy; if it is free, then we should be free; likewise if it is benevolent and forgiving. All our thoughts and behaviour should be shaped on the divine model.

[14] So where to begin? If you are prepared for it, I would say that you need to begin by understanding the meaning of words.

'Are you implying that at present I don't?'

I am.

[15] 'Then how come I use them?'

You use them the way illiterates use written signs, or the way cattle make use of their senses; in other words, it's possible to use them without fully understanding what they mean.

[16] But if you think you really do understand, let's take a few words and test each other's level of understanding.

[17] 'But I'm a grown man who's already been through the wars; exams at my age are an imposition.'

[18] Don't I know it. And after all, you're not here because you think you lack for anything; what could you even imagine that you need? You're rich, you have children, a wife probably, and a sufficiency of slaves; the emperor knows you, you have many friends in Rome, you see to your civic duties, and know how to reward your friends and get even with your enemies. [19] What more could you want? Well, what if I were to show you that all that's missing are the keys to happiness? That your life to date has been devoted to everything except what it ought to be? And what if I were to crown it off by saying that you don't know what God is, or man, or what good and bad are, [20] and – if *that's* not too much to endure – that you don't know who *you* are, either? Could you put up with me, take the criticism, and remain? [21] Hardly; you would be out of here in a huff and a hurry.

And yet I won't have done you any harm – any more than a mirror is to blame when it shows a plain person what they look like; or a doctor is mean if he tells a patient, 'Look, you may think this is insignificant, but you're really sick; no food for you today, only water.' No one thinks, 'How rude!' [22] But say to someone, 'Your desires are unhealthy, your powers of aversion are weak, your plans are incoherent, your impulses are at odds with nature and your system of values is false and confused,' – and off they go alleging slander.

[23] Our condition can be compared to a festival.[37] Cattle are brought in to be sold, and most of the people attend to either buy or sell; but there a few who come simply to see how and why the festival is organized, who put it on, and for what purpose.

[24] It's just the same in this festival here: some people are like the cattle that care only for their feed; those of you focused on wealth, property, a large household, public status – all this is nothing more than cattle fodder. [25] But a few people in the crowd are capable of reflection; what is this world, they want to know, and who runs it? [26] Someone must – for no country or estate can function for any length of time without its governor or steward. And this design, so big, so beautiful and so well planned – can it run on its own, haphazardly?

[27] OK, then, there is a ruler. But who is he, and how does he exercise control? What are we like, who are his descendants, and for what purpose were we born? Shouldn't there be some link between us, some connection?

[28] That's what occupies a few, who spend all their spare time seeing and learning as much as they can about the festival before the time comes to get up and leave. [29] Naturally, they are laughed at by the majority; much the way those who make money at the games laugh at those who are only there to watch. And I suppose if cattle had opinions, they would make fun of anyone interested in anything besides the grass!

II 15 *To people who cling hard to certain of their decisions*

[1] Some people suppose that the virtue of resolution, when considered in connection with the fact that nature made the will free and untrammelled, and everything else blocked, checked, slavish and external, entails that our decisions should all be

honoured to the extent of never backing off from one an inch.
[2] No – the decision first must be well founded. I mean, I like
a body to be strong, but strong with the energy that comes of
good health and training, not the kind that comes of some
manic disorder. [3] If you are taking pride in having the energy
of a lunatic, I have to say, 'Friend, you need a therapist. This is
not strength, but a kind of infirmity.'

[4] In a different sense, this ailment affects the minds of
people who misconstrue our philosophy. A friend of mine, for
instance, arbitrarily decided that he was going to starve himself
to death. [5] When I heard that he was already three days into
his fast, I went and asked him to explain.

'I made my decision,' he said.

[6] 'Yes, but what drove you to it? Look, if it is the right
decision, we are ready to sit by your side and help you make
the passage.³⁸ But if it was a reckless decision, it should be open
to change.'

[7] 'But we must stick with a decision.'

'For heaven's sake, man, that rule only applies to sound
decisions. I suppose next you will decide that it is night now,
and refuse to change your mind because you don't want to.
You will repeat, "We must stick with a decision." [8] Begin
with a firm foundation; evaluate your decision to see if it is
valid – then there will be a basis for this rigid resolve of yours.
[9] If your foundation is rotten or crumbling, not a thing should
be built on it,* and the bigger and grander you make it, the
sooner it will collapse.

[10] 'With no good reason, you are taking the life of an old
friend of mine, one who shares both cities with me, the big one
and the small.³⁹ [11] And while busy killing and doing away
with an innocent man, you keep saying, "We must stick with a
decision." [12] If the idea of killing me should ever occur to
you, would the same principle apply, I wonder?'

[13] Well, with great difficulty the man was finally prevailed
on to relent. But there are some people today whom there is
just no persuading. I have come to understand that saying which

* Reading οὐκ οἰκοδομητέον τι for οὐκ οἰκοδομημάτιον.

I did not fully appreciate until now: 'A fool cannot be convinced or even compelled to renounce his folly.' [14] God save me from fools with a little philosophy – no one is more difficult to reach.

'I've made a decision.'

Yes, so have lunatics. But the more fixed their delusions, the more medication they require. [15] Do what sick people do, call on the doctor and say to him, 'Doctor, I'm sick and need your help. I promise to follow whatever you prescribe.' [16] Similarly, I expect to hear from you, 'I am lost and don't know what I should do. I've come to you to find out.' Instead, I get, 'Talk to me about anything else; in this matter my mind's made up.' [17] What else am I supposed to talk to you about? Nothing is more important than that I cure you of the conviction that 'We must stick with a decision, and never back down' is too crude a law. This is deranged, not healthy, resolution.

[18] 'I want to die, even though I don't have to.'*

Why? What has happened?

'I made that decision.'

[19] Good thing it wasn't me you decided needed to go.

'I don't take money for my services.'

Why not?

'That was my decision.'

Realize that this irrationality means one day you might well switch to accepting money, and with the same degree of passion announce, 'This is my decision.' [20] You're like someone afflicted with certain illnesses, which manifest in different parts of the body at different times. It's the same with the unhealthy mind; what view it will incline to no one can ever guess. And when this arbitrariness is reinforced by strength of purpose, the illness becomes past help or healing.

---

* Reading κ'ἄν με οὐδὲν ἀναγκάζῃ.

II 16 *We do not regularly put our beliefs about good and bad into practice*

[1] Where does the good lie?

'In the will.'

And evil?

'Also in the will.'

And things neither good nor bad –

'. . . lie in whatever is external to the will.'

[2] Very good! But how many of you remember this outside class? Do any of you, on your own, practise formulating answers to common impressions the way you provide answers in a logical drill: 'Is it day?' 'Yes.' 'Is it night then?' 'No.' 'Then are the stars odd or even in number?' 'I cannot say.' [3] When confronted with money, are you trained to give the right response – 'Money is not a good'? Have you practised giving answers like this, or is your training confined to sophisms?

[4] Well, it should come as no surprise to you that you surpass yourself where you are trained, but get nowhere in areas you've ignored. [5] Take the example of a public speaker. He is confident that he has written a good speech, he has committed the thing to memory, and can deliver it smoothly. Still he agonizes, [6] because it's not enough for him to be competent, he also hungers for the crowd's approval. This means that, however well trained he is in the art of public speaking, he has no training in the business of praise and blame. [7] When was he ever questioned as to what praise and blame are, and what is the nature of each; or whether all praise should be welcomed, and all criticism shunned? Did he ever submit to training based on the answers to *those* questions?

[8] It's no wonder now that, having applied himself to oratory, he's better than his contemporaries in that field; but no better than the mass of men in the areas he's overlooked. [9] He is like a musician who knows how to play, who sings well, dresses nicely – and still experiences nerves before taking the stage. Music, he knows; but he does not know what an audience is, or what good and bad reviews amount to. [10] He doesn't

even understand his own anxiety, whether it's our concern or another's, and whether it can be managed. The result is that, if he wins applause, he returns home full of himself; but if he is booed, he shrivels as if the air has been let out of him and sinks down, deflated.

[11] Our case is much the same. What do we value? Externals. What do we look after? Externals. [12] So of course, we are going to experience fear and nervousness. Faced with external circumstances that we judge to be bad, we cannot help but be frightened and apprehensive. [13] 'Please, God,' we say, 'relieve me of my anxiety.' Listen, stupid, you have hands, God gave them to you himself. You might as well get on your knees and pray that your nose won't run. A better idea would be to wipe your nose and forgo the prayer. The point is, isn't there anything God gave you for your present problem? [14] You have the gifts of courage, fortitude and endurance. With 'hands' like these, do you still need somebody to help wipe your nose?

[15] The trouble is, we don't exercise these virtues because we don't appreciate them. Show me one person who cares *how* they act, someone for whom success is less important than the manner in which it is achieved. While out walking, who gives any thought to the act of walking itself? Who pays attention to the process of planning, not just the outcome? [16] If the plan works, of course, a person is overjoyed and says, 'How well we planned it! Didn't I tell you, with brains like ours it couldn't possibly fail?' But a different result leaves the person devastated, incapable of even finding words to explain what happened.

[17] No one ever consults a seer, or spends the night in a temple, out of concern for the means, rather than the ends, of their actions. Find me one such person, I want to see him. This is the person I have looked for a long time, the true genius and aristocrat – I don't care if they be young or old, just find me one.

[18] So how can we possibly wonder, if, having squandered our attention on material things, we act in a way that is mean, shameless, worthless, cowardly, meek – a complete nightmare? We didn't practise, or care about, that. [19] Rather than death

or exile, if we feared fear itself, we would practise avoiding the things we believe to be bad. [20] As it is, in the classroom we're fierce and fluent, quick to answer any little question on these topics, and adept at drawing the right conclusion. But force us to put the principles into practice and we're as good as lost. Let any danger loom and you will discover what we really practised and trained for. [21] Then, because of our negligence, we forever compound our problems and make our situations out to be worse than they actually are. [22] So, for instance, whenever I'm on board ship and gaze into the deep, or look around me and see nothing but ocean, I'm gripped by terror, imagining that if we wreck I will have to swallow all this sea. It doesn't occur to me that around three pints will about do me in. So is it the sea that terrifies me? No, it is my imagination. [23] Again, in an earthquake, I am prone to picture the whole city coming down on top of me, whereas, in fact, a single brick is enough to dash my brains out.

[24] So what oppresses and scares us? It is our own thoughts, obviously. What overwhelms people when they are about to leave friends, family, old haunts and their accustomed way of life? Thoughts. [25] I mean, look at children: their nanny leaves them and they begin to cry; but give them a cake and they've forgotten all about their nanny.

[26] 'Are you saying that we should model ourselves on children?'

No – because I don't think you need a cake, you need correct thoughts.

'What are they?'

[27] Every day you should put the ideas in action that protect against attachment to externals such as individual people, places or institutions – even your own body. Remember the law of God and keep it constantly in view: [28] look to your own means, leave everything that isn't yours alone. Make use of what material advantages you have, don't regret the ones you were not allowed. If any of them are recalled, let go of them willingly, grateful for the time you had to enjoy them – unless you want to be like a child crying for her nurse or mother. [29] After all, what difference does it make what a person is

enslaved to, and cannot live without? You're no different from a teenager mooning over a girl when you ache for your familiar haunts, your club, your old gang of friends and former way of life.

[30] Here is someone distraught because he will no longer drink of the water of Dirce.[40] Is our water here in Rome inferior somehow?

'No, but I had grown used to Dirce's.'

[31] Well, you will get used to ours in time. And once you become used to it, the day may come when you pine for it in turn. You may even try your hand at poetry in imitation of that line in Euripides:

'Ah, for Nero's baths, and the water of Marcia!'[41]

Behold the birth of tragedy: when idiots come face to face with the vicissitudes of life.

[32] 'Will I ever see Athens and the Acropolis again?'

Poor fellow, you're not satisfied with what you see every day? Can you hope for any better vision than the sun, the moon, the stars, all the land and sea? [33] And if you appreciate how God governs them, and carry him around inside you, what attraction can mere marble or fine masonry still have for you? When it is time to leave the sun and moon behind, how will you react? [34] Will you sit down and cry, like an infant? Did nothing that you heard and studied in school get through to you? Why did you advertise yourself as a philosopher when you might have told the truth: 'I made it through a couple of primers, then read a little Chrysippus – but I hardly crossed the threshold of philosophy.' [35] How can you associate yourself with Socrates, who lived and died as he did, or with Diogenes?[42] [36] You cannot imagine either of them reduced to tears or tantrums because they weren't going to see this man, or that woman, or because they had to be in Susa, say, or Ecbatana, rather than Athens or Corinth. [37] Whoever can exit the party at will when the fun begins to fade is not likely to stick around and be bored; he will stay only as long as he is entertained – like a child involved in playing a game. [38] He is hardly the kind to endure permanent exile, or a sentence of exile until death.[43] [39] Like a child, it's high time you were weaned off milk and started taking solid food – or, put another way, it's time you stopped crying for your nurse and mother.*

[40] 'But by leaving them I make them unhappy.'

You think *you* are the cause of their unhappiness? No; the cause of their disturbance is the same as yours: judgements. Overhaul your judgements and, if they're smart, they will overhaul theirs. Otherwise, their unhappiness will be of their own making.

[41] Listen, as the saying goes, it's crisis time: make a last desperate effort to gain freedom and tranquillity – to be Stoic. [42] Lift up your head, like a person finally released from slavery. Dare to face God and say, 'From now on, use me as you like. I am of one mind with you, I am your peer.'† Whatever you decide, I will not shrink from it. You may put me where you like, in any role regardless: officer or citizen, rich man or pauper, here or overseas. [43] They are all just so many opportunities to justify your ways to man, by showing just how little circumstances amount to.

[44] No, instead you keep safe indoors, waiting for mother to come and feed you. What would Heracles have been had he just hung around the house? He would have been Eurystheus[44] – not Heracles at all. Think about how many friends and companions Heracles made in consequence of travelling the world. None, however, was closer to him than Zeus, which is why he was rightly believed to be his son. It was in obedience to him that he went around wiping out crime and injustice.

[45] Well, you are no Heracles, with power to clear away the ills of other people; no, you are not even Theseus, otherwise you might at least relieve Attica of its troubles.[45] Therefore, set your own house in order. Cast out of your mind – not Procrustes or Sciron[46] – but sorrow, fear, lust, envy, spite, greed, petulance and over-indulgence. [46] Getting rid of these, too, requires looking to God for help, trusting him alone, and submitting to his direction. [47] Then if you're not willing to do this – all tears and agitation – you will serve someone physically more

* Deleting γραῶν ἀποκλαύματα.
† Retaining ἴσος, the reading of the MSS.

powerful than you, and continue to look outside yourself for happiness, fated never to find it. And that is because you look for it in the wrong place, forgetting to look where it really lies.

II 17 *How to adapt preconceptions to everyday instances*

[1] The first thing a pretender to philosophy must do is get rid of their presuppositions; a person is not going to undertake to learn anything that they think they already know. [2] We come to the study of philosophy rattling off what should and should not be done, what's good, what's bad, and what's disgraceful. On this basis, we are quite prepared to pass out praise, blame, censure, or condemnation, subtly distinguishing good habits from bad.

[3] So what do we need philosophers for, if we know it all already? We want to learn what we don't presume to know – namely, problems of logic. We want to learn what those philosophers teach because it is supposed to be keen and clever.* [5] Well, it is ridiculous to imagine that you will learn anything but what you want to learn; in other words, you can't hope to make progress in areas where you have made no application.

Many people, however, make the same mistake as the orator Theopompus. He criticized Plato for wanting to define every little thing.[47] [6] 'Did no one before you,' he says, 'use the words "good" and "just"? Or if we did, were we ignorant of what each of them meant – were we making empty sounds bereft of sense?' [7] Look, Theopompus, no one denies that we had an inborn idea and preconception of these terms. What we lacked was the ability to apply them correctly. We had not yet organized them with a view to determining the class of things each of them belongs to.

[8] You might as well put the same challenge to doctors:

---

* Omitting οἱ δ' ἵν' ἀπ' αὐτῶν περιποιήσονται from the translation.

'Didn't we use the words "sick" and "healthy" before Hippocrates came along, or were we talking nonsense?' [9] Well, we had a concept of what 'healthy' means, yes, but even now we can't agree on how to adapt it. There's one doctor who says, 'Withhold his food,' while another says, 'Make him eat.' One says, 'Bleed her,' another says, 'She needs a transfusion.' And the cause of this chaos is none other than our still-unrealized ability to apply the concept of 'healthy' to particular cases.

[10] The same problem occurs in the conduct of life. 'Good', 'bad', 'useful', 'harmful' – these words are part of everyone's vocabulary, we all have a preconception of what they signify. But is it developed and complete? [11] Prove it – apply it correctly to particular things. Now Plato, for his part, associates definitions with his preconception of what is 'useful'; you, however, categorize them as useless. [12] Both of you cannot be right. Some people associate the idea of the good with wealth, or pleasure, or health; others plainly do not. [13] Because if all of us who use these words are not just blowing smoke, and we don't need help clarifying their preconceptions, why is there any misunderstanding, conflict or blame on either side?

[14] But why refer to conflict between different people, and bring up that? Just take yourself – if you are good at applying your preconceptions, why are you internally conflicted and confused? [15] We will ignore for now the second field of study, to do with impulse and the art of applying impulse to appropriate acts.[48] Let's skip the third field too, concerning assent – [16] I'll give you a pass on both. Let's stay with the first; it furnishes almost tangible proof that you are not good at applying preconceptions. [17] If your present desires are realistic – realistic for you personally – why are you frustrated and unhappy? If you are not trying to escape the inevitable, then why do you continue to meet with accident and misfortune? Why do you get what you do not want, and don't get what you do? [18] This is categorical proof of inner confusion and unhappiness. I want something to happen, and it fails to happen, or I don't want something to happen, and it does – and can any creature be more miserable than I?

[19] It is just this that Medea could not tolerate, and which

drove her to slay her children – a magnificent act from one point of view, it shows she had the right idea of what it means to have one's desires dashed.[49] [20] 'I'll have my revenge on the man who hurt and humiliated me. But what good are the usual types of punishment? How should it happen then? I will kill my children. But I will punish myself in the process . . . [21] Well – what of it?'

Behold the ruin of a noble soul. She did not know, in effect, that obtaining our desire is not done by looking outside ourselves for help, or by changing or rearranging circumstance. [22] Don't want your husband, and nothing that you want will fail to come. Don't want to stay with him at any price, don't wish to stay in Corinth – in short, don't want anything except what God wants, and no one will stop or stay you, any more than they can stand in the way of God. [23] When you have him as your leader, and conform your will and desire to his, what fear of failure can you have?

[24] Attach your desire to wealth and your aversion to poverty: you won't get the former, but you could well end up with the latter. You will fare no better putting your faith in health, status, exile – any external you care to name. [25] Hand your will over to Zeus and the gods, let them administer it; in their keeping, your happiness is assured.

[26] But please stop representing yourself as a philosopher, you affected fool! You still experience envy, pity, jealousy and fear, and hardly a day passes that you don't whine to the gods about your life. [27] Some philosopher! You learned syllogisms and changing arguments. Good, now try unlearning them, if you can, and make a fresh start. Wake up to the fact that so far you have barely touched the subject. [28] Begin to fashion your future in such a way that nothing happens contrary to your desire and nothing that you desire fails to materialize.

[29] Give me one student with *that* ambition when he presents himself at school, one committed to *that* kind of training, one who says, 'To me those other things are worthless; it's enough if one day I can live without sorrow and frustration, if I can lift up my head like a free person in the face of circumstance and look to heaven as a friend of God, without fear of

anything that might happen.' [30] Show me such a person, so I can say, 'Come, child, take what you deserve. You were born to honour philosophy with your patronage – these halls, these books, these lectures, they all belong to you.' [31] Then, after he's tackled and mastered this field of study, I will wait until he returns and says, 'I want to be free from fear and emotion, but at the same time I want to be a concerned citizen and philosopher, and attentive to my other duties, toward God, my parents, my siblings, my country, and my guests.' [32] Welcome to the second field of study, this is yours as well. [33] 'But I've already mastered the second field of study; I want to be faultless and unshakeable, not just when I'm awake, but even when I'm sleeping, even when I'm drunk or delirious.'[50] You are a god, my child, you are headed for the stars.

[34] But no, what I get instead is, 'I want to read Chrysippus' treatise on the Liar.'[51] Is that your plan? Then go and jump in the lake and take your ridiculous plan with you. What good could come of it? Your unhappiness will persist the whole time you are reading it, and your anxiety will not abate a bit during a reading of the thing before an audience.

[35] Here's how you behave: 'Shall I read to you, brother, then you to me?'

'Man, it's marvellous the way you write.'

'Well, it's uncanny how you capture Xenophon's style.'

[36] 'And *you* have caught Plato's manner.'

'And you Antisthenes'!'[52]

Then, having indulged each other in your fatuous fancies, you go back to your former habits: your desires and aversions are as they were, your impulses, designs and plans remain unchanged, you pray and care for the same old things. [37] And so far from looking for someone to bring you to your senses, you are distinctly offended by any advice or correction. You say, 'He's nothing but a mean old man; when I left him he showed no sign of sorrow. He didn't say, "My, it's a dangerous journey you're going on, child, I'll light a candle if you come through safely." [38] That's what he would say if the man had any compassion.' And what a blessing it would be for a person like you to come through safely, calling for many candles to be lit! Really, you deserve to be immortal and impervious to misfortune.

[39] As I said, then, this presumption that you possess knowledge of any use has to be dropped before you approach philosophy – just as if we were enrolling in a school of music or mathematics. [40] Otherwise we won't come close to making progress – not even if we work our way through the collected works of Chrysippus, with those of Antipater[53] and Archedemus thrown in for good measure.

II 18 *How to fight against impressions*

[1] Every habit and faculty is formed or strengthened by the corresponding act – walking makes you walk better, running makes you a better runner. [2] If you want to be literate, read, if you want to be a painter, paint. Go a month without reading, occupied with something else, and you'll see what the result is. [3] And if you're laid up a mere ten days, when you get up and try to walk any distance you'll find your legs barely able to support you. [4] So if you like doing something, do it regularly; if you don't like doing something, make a habit of doing something different.

[5] The same goes for moral inclinations. When you get angry, you should know that you aren't guilty of an isolated lapse, you've encouraged a trend and thrown fuel on the fire. [6] When you can't resist sex with someone, don't think of it as a temporary setback; you've fed your weakness and made it harder to uproot. [7] It is inevitable that continuous behaviour of any one kind is going to instil new habits and tendencies, while steadily confirming old ones.

[8] And as philosophers point out, this, of course, is how moral infirmities develop also. If you are seized by greed on some occasion, reason can be invoked to alert you to the danger. Then the passion will abate and the mind will be restored to its former balance. [9] But if you don't bring anything by way of relief, the mind will not return to normal; when it's inflamed

by an impression, it will yield to passion more quickly the next time. Keep it up, and the mind grows inured to vice; eventually the love of money is entrenched. [10] When someone contracts smallpox, if he lives he is not the same as he was before the illness, unless the recovery is complete. [11] It's the same with the passions of the soul; they leave certain scars and blisters behind. And unless you remove them well, the next time you're flogged on the same spot those blisters will be open wounds.

[12] So if you don't want to be cantankerous, don't feed your temper, or multiply incidents of anger. Suppress the first impulse to be angry, then begin to count the days on which you don't get mad. [13] 'I used to be angry every day, then only every other day, then every third . . .' If you resist it a whole month, offer God a sacrifice, because the vice begins to weaken from day one, until it is wiped out altogether. [14] 'I didn't lose my temper this day, or the next, and not for two, then three months in succession.' If you can say that, you are now in excellent health, believe me.

[15] Today, when I saw a good-looking girl, I didn't say to myself, 'It would be nice to sleep with her,' or 'Her husband's one lucky guy.' Because that's tantamount to saying, 'Anyone would be lucky to sleep with her, even in adultery.' [16] Nor do I fantasize about what comes next – the woman undressing in front of me, then joining me in bed. [17] I pat myself on the back and say, 'Well done, Epictetus, you've solved a devilishly difficult problem, much harder than the Master Argument itself.'⁵⁴ [18] But if the woman is willing, if she calls to me or gives me a nod, if she takes me by the arm, and begins to rub up against me – and still I overcome my lust – well, that's a test far harder than the Liar paradox, it even beats the Quiescent.⁵⁵ That's the sort of thing to boast about – not propounding the Master.

[19] So how does one get there? Start by wanting to please yourself, for a change, and appear worthy in the eyes of God. Desire to become pure, and, once pure, you will be at ease with yourself, and comfortable in the company of God. [20] Then, as Plato said, when a dangerous impression confronts you, go and expiate the gods with sacrifice, go to the temples to suppli-

cate the gods for protection. [21] It will even do to socialize with men of good character, in order to model your life on theirs, whether you choose someone living or someone from the past.[56]

[22] Consider Socrates; look how he lay next to Alcibiades and merely teased him about his youthful beauty.[57] Think how proud he must have been to have won that victory over himself – an Olympic-sized victory, and one worthy of a successor to Heracles;[58] so, really, he's the one who deserves to be addressed, 'Greetings, hero' – not these grimy boxers and pancratiasts[59] or gladiators, their current counterparts.

[23] With these thoughts to defend you, you should triumph over any impression and not be dragged away. [24] Don't let the force of the impression when first it hits you knock you off your feet; just say to it, 'Hold on a moment; let me see who you are and what you represent. Let me put you to the test.' Next, don't let it pull you in by picturing to yourself the pleasures that await you. [25] Otherwise it will lead you by the nose wherever it wants. Oppose it with some good and honourable thought, and put the dirty one to rout. [26] Practise this regularly, and you'll see what shoulders, what muscles, what stamina you acquire. Today people care only for academic discussion, nothing beyond that. [27] But I'm presenting to you the real athlete, namely the one training to face off against the most formidable of impressions.

Steady now, poor man, don't let impressions sweep you off your feet. [28] It's a great battle, and God's work. It's a fight for autonomy, freedom, happiness and peace. [29] Remember God, ask him to be your helper and protector, as sailors pray to the Dioscuri[60] for help in a storm. Is there any storm greater than the storm of forceful impressions that can put reason to flight? What is a real storm except just another impression? [30] Put away the fear of death, and however much thunder and lightning you have to face, you will find the mind capable of remaining calm and composed regardless.

[31] If you lose the struggle once, but insist that next time it will be different, then repeat the same routine – be sure that in the end you will be in so sad and weakened a condition that

you won't even realize your mistakes, you'll begin to rationalize your misbehaviour. [32] You will be living testimony to Hesiod's verse:

'*Make a bad beginning and you'll contend with troubles ever after.*'[61]

II 19 *To those who tackle philosophy just to be able to talk about it*

[1] The Master Argument[62] is evidently based on the mutual incompatibility of the following three principles: 1) everything past that is true is necessary; 2) an impossibility cannot follow a possibility; 3) something which is neither true nor ever will be true is possible.

Diodorus saw the inconsistency; his solution was to concede the truth of the first pair of propositions, but maintain (in defiance of the third) that nothing is possible which neither is nor ever will be true. [2] He was followed by someone who maintained the truth of the other two: 3) that something is possible which neither is true now nor ever will be, and 2) that an impossibility does not follow a possibility – but not 1) that everything past that is true is necessary. Cleanthes' school, in fact, seems to have upheld the latter view, and Antipater[63] mainly agreed with him. [3] And some defend the other set of principles: 3) that something is possible which neither is true nor ever will be, and 1) everything past that is true is necessary – but, in opposition to 2), assert that an impossibility can follow a possibility. [4] To retain all three, though, is impossible because they are mutually incompatible.

[5] Then, if someone asks me which of these propositions I approve myself, I will answer him, 'I don't know, but I *can* report that Diodorus held this opinion about them, the followers of Panthoides, I believe, and those of Cleanthes, held that one, and the school of Chrysippus advocated the third.'

[6] 'Yes, but what about *you*?'

'Look, I wasn't born for this – to test my impressions, compare what people say and form my *own* opinion on the subject.'[64]

Which is to say, I'm no different from a student of literature.

[7] 'Who was Hector's father?'

'Priam.'

'Who were his brothers?'

'Alexander and Deiphobus.'

'And who was their mother?'

'Hecuba. Or so I've read.'

'Where?'

'In Homer. But I believe Hellanicus,[65] too, has written on these very same questions, and there may be one or two others . . .'

[8] It's the same with me and the Master Argument; what can I add to what's already been said? If I am vain, however, and want to impress people, especially at a party, I can catalogue exactly who said what: [9] '. . . And Chrysippus has written splendidly on the subject in the first chapter of his book *On Possibles*. Cleanthes devoted a whole treatise to the topic, Archedemus too. And then there are Antipater's contributions, not only in his book *On Possibles*, but in his special monograph on the Master Argument. [10] Haven't you read it?'

'No, I have not.'

'Oh, read it by all means!'

And what will he gain by reading it? He'll just be harder to shut up than he is already. I mean, what did *you* gain by reading it? What opinion did you formulate on the subject? Of course, you will tell us all about Helen and Priam and the island of Calypso – things which neither exist nor ever will.[66]

[11] In literature, too, it is no great achievement to memorize what you have read while not formulating an opinion of your own. In ethics, we do the same thing, only it's much worse.

[12] 'Tell me what's good and bad.'

'Listen: "The wind carrying me from Troy brought me to the Ciconians."[67] [13] Everything can be classified as good, bad or indifferent. The virtues, and the things that share in them, are good. The vices and what shares in them are bad. Everything in between is indifferent, like wealth, health, life, death and poverty.'

[14] 'What's your source for that?'

'Hellanicus says it in his book on Egypt.'

I mean, how is this any different from saying, 'Diogenes[68] – or Chrysippus, or Cleanthes – says so in their *Ethics*'? Have you evaluated what they have said, or made up your own mind about it? [15] Let's see how you handle a storm while on board ship. Do you still maintain these distinctions when the sails are flapping madly and you're crying out to heaven? Suppose some joker sidles up and says, 'Please be so kind as to remind me of what you were saying the other day: A shipwreck is nothing bad – that was it, wasn't it? – and doesn't have anything bad about it?' [16] Aren't you inclined to grab an oar and brain the man with it? 'Why are you tormenting me, pal? We're about to die and you come along offering nothing but jokes and ridicule?'

[17] If the emperor summons you to answer a charge, do you remember these same distinctions when you show up pale and shaking? Suppose someone comes up to you and says, 'What are you afraid of, friend? What significance does this accusation have for *you*? After all, it isn't virtue or vice that Caesar hands out in his chamber.' [18] 'Why do you have to add to my troubles with your sarcasm?' 'Tell me, anyway, philosopher, what are you scared of? You're only in danger of death, prison, torture, exile or disgrace – that's all. Are any of these a vice, or is there anything vicious about them? What did you personally used to call such things?' [19] 'Why are you pestering me, pal? My own evils are enough for me.'

'Evils' is right: you have enough evils in the way of hypocrisy, cowardice and the moral pretension you affected while sitting in the classroom, dressed up in borrowed colours. Why did you used to call yourself a Stoic?

[20] Just pay attention to the way you behave and you will discover the school of philosophy you really belong to. You'll discover that the majority of you are Epicureans, a few Peripatetics[69] – but these grown soft. [21] After all, where should we look to prove that, in actual fact, you regard virtue as equal to,

or even more important than, everything else? Show me a Stoic, if you know of one.

[22] Where or how? Of course, you can produce thousands who talk the Stoic talk; they are the same ones who are no less conversant in Epicurean principles, and can give you an expert account of Peripatetic doctrine too. [23] Well, who is a Stoic, then? We call a statue Phidian if it is characterized by Phidias' style. So show me someone characterized by the beliefs that he espouses. [24] Show me someone untroubled with disturbing thoughts about illness, danger, death, exile or loss of reputation. By all the gods, I want to see a Stoic!

[25] OK, you may not know of one perfectly formed; at least show me someone in the way of becoming one – somebody pointed in the right direction. Do me this one favour; don't grudge an old man the sight of something he has yet to see. [26] Do you plan to show us the Zeus of Phidias, or his Athena – objects made of ivory and gold? It's a living soul I want one of you to show me, the soul of a person willing to work with, and never criticize, either God or a fellow human being. One who will never fail, or have experiences he does not want; who will never give in to anger, jealousy or the desire to dominate others.

But rather than try to describe him in detail [27] I will define him simply as someone set on becoming a god rather than a man. Even in this body of death his mind is focused on communion with God. Show me this person. [28] But you can't. So stop kidding yourselves and deceiving others about what's most important.* And stop assuming an identity that's not your own; you're all thieves and robbers at large of deeds and titles that don't in the least pertain to you.

[29] Well, I am your teacher now, and you have come to me to be educated. This is my ambition: I aspire to make you proof against force, obstruction and disappointment; free, content and happy, with your attention fixed on God in every matter great and small. Learning and putting these goals into practice, in the meantime, is the reason *you* are here. [30] So why can't you do it, if you have the right ambition, and I, in turn, have

---

* Adopting the addition of τί περὶ τὰ μέγιστα before κυβεύετε.

the proper training? What's missing? [31] Whenever I see that a worker has the right material, I expect the work to be done. Well, now, we have a workman here, and we have the material. What are we missing? [32] Cannot the thing be taught? It can. Well, then, isn't it within our power? On the contrary, it's the *only* thing within our power. Wealth is not, nor is health or fame – nothing, in a word, is within our power except using impressions correctly; by nature this alone cannot be interfered with or impeded.

[33] So tell me the reason why you don't succeed. Look, either it's my fault, or it's yours, or the fault lies in the nature of the thing. But since the thing itself is manageable and alone is within our power, it follows that either I'm at fault or you are – or, more likely, that we both must share the blame.

[34] So what do you say? Are you prepared at last to get down to business? Let's make a fresh start. Just begin, believe me, and you will see the truth of what I've been saying.

II 20 *Against the Epicureans and Academics*

[1] Even people who deny that statements can be valid or impressions clear are obliged to make use of both. You might almost say that nothing proves the validity of a statement more than finding someone forced to use it while at the same time denying that it is sound. [2] If, for instance, somebody were to deny that there is anything universally true, obviously he would have to make a statement to that effect: 'Nothing is universally true.' You don't see the contradiction? [3] It's the same as if they were to say, 'If any truth is universal, it is false.' [4] Or if someone were to say to you, 'Know this, nothing is knowable, everything is in doubt.' Or, 'Trust me on this one, you'll be glad you did: Nobody but nobody can be trusted.' Or, 'You learned it here first, my friend: There is nothing capable of being learned. [5] I not only tell you this, I'll prove it to you if you like.' So how – to get to the point – are these so-called Academics any different? They say, 'Believe me, everyone, noth-

ing can be believed with any certainty. Be certain of this: you cannot be certain of anything.'[70]*

[6] Epicurus is the same way. In his effort to expunge the natural good will that men have for each other, he demonstrates the principle that he aims to destroy. [7] This is what he says: 'Don't be idiots, everyone, refuse to be fooled or misled: rational beings have no natural good will toward one another, believe me. Anyone who says different is trying to trick you and lead you astray.' [8] Well, why do you care? Let us be tricked. After all, *you* won't be any the worse if all the rest of us are convinced that good will towards one another *does* exist by nature, and that saving, not destroying, it is a primary obligation. Actually, you'd be much better off and more secure.

[9] So why, my friend, do you concern yourself with us, burning the midnight oil and rising at dawn, to write those interminable books? Is it because you're worried that one of us might be misled into thinking that the gods actually care for mankind, or mistake the essence of the good for something besides pleasure? [10] Because if that's the case, drop everything and go to bed; make like the animal you've judged yourself worthy to be: eat, drink, copulate, defecate and snore. [11] The views of others on the important questions, whether right or wrong, should hold no interest for you. What are we to you anyway? Now, sheep, of course, you have an interest in, inasmuch as they allow themselves to be shorn and milked and ultimately led to slaughter. [12] Wouldn't it be nice if human beings, tranquillized and sedated by Stoic doctrine, could likewise submit to you and your kind to be shorn and milked? [13] You should have reserved your teachings for your fellow Epicureans and kept them out of the hands of us Stoics; instead you should try and convince us that nature intends us for fellowship, and that virtue is a good thing, so that you can keep everything for yourself. [14] Perhaps this sociability should be extended to some, but not others. Well, who deserves it – people who reciprocate it, or people who hold it in contempt? And no

* Emending οὐδεὶς συγκατατίθεται το οὐ δεῖ συγκατατίθεσθαι and οὐδεὶς πιστεύει το οὐ δεῖ πιστεύειν.

one holds it in more contempt than you who make such a distinction.[71]

[15] What urged him to get out of bed and write the things he wrote was, of course, the strongest element in a human being – nature – which subjected him to her will despite his loud resistance. [16] 'Since you hold these asocial opinions,' she told him, 'write them down for others to read, lose sleep in the process and by your own behaviour belie your doctrines.' [17] We hear of Orestes being hounded by the Furies, who wouldn't let him sleep; but for Epicurus the Furies and Avengers were much harsher. They woke him when he slept and wouldn't allow him a moment's peace, forcing him to make public his horrid views the way drunken madness goads the priests of Cybele – [18] human nature is just that irresistible.[72] A vine cannot behave olively, nor an olive tree vinely – it is impossible, inconceivable. [19] No more can a human being wholly efface his native disposition; a eunuch may castrate himself but cannot completely excise the urges that, as a man, he continues to experience. [20] And so Epicurus removed everything that characterizes a man, the head of a family, a citizen and a friend, but he did not remove our human instincts, and could not – any more than lazy Academics can dispose of or negate their own senses, although most of their energy has gone into trying to do just that. [21] It's too bad, really. Nature gives a person rules and guidelines to discover the truth, and instead of trying to complement and improve on them, they devote themselves to impugning and rejecting the least little thing that could assist them in the effort. [22] Tell us, philosopher, what you think of piety and devotion to the gods.

'I will prove that it's a good thing, if you like.'

'Yes, prove it, so that our citizens may turn and honor the divine, and put an end to their ambivalence about matters that are most important.'

'Well, are you armed with the appropriate proofs?'

'I am, thankfully.'

[23] 'Well, then, since you're satisfied with them, here come the refutations:[73] The gods do not exist, and even if they exist they do not trouble themselves about people, and we have

nothing in common with them. The piety and devotion to the gods that the majority of people invoke is a lie devised by swindlers and con men and, if you can believe it, by legislators, to keep criminals in line by putting the fear of God into them.'

[24] Nice job, philosopher, you have rendered the citizenry a valuable service by rescuing youth already dangerously liable to hold the gods in contempt.

[25] 'What, you mean you don't care for those particular ideas? Just wait: now I'll prove that justice is nothing, that honesty is stupidity, that being a father means nothing, that being a son means nothing.'

[26] That's good, philosopher, keep it up, and win over the young people so that we'll have more with the same feelings and beliefs as you. It's these opinions that produced our well-regulated cities. Sparta owes its existence to such ideas. And through his laws and system of training Lycurgus instilled his people with the following convictions: slavery is no more bad than good, and being free is no more good than it is bad. The fallen of Thermopylae died for these doctrines; and what other opinions but these motivated the Athenians to quit their city?[74] [27] And advocates of such ideas proceed to marry, have children, become leaders in their community, priests or prophets – of gods who don't exist, of course. And they consult the priest of Apollo in order to be told lies in the form of false oracles that we then impose on others.

What a travesty! [28] What are you doing? You prove yourself wrong on a daily basis and still you won't give up these idle efforts. When you eat, where do you bring your hand – to your mouth, or to your eye? What do you step into when you bathe? When did you ever mistake your saucepan for a dish, or your serving spoon for a skewer?

[29] If I were slave to one of these philosophers I would taunt him constantly, even if I got a beating every day in consequence. If he said, 'Put some oil in the bath, boy,' I'd go grab the fish sauce and pour it over his head.

'What the . . . ?'

'Pardon me, I received an impression – identical, indistinguishable, I swear to you – of olive oil.'

'Bring me the cereal.'

[30] I'd bring him a cruet full of vinegar.

'Didn't I ask for the cereal?'

'Yes, sir. This is cereal.'

'It's not vinegar?'

'Why vinegar any more than cereal?'

'Well, here, smell it and taste it.'

'How do you know if the senses don't deceive us too?'

[31] Give me three or four fellow slaves in on the game, and I would make him either renounce his way of thinking – or hang himself in exasperation. But in fact it is they who are making fun of us, by enjoying all the resources that nature provides while trying to discredit them in their philosophy. [32] What they lack in gratitude they make up for in gall. To cite just one example; although every day they eat bread, they have the nerve to say, 'We do not know if there is a Demeter, a Persephone, or a Pluto.'[75]

[33] I hardly need add that they enjoy night as well as day, the cycle of seasons, the stars, sea and land, and the assistance of their fellow human beings, without giving any of them a thought; they only want to cough up their little argument and head off to the bath after thereby giving their stomach a work-out. [34] Nor are they particular about what they say, or with whom; or stop to consider how their opinions could influence others. I wonder what the effect of hearing them might have on a youth who shows promise; his potential might be completely undermined. [35] We could give adulterers grounds for rationalizing their behaviour; such arguments could provide pretexts to misappropriate state funds; a rebellious young man could be emboldened further to rebel against his parents. So what, according to you, is good or bad, virtuous or vicious – this or that? [36] What point is there in trying to refute one of these philosophers, arguing with them, or trying to alter their opinion? [37] You'd have a better chance persuading someone to change their sexual orientation than reaching people who have rendered themselves so deaf and blind.

II 21 *On inconsistency*

[1] People are ready to acknowledge some of their faults, but will admit to others only with reluctance. No one, at any rate,* will admit to being stupid or obtuse. On the contrary, you hear people on every side saying, 'If only I had as much luck as I have sense.' [2] Shyness they will concede, saying, 'I'm a bit timid, I know; but I'm nobody's fool for all that.' [3] Hardly anyone admits to a lack of self-control, no one at all will admit to being unjust, few will say that they are nosy or envious, but most will allow that they are liable to feel pity.[76]

[4] What's the cause of all this? Mainly it's inconsistency and confusion with regard to what is good and bad. But though values differ, as a rule people will admit to practically nothing that they regard as dishonourable. [5] Timidity they take to be the sign of a sensitive nature, pity too; but stupidity they look on as the mark of a slave. Nor are they quick to confess to selfish or asocial behaviour.

[6] In general, where people are led to acknowledge a fault it is because they imagine there is something involuntary about it. So it is with shyness and pity. [7] Even if they confess to a lack of self-control, love is usually blamed, to gain sympathy for something supposedly beyond our control. Injustice, on the other hand, they don't consider involuntary in any sense. But jealousy, in their view, has an instinctive air about it, so they will own up to that too.

[8] Surrounded as we are by such people – so confused, so ignorant of what they're saying and of whatever faults they may or may not have, where those faults came from and how to get rid of them – I think we too should make a habit of asking ourselves, 'Could it be that I'm one of them too? [9] What illusion about myself do I entertain? How do I regard myself – as another wise man, as someone with perfect self-control? Do I, too, ever make that boast about being prepared

---

* Reading γοῦν for οὖν.

for whatever may happen? [10] If I don't know something, am I properly aware that I don't know it? Do I come to a teacher as ready to submit to his instruction as if it issued from an oracle? Or am I one of those little snots who attends school for the sole purpose of memorizing its doctrines and becoming familiar with books previously unknown to me, so that – God willing – I can lecture on them to others?'

[11] Look, back home you and your slave have come to blows, your whole household is in disarray, and you're practically at war with your neighbours. Now you come to me all dignified and scholarly and take your seat to give a critique of my commentary on the text, or, shall I say, of whatever non-sense came into my head to say on that score. [12] You arrived full of envy and embarrassment because you're not getting an allowance from home and sit through the round of lectures and discussion thinking about nothing except how things stand between you and your father or brother: [13] 'How are the people back home talking about me? Even now they imagine that I'm making progress in my studies and are saying, "He'll come back knowing everything." [14] Well, I guess at one time I had hoped that I *would* know everything by the time I got back – but it requires a lot of work, and I never get any help from home, and the public baths here in Nicopolis are filthy . . . Things are no better here than home.'

[15] So next they start saying, 'No one is better off for attending school.' Yes, well, who is it that goes to school any-way? Who goes to become a better person? Who goes prepared to have their opinions overhauled, and to learn which ones need to be? [16] So don't be disappointed if you return home with the very same set of ideas you arrived with. Because you had no intention of changing, correcting or adopting others in their place. [17] Come, you weren't close to holding that intention. So at least consider this – are you getting what you *did* come for? You want to be able to hold forth on speculative topics. Well, aren't you becoming more facile every day? And these topics, don't they furnish you with enough material to make an impression in public? You're analysing syllogisms and changing arguments. You're exploring the premises of the Liar

Argument, and hypotheticals. So what's left to complain about if you have what you're here for?

[18] 'Yes, but what good will all this do me when a child of mine dies, or if my brother, or I myself, have to die or be tortured?'

[19] Nothing. Because that's not why you came, not why you took your seat in front of me, not the reason you sometimes sacrificed sleep to study by lamplight.

Did you ever go out into the courtyard and challenge yourself with an external impression in place of a syllogism, and work through it in public? [20] Did you ever do that? Then you say the speculative topics are useless. Useless to whom? Only to people who don't use them as they should. I mean, salves and ointments are not useless to people who apply them when and how they're supposed to; weights are not useless in themselves, they're useful to some people, worthless to others. [21] Now, ask me whether syllogisms are useful, and I'll tell you that they are, and, if you like, I'll demonstrate why.

'What good have they done me?'

But you didn't ask if they were useful to you personally, but useful in general. [22] Let somebody suffering from indigestion ask me whether vinegar is useful, I will say yes.

'So is it useful to me?'

To you, no. You need to have the discharge from your eyes stopped first, and your skin lesions healed. All of you, first attend to your wounds, stanch the bleeding, calm your mind, bring it to school when it is free of distraction. Only then will you be in a position to realize reason's potential.

II 22 *Of love and friendship*

[1] Whatever you show consideration for, you are naturally inclined to love. Now no one, of course, shows consideration for what's bad, any more than they do for things that they have no connection with. [2] It follows that people only show consideration for what is good. [3] And if they show consideration

for it, they must also love it. So the person who knows what is good is also the person who knows how to love. But if someone is incapable of distinguishing good things from bad and neutral things from either – well, how could such a person be capable of love? The power to love, then, belongs only to the wise man.

[4] 'Wait a minute,' I hear someone say, 'I'm no "wise man", but I love my child none the less.'

[5] First of all, I am surprised, I must say, that you would admit to not being wise. After all, what's missing? Your senses are in working order, you differentiate among impressions, and you give your body the right food, clothing and housing. [6] So how is it you say you aren't wise?

I'll tell you myself. It's because you are frequently dazed or disturbed by certain sense impressions whose appearance of truth gets the better of you. Sometimes you think that some things are good, then you consider the same things bad, and later you decide that they're indifferent. In other words, you're subject to sorrow, fear, jealousy, anger and inconsistency. That's the real reason you should admit that you are not wise.

[7] In love and friendship you are also inconsistent, are you not? I mean, money, pleasure and the rest you sometimes take to be good, at other times bad. Isn't it the same with people? Don't you regard the same ones as good and bad at varying times? Sometimes they're your friend, later your enemy; and you sing their praises only later to run them down.

'Yes, I admit to that too.'

[8] So, do you think that you can be the friend of someone if you hold the wrong opinion about them?

'Naturally, no.'

What if your opinion of them is subject to change* – can your relations be warm?

'No again.'

And if you alternate praise of them with disparagement?

'No, not then either.'

[9] All right, no doubt you have seen dogs playing with, and

* Emending αὐτόν το γνωμήν.

fawning before, each other, and thought, 'Nothing could be
friendlier.' But just throw some meat in the middle, and then
you'll know what friendship amounts to. [10] Put a piece of
real estate in the centre between you and your son, and you'll
know how impatient he is to bury you, and how even you are
wishing your son were dead. Then you say, 'Some child I raised
– he's been planning my funeral for years.' [11] Place a pretty
girl in the middle, and the old man falls for her as hard as the
boy. Or dangle some honour or another before the two of you.
If you have to risk your life you'll repeat the words of Admetus'
father: '*You want to see the light, don't you imagine your father
does too?*'[77] [12] Don't you think he loved his son when the
boy was small, suffered when he was sick, and could be heard
saying, 'If only I could be sick in his place'? But, faced with a
genuine choice, they have only insults to exchange, as you see.
[13] Eteocles and Polyneices – didn't they share the same mother
and father? They were reared together, lived, drank, slept
together and often exchanged an intimate kiss. Anyone seeing
them would almost certainly have mocked the philosophers
with their notorious views on friendship.[78] [14] Yet when the
question came up between them of who would be king, it was
like meat thrown before a pack of dogs. Here is what they said:

'*Where before the tower do you intend to stand?*'
'*What business is that of yours?*'
'*I want to be directly opposite so that I can kill you per-
sonally.*'
'*And I am seized by the same desire.*'[79]

They even petition the gods for that favour.

[15] It is a universal law – have no illusions – that every
creature alive is attached to nothing so much as to its own
self-interest. Whatever threatens to stand in the way of that –
be it brother, father, child or sweetheart – he will hate, curse
and prosecute, [16] because he is naturally disposed to favour
primarily his own interest. *This* is his father, his brother, his
relations, his country and his god. [17] If we believe the gods
to be hostile to our individual interest, then we are as ready to
turn on them as on the others, knocking their statues over and

burning down their temples. Witness Alexander, who ordered the shrines of Asclepius torched after his beloved[80] died.

[18] The upshot is that if you identify self-interest with piety, honesty, country, parents and friends, then they are all secure. But separate them, and friends, family, country and morality itself all come to nothing, outweighed by self-interest. [19] Wherever 'me' and 'mine' are, that's where every creature necessarily tends. If we locate them in the body, then the body will be the dominant force in our lives. If it's in our faculty of will, then that will dominate. Likewise with externals. [20] But only if I identify with my will can I be someone's friend – or son, or father – in the true sense, because only then will my self-interest be served by remaining loyal, honest, patient, tolerant and supportive, and by maintaining my social relations. [21] If I put myself one place, and put honour anywhere else, the consequence will be to strengthen the view of Epicurus, as set forth in his declaration that 'Honour is nothing, and if it does exist, it is only what is generally approved.'[81]

[22] Ignorance of this made the Athenians turn on the Spartans, and the Thebans on both; made the Persian king invade Greece and the Macedonians invade both; and now the Romans have been induced to turn against the Getae. Going further back, it was the cause of the Trojan War. [23] Paris was Menelaus' guest, and anyone who saw how well they treated each other would have laughed at anyone who said they weren't friends. But between the two a bit of temptation was thrown in the form of a beautiful woman, and over that there arose war.

[24] So now if you see friends, or brothers, who appear to be of like mind, don't draw any conclusions about their friendship right away, even if they swear oaths and say that neither can live one without the other. [25] A bad person's character cannot be trusted, it's weak and indecisive, easily won over by different impressions at different times. [26] Don't make the common mistake of only asking, 'Do they share parents?', or, 'Did they grow up together?', or, 'Did they attend the same school?' Just ask whether they put their self-interest in externals or in moral choice. [27] If it's in externals, you cannot call them friends, any more than you can call them trustworthy,

consistent, courageous or free. You cannot even call them human beings, if you think about it. [28] Because it is no human frame of mind that makes people snap at others and insult them, or take to the marketplace the way bandits take to the desert or mountains,* and behave like bandits in court; or that turns them into depraved lechers and adulterers; or is responsible for all other crimes that people commit against each other.

Their only cause is the frame of mind that sets the self and its interests anywhere except in the realm of choice. [29] But if you hear of people who are sincere in identifying virtue with choice and the use of impressions, don't bother with whether they are members of the same family, or friends who've run together a long time; knowing this is enough to say with confidence that they are friends, just as it's enough to judge them fair and reliable. [30] For where else is friendship found if not with fairness, reliability and respect for virtue only?

[31] 'But she has looked after me for such a long time; did she not love me?'

'How do you know, stupid, if she hasn't looked after you the way she polishes her shoes, say, or tends to her farm animals? How do you know she won't discard you like a broken glass once your value as a utensil is used up?'

[32] 'But she's also my wife, and we have lived together for years.'

'And Eriphyle, how long was she with Amphiaraus, the mother, too, of his many children? But a necklace came between them.[82] [33] And by "necklace", I mean her whole attitude toward externals. That was the inhuman factor that destroyed their love, and would not permit the woman to remain a wife, or the mother to remain a mother.† [34] If any of you are serious about being a friend, rid yourself of such attitudes, condemn them and drive them out of your mind. [35] That way, you won't be hard on yourself, or be forever fighting, second-guessing and tormenting yourself. [36] And then you

---

* Reading τὰς ἀγορὰς καταλαμβάνειν ὡς τὰς ἐρεμίας ἢ τὰ ὄρη.
† Reading τὴν γυναῖκα and τὴν μητέρα with some manuscripts.

will be in a condition to befriend others – forming easy and natural relationships with like-minded people, but capable too of treating unenlightened souls with sympathy and indulgence, remembering that they are ignorant or mistaken about what's most important. Never be harsh, remember Plato's dictum: 'Every soul is deprived of the truth against its will.'[83]

[37] If you don't get rid of these attitudes, however, you may do all the things friends typically do together, like drink, board, and travel, you can even have the same ancestry – but so can snakes. They can never be friends, though, and neither can you, as long as you hold on to these hateful and inhuman judgements.

II 23 *On the art of expression*

[1] Everyone would read with greater ease and pleasure a book written in a legible hand. And so it is with a speech: everyone would listen with greater ease to one composed in well-wrought and well-organized prose. [2] So we must not say that there is no such thing as a faculty of expression. That would mark us out as lazy as well as ungrateful – ungrateful, because it scorns God's gifts, just the same as if one were to deny the value of the power of sight, of hearing, or of speech itself.

[3] Was it for nothing that God gave you eyes and endowed them with breath so keen and refined that it spans the distance to objects, and assumes their shape?[84] [4] Do you know of any messenger that's as fast or accurate? And was it for nothing that he made the air between responsive and elastic enough to permit vision to pass through it? And what of light, without which the rest would be useless – was it for nothing that he created that too?

[5] So don't be ungrateful for these gifts, but at the same time don't forget that there are others superior to them. Give thanks to God for sight, for hearing, for life itself and the means provided to support it, like grain, wine and oil. [6] But remember that he has given you something superior to all these, the faculty intended to use them, to test them, and to judge their

relative worth. [7] After all, what is it that determines in the case of each of these faculties what value to assign them? You've never heard sight speak up for itself, or hearing*; both have been appointed to be slaves and subordinates to the faculty of using impressions. [8] What other faculty do you consult to learn what each thing is worth? What faculty can be superior to this one, which employs the others in a subordinate capacity, testing and passing judgement on each? [9] None of the others knows what it is or what it is worth, when it should or should not be used. What faculty is responsible for opening and closing the eyes, depending on whether or not it judges a thing worthy of being seen? Sight itself? No, it is the will. What opens or stops our ears, [10] making us either receptive to a speech or unmoved by it? Not hearing; it is the will and the will alone.

[11] Well now; the will looks around and finds itself in the company of faculties that are deaf and blind, incapable of looking after anything except the business that they were appointed to care for under will's own direction. Only the will is discerning enough to look after them, in proportion to their value, and supervise itself at the same time. Realizing this, is the will likely to declare anything other than itself supreme? An eye, when open, has no option but to see. [12] The decision whether to look at a particular man's wife, however, and how, belongs to the will. [13] And the determination whether to trust what someone says, and then, if we trust them, whether we should be angered by it – that also belongs to the will.

[14] This faculty of expression and arranging words – if it really is a faculty – does nothing more than dress up and organize words on a given topic, the way a hairdresser arranges hair. [15] But whether to speak at all or remain silent, and then, if the former, whether it is better to speak this way or that, and if this is or is not appropriate – in short, determining the right time and utility for every speech – all these are the province of the will. So don't expect it to come forward and vote for anything but itself.

[16] 'But what if all this is true, and the subordinate element

---

* Omitting μή τι πυρῶν . . . μή τι κυνός with most editors.

can still be superior to what it serves, as, for instance, the horse to the rider, the dog to the hunter, the instrument to the musician, or a subject to his king?' Look, what puts the other faculties to use? The will. What administers all of them? [17] Then, what destroys the person as a whole, sometimes by hunger, sometimes by hanging, sometimes by jumping off a cliff? The will. [18] Is there anything in the human sphere, then, that takes precedence? How can anything subject to obstruction be stronger than something that is not? [19] Now both the will and externals are fitted by nature to obstruct the power of sight, as well as speech and hearing. But what can obstruct the will? Nothing external; only the will can turn back on, and obstruct, itself. Which is why virtue and vice apply to it and it alone.

[20] Now let's see so great a faculty, the one put in charge of all the rest, come forward and say that the flesh is the element that rules over everything. Such a claim to prominence would be intolerable even from the flesh itself. [21] Come, Epicurus, which part of you was it that was responsible for making such a pronouncement? Which part authored works on *The End*, on *Physics*, and on *The Criterion of Truth*? Which part let your beard grow long?[85] Or described yourself, at the hour of death, 'as passing a most happy day, which also happens to be our last'? [22] Was it flesh – or the will? Only madness could get you to acknowledge any faculty of greater authority than the will. Or are you really that deaf and blind?

[23] Does this mean that our other faculties should be despised? Of course not. We certainly do not say that there is nothing to be used or gained apart from the will; that is stupid, besides being impious and ungrateful to God. Each thing must be given its due. [24] Even a donkey has some utility, only not as much as an ox. There is some use in a dog, but not as much as in a slave. There is use in slaves, but not so much as in free citizens. There is use in them, too, but not so much as in the people who rule over them. [25] If some things are of greater value, however, that does not mean we should slight the contribution of the others. The faculty of expression has its utility, even if it is less than the power of the will. [26] So let no one suppose that, in saying this, I am suggesting that you should be

careless of how you express yourself, any more than you should neglect your eyes, ears, hands, feet, clothes or shoes. [27] But if I'm asked to name the greatest element of all, what am I to say? The faculty of speech? I cannot. It is the faculty of the will, when rightly applied, [28] since it controls speech as well as every other faculty, great and small. It is by putting this right that a good person becomes good; when its purpose fails, he turns bad. [29] It determines whether we are to know happiness or not, and whether we will be on hostile or amicable terms with our neighbours. Simply put – ignore it and unhappiness results, give it your attention and your happiness is assured. [30] Yet to try to efface the faculty of eloquence and say that there is no such thing, this really betrays a kind of cowardice, besides ingratitude toward those who have given it. [31] It seems to me that someone with such an attitude is afraid that, if a faculty of expression does exist, we won't be able to ignore it. [32] It's like people who pretend that there is no difference between ugliness and beauty. Seeing Thersites, then, affected people the same as seeing Achilles; and Helen made no greater impression than the sight of the average woman? [33] That, too, is an ignorant and boorish attitude, characteristic of people with no power of discernment; they're afraid that if they begin to notice the difference, right away they'll lose control and fall under the sway of beauty altogether. [34] The important thing is this: allow everyone their particular gift or talent, but step back and look at what it's worth. Then come to recognition of the faculty that rules them. Make that the object of your avid pursuit and relegate the others to a secondary role, while still giving them what attention you can spare. [35] Take the eyes: they demand attention, but not because they are of primary importance, but for the sake of what actually is; because the ruling faculty cannot function as nature intended it unless it makes judicious use of the eyes, in making choice among particulars.

[36] But here's what happens: people act like a traveller headed for home who stops at an inn and, finding it comfortable, decides to remain there. [37] You've lost sight of your goal, man. You were supposed to drive through the inn, not park there.

'But it's nice here.'

Look, there are plenty of nice inns in addition to that one, plenty of nice resorts* – [38] but they are only way stations. Your goal was different: to return to your native community, help insure the safety of the citizenry, then turn your attention to acting the part of a citizen yourself.[86] Get married, raise children, and be prepared to hold the usual public offices. [39] You see, you didn't come with the option of choosing one of those pleasanter places; you are meant to live and go about your business in the place where you were born and made citizen.

Well, something analogous goes on in our school here. [40] Since you can't make progress towards your ideal without the benefit of teaching based on the spoken word, and since the same goes for purifying the will and correcting the power of using impressions; and since communicating our principal doctrines requires the use of careful diction, and a certain variety and forcefulness of style, [41] some students become captivated by all these things and don't want to proceed further. One is captivated by diction, another by deductive or equivocal arguments, someone else by yet another 'inn' of this kind; and there they stay and rot as if seduced by the Sirens.

[42] Your objective, my friend, was to see to it that you make natural use of whatever impressions come your way; that you do not fail in your desires, or have experiences you don't want; that you never be unfortunate or unhappy, but free, unrestricted and unrestrained; in sympathy with God's rule, which you submit to cheerfully; at odds with no one, no one's accuser; able in all sincerity to speak Cleanthes' line:

'Lead me, Zeus, lead me, Destiny.'[87]

[43] But though this is the goal you're given, next thing you know a turn of phrase catches your fancy, or certain abstract propositions, and there you call halt and decide to pitch camp. You've forgotten all about your obligations back home, announcing, 'It's pleasant here.' Well, who says otherwise? But pleasant as a way station, as an inn. [44] What's to keep you

* Reading λίμενες for λείμονες.

from speaking like Demosthenes[88] and still being unhappy? Or analysing arguments like Chrysippus while still uneasy, still subject to envy and irritation – still distressed and downhearted, in other words? Nothing. [45] So, you see, those inns were not without value,* but your goal lay elsewhere.

[46] When I say this to some people, they imagine that I am denouncing rhetoric, or care in the presentation of principles. But I'm not one of those who denounce it, only the obsessive devotion to it, and making it the focus of one's hopes and expectations. [47] If someone who advocates this view does his listeners a disservice, then set me down as one of the offenders. When I see that one thing is supreme and most important, I cannot say that something else is, just to make you happy.

* Reading οὐκ οὐδενός for οὐδενός.

BOOK III

III 3 *What is the material proper to the good person and what is the goal they should strive to achieve*

[1] The body is the raw material of the doctor and physical therapist. Land is the farmer's raw material. The raw material of the good man is his mind – his goal being to respond to impressions the way nature intended. [2] As a general rule, nature designed the mind to assent to what is true, dissent from what is false and suspend judgement in doubtful cases. Similarly, it conditioned the mind to desire what is good, to reject what is bad and to regard with indifference what is neither one nor the other. [3] Just as it is not in the power of a banker or retailer to reject Caesar's money – they are forced to make a proportional exchange whether they want to or not – so it is with the soul: [4] when presented with something good it gravitates toward it immediately, as it recoils from anything bad. The soul will never reject a clear impression of good, any more than Caesar's coin can be refused. The actions of gods as well as men are entirely based on this principle.

[5] It follows that the good is preferred over every human association. I care nothing for my father – only for the good.

'Are you that unfeeling?'

I am that way designed; it is the currency God gave me. [6] The upshot is that, if the good turns out to be something other than decency and fairness, then father, brother, country and the rest can all go hang. [7] Now look, am I supposed to step aside and abandon my good just so you can have yours? Why?

'Because I'm your father.'

But not the good.

'I'm your brother.'

But not the good.

[8] If, however, we locate the good in soundness of character, then it becomes good to maintain these relationships. Whoever gives up some material things also wins the good.

[9] 'My father is laying waste to my inheritance.'

But not harming you.

'My brother will claim more than his share.'

He's welcome to as much as he likes. Will he take a greater share of honesty, loyalty and brotherly love? [10] No; even Zeus cannot deprive you of that fortune – because he chose not to be able to. He entrusted it to me and gave me a share equal to his own – free, clear and unencumbered.

[11] If people have a different currency, just flash it, and whatever is for sale there will be yours in exchange. [12] A corrupt governor has come to power in our province. What currency does he recognize? Silver. Show him silver, then, and you can cart off what you like. Here is an adulterer. His currency takes the form of pretty girls. 'Take the money, and sell me the merchandise.' In this way they are bought and sold. [13] Here is one whose taste runs to boys. Procure him his currency and you can take what you please. Another is devoted to the hunt. Offer him some handsome horse or dog, and he will groan and complain, but in the end sell off whatever he has in order to make your price. You see, another from within[1] forces him to act like this, ever since he designated this his currency.

[14] Here is the primary means of training yourself: as soon as you leave in the morning, subject whatever you see or hear to close study. Then formulate answers as if they were posing questions. Today what did you see – some beautiful woman or handsome man? Test them by your rule – does their beauty have any bearing on your character? If not, forget them. What else did you see? [15] Someone in mourning for the death of a child? Apply your rule. Death too is indifferent, so dismiss it from your mind. A consul crossed your path; apply your rule. What category of thing is a consulship – a good of the mind or

one of matter? If it's the latter, then out with it, it failed our test. If it is nothing to you, reject it.

[16] Now, if we continued to practise this discipline every day from morning to night, we would see some results, by God. [17] As it is, though, we are overcome by every impression that we meet. Only in school – if even there – does our brain briefly come to life. Outside school, whenever we see a person in mourning, we think to ourselves, 'She's crushed.' If we happen to spy a consul, we think, 'There goes one lucky man.' The sight of a person in exile elicits 'How tragic' in response; a beggar prompts us to think, 'Poor guy, he doesn't even have money enough for food.' [18] These are the insidious opinions we need to concentrate hard to expunge. What, after all, are sighing and crying, except opinions? What is 'misfortune'? An opinion. And sectarian strife, dissension, blame and accusation, ranting and raving – [19] they all are mere opinion, the opinion that good and bad lie outside us. Let someone transfer these opinions to the workings of the will, and I personally guarantee his peace of mind, no matter what his outward circumstances are like.

[20] The soul is like a bowl of water, with the soul's impressions like the rays of light that strike the water. [21] Now, if the water is disturbed, the light appears to be disturbed together with it – though of course it is not. [22] So when someone loses consciousness, it is not the person's knowledge and virtues that are impaired, it is the breath[2] that contains them. Once the breath returns to normal, knowledge and the virtues are restored to normal also.[3]

III 4 *To someone who became a little too excited in the theatre*

[1] When the governor of Epirus was too demonstrative for some in his support of a certain comic actor in the theatre, he came to Epictetus to share with him how peeved he was with his detractors.

Well, said Epictetus, what fault did they commit? They were only showing their enthusiasm the same way you did.

[2] 'And this is how they demonstrate their loyalties?' he asked.

Yes, Epictetus said; when they saw you, their governor, the friend and official of Caesar, making a flagrant display of partiality, naturally they were inclined to take sides too. [3] If it isn't right to cheer so loud, stop doing it yourself; but if it is allowable, why be upset if you find them imitating you? Who, after all, should the masses imitate, if not you, their superior? Who else are they going to fix their eyes on? [4] 'Look how the procurator of Caesar behaves,' they say. 'He's shouting; in that case I'll shout too. He's leaping out of his seat; I think I'll leap out of mine. His claque of slaves is shouting from every corner of the arena; I don't have slaves, but I'll make up for it by yelling louder than all of them.'

[5] You have to realize that, when you go to the theatre, you serve as a model and standard of conduct for the rest of the crowd. [6] The question, then, is why they should have faulted you. It's because everyone hates the thing that stands in their way. They wanted one actor crowned, you wanted a different one: they stood in your way and you in theirs. They saw you win owing to your influence. So they did the only thing left for them to do, they ranted against the thing that stood in their way. [7] Don't expect to get your wish and not get an earful concerning what *they* wished had happened.

The way they carry on should come as no surprise. I mean, don't farmers and sailors rage against Zeus when he stands in their way? The emperor is railed against constantly. And don't think the two of them are unaware of it. [8] Caesar's spies report back to him whatever they overhear. And what is his response? He knows that if he punished every person who ever said something bad about him, he would have no one left to rule. [9] As far as you're concerned, when you attend the theatre, don't say, 'Come on, Sophron, win the crown!' Instead, say, 'I pray that my will remains in tune with nature here; because no actor means more to me than I do to myself. [10] It's absurd that I should lose, just so that someone else can win a prize for comic acting.'

[11] 'So who should I hope wins? The winner. That way the victory is always exactly what I hoped for.'

'But I want Sophron to be crowned.'

Then hold all the contests you want at your own house, and you can proclaim him victor in the Nemean, Pythian, Isthmian and Olympic Games conjointly.[4] But out in public don't ask for too much by hoping to gain a monopoly on a privilege shared by all – [12] otherwise get used to being vilified. Because when you engage in the same things as the masses, you lower yourself to their level.

III 5 *To students who leave school for reasons of ill health*

[1] 'I am ill here,' said a student, 'and want to go home.'

[2] Because you were never ill at home, I suppose? Consider whether you are doing anything here to improve your will. Because if you aren't achieving anything, you arrived for no good reason to begin with. [3] Leave, attend to your affairs at home; if your governing principle cannot be brought into line with nature, maybe your patch of land can, at least. You will add to your savings, look after your ageing father, frequent the law-courts, serve as a magistrate, and do whatever comes next – you sorry creature, in your sad and sorry way.

[4] But if you understand that you are getting rid of bad judgements and gaining others in their place, that you have transferred your attention from things outside control of the will to things within, and that now if you cry 'Poor me!' it is not for your father or your brother's sake but your own, then why should sickness concern you any more? [5] You must realize that death and illness are bound to overtake us whatever it is we're doing. They overtake the farmer at the plough, the sailor at the helm; [6] what do you want to be doing when they come upon you? Because you have to be doing something when you go; and if you can find anything better than this to be doing, then do it by all means.

[7] Speaking for myself, I hope death overtakes me when I'm occupied solely with the care of my character, in an effort to make it passionless, free, unrestricted and unrestrained. [8] That's how I'd like to be engaged, because then I can say to God, Is there any way I violated your commands? Or misapplied the gifts I received from you? Or used my senses and preconceptions unproductively? Did I ever blame you? Did I ever find fault with your administration? [9] I fell sick when you wanted it: so did others, but I did not complain. I became poor when you wanted, again without complaint. I did not hold office, because you did not want it; and never desired to hold office. Did you ever find me angry for that reason? Did you ever see me any way but with a smile on my face, ready to obey any orders that you had for me? [10] Now you want me to leave the fair, so I go, feeling nothing but gratitude for having been allowed to share with you in the celebration, to get to see your works and comprehend your rule.

[11] Let these be my thoughts, these my studies, whether writing or reading, when death overtakes me.

[12] 'But my mother won't be here to hold my head while I am ill.'

Well then go to your mother. You deserve, in fact, to be held by her whenever you're ill.

[13] 'But I had a nice little bed to lie on at home.'

Go to your nice bed, then; sick or well you deserve to lie on a bed like that. Please don't miss out on whatever you can do there on my account.

[14] What does Socrates say? 'One person likes tending to his farm, another to his horse; I like to daily monitor my self-improvement.'[5]

[15] 'In what? Little phrases?'

Hush.

'Clever theories, then?'

Don't be absurd.

[16] 'Well, as far as I can see, philosophers don't busy themselves with anything but.'

It's no small thing – can we agree? – never to accuse anyone, God or man, never to blame anyone, and to have the same countenance going in or out. [17] These are the things that Socrates knew, and yet he never said that he knew or taught anything; and if anyone came looking for phrases or theories he would escort them to either Protagoras or Hippias.[6] He would have escorted someone looking for vegetables to a green-grocer in exactly the same way. Which of you has the same attitude? [18] If you did, you would gladly put up with illness, hunger and death. [19] Any of you who have been in love with some girl or other knows I speak the truth.

III 8 *Why training for impressions is necessary*

[1] Just as we practise answering sophistic questions, so should we train for impressions every day, [2] as they implicitly pose their own questions.

'So-and-so's son died.' ('The question').

Answer: 'Since it's nothing he can control, it isn't bad.'

'So and so's father left his son nothing when he died.'

'Not something the son can control, so not bad.'

'Caesar condemned him.'

'Outside his control – not bad.'

[3] 'He lamented these events.'

'That *is* in his control – and bad.'

'He withstood it like a man.'

'That is in his control – and good.'

[4] If we make a habit of such analysis, we will make progress, because we will never assent to anything unless it involves a cognitive impression.[7]

[5] 'His son died.'

What happened? His son died.

'Nothing else?'

Nothing.

'The ship was lost.'

What happened? The ship was lost.

'He was thrown into jail.'

What happened? He was thrown into jail. 'He's in a bad

situation' is a stock comment that everyone adds on their own account.

[6] 'But it's not right of Zeus to do this.'

Why? Because he made you tough and proud, removed the stigma of evil from these circumstances and made it possible for you to be happy despite them? Or because he left the door open when things finally don't agree with you? Friend, take advantage of it, and stop blaming God.

[7] If you care to know what the Romans think of philosophers, just listen. Italicus, who was reputed to be one of their finest philosophers, was angry with his friends once when I happened to be by. 'I can't stand it any more,' he said, as though he were *in extremis*, 'you're killing me. You want me to end up' – and here he pointed in my direction – 'like him!'[8]

III 16 *That one should be careful about entering into social relations*

[1] It is inevitable if you enter into relations with people on a regular basis, either for conversation, dining or simple friendship, that you will grow to be like them, unless you can get them to emulate *you*. [2] Place an extinguished piece of coal next to a live one, and either it will cause the other one to die out, or the live one will make the other reignite. [3] Since a lot is at stake, you should be careful about fraternizing with non-philosophers in these contexts; remember that if you consort with someone covered in dirt you can hardly avoid getting a little grimy yourself.

[4] I mean, what are you going to do if your friend starts nattering about gladiators, horses and sports stars; or, even worse, if he starts gossiping about shared acquaintances: 'He's good, she's bad, it's good this happened, it's too bad about that . . .'? What if he sneers, ridicules and even plays low-down tricks? [5] Do any of you have the musician's ability to pick up an instrument, immediately identify which strings need attention, and bring the whole instrument into tune? Or Socrates'

gift in every setting of winning over the company to his side? Not likely. [6] Inevitably you are going to adopt the common person's mentality instead.

[7] So why are they stronger than you? Because they talk such garbage from conviction, whereas your fine talk is no more than lip service. It lacks life and vigour; anyone listening to your speeches might well come to hate that damned 'virtue' you keep proclaiming. [8] *That's* why those fools get the better of you. Conviction is quite a potent and irresistible force. [9] So until those fine principles take root in you so that you can begin to rely on them a little, I advise you to use discretion in associating with such people. Otherwise whatever you write down in class will melt away like wax in the sun. [10] Keep well out of the sun, then, so long as your principles are as pliant as wax.

[11] This is why philosophers say that we should even leave our native land, since old habits pull us back and make it hard to embark on a new routine; also, we can't stand running into people who say, 'Look at him, this so-and-so, trying to become a philosopher.' [12] Similarly, doctors, for good reason, send their most chronic patients away to a different environment and a different climate. [13] Adopt new habits yourself: consolidate your principles by putting them into practice.

[14] No. Instead from school it's straight off to the theatre, to a gladiatorial game, to an athletic show or the circus. Then from there you come back here, and from here, off you go again, the same people, the same pursuits – [15] you show no serious discipline, concern, or care for yourself. 'How do I handle chance impressions, naturally or unnaturally? Do I respond to them as I should, or don't I?* Do I tell externals that they are nothing to me?' [16] Unless this describes you, forsake your old habits, and your non-philosophical friends, if you hope to amount to anything.

---

* Reading ἀποκρίνομαι with some MSS. for ἀποκρίνωμαι.

III 20 *Every circumstance represents an opportunity*

[1] Just about everyone agrees that 'good' or 'bad' in the case
of objective judgements applies to us, not to things outside us.
[2] No one calls 'good' the fact that it is day, or 'bad' that it is
night, or 'the greatest of evils' that three is equal to four. [3]
No, they call correct judgement good and incorrect judgement
bad – the consequence being that good even comes of error,
when we recognize the error as such.

[4] And so it should be in life. 'Being healthy is good, being
sick is bad.' No, my friend: enjoying health in the right way is
good; making bad use of your health is bad. 'So even illness
can benefit us?' [5] Why not, if even death and disability can?
It was no small advantage Menoeceus derived from his dying,
after all.⁹ 'Whoever says so is welcome to the same advantages!'
Come, by his sacrifice didn't he save himself – that is, the patriot
in him, the benefactor, the man of honour, the man of his word
– all of whom would have died had he survived? [6] Conversely,
he would have acquired the reputation for being timid, mean,
treacherous and weak.

Well – do you think his death did him hardly any good? [7]
I suppose the father of Admetus¹⁰ greatly enjoyed living on such
base and despicable terms, [8] who afterward died all the same.
For God's sake, stop honouring externals, quit turning yourself
into the tool of mere matter, or of people who can supply you
or deny you those material things. [9] So is it possible to benefit
from these circumstances? Yes, from *every* circumstance, even
abuse and slander. A boxer derives the greatest advantage from
his sparring partner – and my accuser is my sparring partner.
He trains me in patience, civility and even temper. [10] I mean,
a doctor who puts me in a headlock and sets a dislocated pelvis
or shoulder – he benefits me, however painful the procedure.
So too does a trainer when he commands me to 'lift the weight
with both your hands' – and the heavier it is, the greater the
benefit to me.

Well, if someone trains me to be even-tempered, am I not
benefited in that case? [11] This shows you do not know how

to be helped by your fellow man. I have a bad neighbour – bad, that is, for himself. For me, though, he is good: he exercises my powers of fairness and sociability. A bad father, likewise, is bad for himself, but for me represents a blessing. [12] The wand of Hermes promises that 'whatever you touch will turn to gold'. For my part, I can say, 'bring what challenge you please and I will turn it to good account: bring illness, death, poverty, slander, a judgement of death: they will all be converted to advantage by my wand of Hermes.'

[13] 'What good will you get from death?'

'I will make it your glory, or the occasion for you to show how a person obeys the will of nature.'

[14] 'What will you make of illness?'

'I will expose its true nature by outdoing myself in calmness and serenity; I will neither beg the doctor's help, nor pray for death. [15] What more could you ask? Everything, you see, that you throw at me I will transform into a blessing, a boon – something dignified, even enviable.'

[16] But no. Instead, you say, 'Be careful that you don't get ill: it's bad.' Which is like saying, 'Guard against ever entertaining the idea that three is equivalent to four: it's bad.' How is it bad? If I weigh the statement correctly, what harm can it do me? It is more likely to help. [17] Similarly, it is enough if I hold the right idea about poverty, illness and removal from office: all such challenges will only serve my turn. No more, then, should I look for bad, and good, in external conditions.

[18] Ah, but these principles never leave the school, no one takes them with him when he goes back home. Instead, war immediately breaks out – with your slave, your neighbours, with people who scoff at these principles and make fun of you. [19] For my part, I bless Lesbios for daily reminding me that I know nothing.[11]

III 22 On Cynicism[12]

[1] An acquaintance, evidently attracted to Cynicism, wanted to know who was qualified to be a Cynic and what one could expect from it.

'We will consider the topic at length,' Epictetus said. [2] But this much I can tell you already: whoever undertakes the project without God's approval is inviting God's anger and will only make a public spectacle of himself. [3] I mean, in a well-run household you don't find just anybody presuming to think, 'I should be running the place.' Otherwise the owner, when he turns around and sees someone insolently giving orders, will haul him outside and have him whipped. [4] It's no different in the community of God and men: here too there is a master who assigns everything its place. [5] 'You are the sun. You are empowered as you move to make the year and the seasons, cause plants to grow and flourish, rouse the winds or calm them, and keep men's bodies sufficiently warm. Go, revolve, put everything, great and small, into motion.

[6] 'You are a cow. When a lion appears you know what to do, or you won't even survive to regret it. You are a bull: step out and face the lion, it's your job. It suits you and you have what it takes.

[7] 'You can lead the army to Troy: be Agamemnon. *You* can take on Hector in single combat: be Achilles.' [8] If Thersites had presumed to ask for command, either he would have been turned down flat, or he would have made an ass of himself in front of hundreds of witnesses.

[9] You need to consider the present business carefully because it isn't what you think.

[10] 'Already I wear a tattered coat like the Cynic's, and I already sleep on the ground, just as I will when I go Cynic. I have but to add a satchel and a staff to become an itinerant beggar who hectors everyone crossing his path. If I see a man who shaves his body hair, I'll be sure to lay into him, just like someone elaborately coiffed, or seen strutting around in finery.' [11] If that's how you picture Cynicism, it's better that you keep

your distance. In fact, don't go anywhere near it, the position is not for you.

[12] If you picture it realistically, however, and don't think yourself unworthy, consider next the project's scale. [13] To begin with, you have to set a different example with your behaviour. No more blaming God or man. Suspend desire completely, train aversion only on things under your control. Banish anger, rage, jealousy and pity. Be indifferent to women, fame, boys and tempting foods. [14] Other people indulge in these things protected by walls or the gloom of night. They have many ways of hiding; they can lock the gate and station someone outside their chamber: 'If anyone comes, tell them, "The master's out," or, "He's occupied."'

[15] The Cynic, in contrast, only has his honour to protect him. Without it he will be exposed to shame – naked, and out of doors. Honour is his house, his gate, his guards, his cloak of darkness. [16] He must not have anything personal he wants to hide; otherwise, so long – he has killed the Cynic, the free spirit, the man of the open air. He has begun to fear factors outside his control and crave concealment – which he cannot have even if he tries, because he has no place or means to hide. [17] If this teacher and trainer at large has the bad fortune to fail, what mortification must he feel! [18] With all this weighing on his conscience, how is he going to find the complete confidence he needs to give other people advice? There's no way, it just is not possible.

[19] To begin with, then, you must purify your intellect by training your thoughts: [20] 'My mind represents for me my medium – like wood to a carpenter, or leather to a shoemaker. The goal in my case is the correct use of impressions. [21] The body is irrelevant to me, as are its members. Death, too, whether of the whole body or a part, can come when it likes. [22] And exile? Where can they send me? Nowhere outside the world, since wherever I end up, the sun will be there, as will the moon and stars. There will still be dreams, birds of augury, and other means of staying in touch with the gods.'

[23] Disciplining the mind, though, is just the start of the true Cynic's duty. He has to realize that he has been sent by

God as a messenger for the benefit of others, by bringing them to an awareness of how confused they are about what is good and bad, and how this causes them to look for the good in vain, having no clue as to its true location. The Cynic should realize that in addition to being a messenger he is also a spy.[13] [24] He needs to be like Diogenes, when he was captured in the battle of Chaeronea, and dragged before Philip.[14] [25] The Cynic is a bona fide spy; he reports back on who is friend or foe. He must check and double-check before he returns with the truth, to guard against fear and false reports.

[26] He should be prepared, if necessary, to mount the podium and, like Socrates, say, 'Where are you going, you poor souls, and what are you doing? You drift about as if you were blind. You forsake the right road for a cul-de-sac. You look for peace and happiness in the wrong places; and you're suspicious of anyone who tries to point you in the right direction.' [27] Don't look for it in externals; it isn't in the body, and, if you doubt me, just look at Myron or Ophellius. It isn't in wealth, look at Croesus, or look at the rich of today: you'll see how unhappy they are. It doesn't lie in office, otherwise those who have been consuls multiple times would be happy – which they are not.[15] [28] Whom are we going to trust on this score – you, who see only the surface and are dazzled by wealth and power – or these people personally? What do *they* tell us? [29] Just hear them groan and complain; they say their lives are worse and less safe for having been consul more than once, thereby attracting fame and notoriety. [30] Being king is not the answer either; otherwise it would have made Nero and Sardanapalus[16] happy. Even Agamemnon, a better ruler than either of them, was not therefore happy. When his men were still snoring away, what was he doing?

He pulled many a hair from his head, roots and all.

What did he say?

I pace up and down . . . My spirit is troubled, and my heart is pounding right out of my chest.[17]

[31] Poor man, what's worrying you? It can't be money, *You are rich in gold and bronze.*[18] Nor can it be your health, you're fine. Your problem is that you have neglected and ruined the

faculty with which we exercise the will to get or to avoid, to act or not to act. How? [32] By not learning the true nature of the good to which it is born and of the nature of evil, or learning where its interest lies. Whenever something that is none of its interest goes awry, it thinks, 'Poor me, the Greeks are under attack.'

[33] 'Too bad for your mind, rather – the one thing you have neglected from indifference.'

'They are going to die at the Trojans' hands.'

'And if they are not killed by the Trojans, won't they die regardless?'

'Yes, but not all at once.'

'What difference does that make? If death is wrong, then it is wrong whether they go singly or together. And after all, death signifies nothing more than the separation of body and soul. [34] And if the Greeks die, do they close the door behind them? Isn't death in your power too?'

'It is.'

'So why complain, "Alas, to be king and have to carry Zeus' sceptre"? A king can no more be unfortunate than God. So what does that make you? [35] Right, a shepherd – that is how you react, anyway, like a shepherd whining when a wolf snatches one of his sheep. And your subjects too – alas, they are sheep for real.

[36] 'Why did you come? Your desire was not in danger, was it, or your choice, impulse or aversion?'

'No, Paris ran off with my brother's wife.'

[37] 'Wasn't that a blessing in disguise, to rid your brother of his little wench of a wife?'

'Well, should we just let the Trojans insult us?'

'Are the Trojans wise or foolish? If they are wise, do not quarrel with them; if they are fools, ignore them.'

[38] 'If it's not in any of these things I've been protecting, then where is the good located? Pray tell us, Great Messenger and Spy.'

'It's where you don't think or care to look. Otherwise, you would find that it's within you; and you wouldn't go wandering off among externals, which are none of yours. [39] Turn your attention on yourself – examine your belief system. What is the good as you feature it?'

'It means serenity, happiness and independence.'

'Very good. [40] But doesn't it also appear naturally great in your imagination, priceless and invulnerable to harm? Where are you going to find serenity and independence – in something free, or something enslaved?'

'Free.'

'And your body – is it free or slave?'

'I don't know.'

'You are aware, I presume, that it is subject to fever, gout, rheum and dysentery, not to mention despots, fires and weapons – anything, in a word, that is physically stronger?'

'I agree, it is subject to these.'

[41] 'So how can the body or any of its parts be considered free – or great, or priceless? In essence it is a corpse, a thing of mud and dust. Do you have anything that *is* free?'

[42] 'Now I'm inclined to think not.'

'Look, can you be forced to assent to what appears to you wrong?'

'No.'

'Or to dissent from the plain truth?'

'No.'

'Then you see you do have within you a share of freedom. [43] And can any of you have the will to desire or avoid, choose or refuse, plan or anticipate, if you don't first formulate the impression of something advantageous or improper?'

'No.'

'So here, too, you have a measure of freedom and independence. [44] Poor devil, why not try focusing on that, why not look after that, for a change; that's where you should go looking for the good.'

[45] How can someone who has nothing – no clothes, no hearth or home, no luxuries, no slaves, no city he can call his own – how is it possible for a person like that to be happy? [46] Well, God has sent among you a person who will prove by example that it can be done. [47] 'Look at me, I have no home, no city, no property, no slave; I sleep on the ground;

I haven't a wife or children, no officer's quarters – just earth, and sky, and one lousy cloak. What more do I need? [48] I am cheerful, I am tranquil and I am free. You've never seen me fail to get what I want, or get what I try to avoid. I have never been angry with God or another human being; I've never yelled at anyone. Have you ever seen me with a sad expression? [49] The people before whom you bow and tremble – when *I* meet them, I treat them as if they were slaves. In fact, whenever they see me, they all without exception think that they are in the presence of their lord and master.'

[50] There you have the words of the authentic Cynic, words that faithfully reflect his purpose and personality. Most of you, however, identify the Cynic with minor details like his satchel, his stick and large jaws – large, I suppose, the better to wolf down the food he's given (if he doesn't hoard it) – or with his embarrassing habit of shouting abuse at passers-by, or with the broad shoulder he leaves bare.[19]

[51] You see how big the project is that you propose to take on. First, get a mirror – look at your shoulders, check out your loins, examine your thighs; you are about to sign up for the Olympics, not some desultory, imaginary match. [52] If you lose at the Olympics you cannot just leave, you have to suffer the indignity of having the whole world watch – not just Athenians, Spartans or the citizens of Nicopolis – everyone. A casual contestant will be trounced, but not before he suffers thirst, endures heat exhaustion and swallows handfuls of sand.

[53] Plan carefully, know your limits, be reasonable and don't go forward without God's say-so. If he picks you, be aware that in addition to greatness his plans for you entail a good deal of discomfort. [54] Because this is a particularly charming clause in the Cynic contract: you are going to be beaten like a donkey, and must love your tormentors as if you were their father or brother.

[55] Or would you rather invoke the emperor in their presence: 'Caesar, you may have brought peace to the world, but look at the violence *I* have to put up with! Take me to the proconsul at once.'[20] [56] Caesar and the proconsul mean nothing to the Cynic; he only calls upon Zeus, whom he serves as

ambassador. If he suffers some hardship, he is confident that it is only Zeus putting him through his paces. [57] I mean, Heracles did not wallow in self-pity when he performed his labours for Eurystheus; he did what he was told without reluctance. So the Cynic, who takes his orders from Zeus, and has earned the right to carry the staff of Diogenes – should we expect him to hesitate or complain?

[58] Listen to how Diogenes, laid low with fever, still lectured passers-by: 'Idiots, where are you going in such a hurry? You are going a great distance to see those damned athletes compete;* why not stop a bit to see a man do combat with illness?' [59] A man of his mettle is not one to accuse God, who chose him, of unfairness in making him ill. He positively prides himself on his hardships and is bold enough to be a roadside attraction. What would he blame God *for*? That he cuts such an admirable figure? What would the charge be? That his virtue is too glaringly bright? [60] Here, just remember what he says about poverty, death and pain; how he compares his happiness with that of the Great King.[21] Or rather, he doesn't think there is any comparison. [61] For where you find unrest, grief, fear, frustrated desire, failed aversion, jealousy and envy, happiness has no room for admittance. And where values are false, these passions inevitably follow.

[62] The young man asked, if he got sick, whether as a Cynic he should consent to receive a friend to help take care of him.

Yes, but where are you going to find a Cynic's friend? [63] He would have to be someone just like him, to be worthy of being called his friend. He would have to share equally in the sceptre and the kingdom.[22] It is a worthy minister indeed who deserves a Cynic's friendship, as Diogenes was worthy of Antisthenes, and Crates of Diogenes. [64] Don't imagine that it is enough to become his friend and be accepted into his home [65] just to go up to a Cynic and introduce yourself. If that's your plan, better start looking for a nice rubbish dump in the event of illness – one protected from the north wind, so you don't catch your death of cold. [66] Friendship, it seems to me,

---

* The translation follows Blass in deleting ἢ before μαχήν.

means no more to you than moving in with somebody and sponging off him or her indefinitely.[23] You have no business contemplating so great a project as Cynicism.

[67] 'Well,' the young man said, 'what about marriage and children – will the Cynic choose to take these duties on?'

Give me a state composed of wise men, and you may not be able to find a single person adopting the profession of Cynic. For whose sake, after all, would one take on so rigorous a way of life? [68] Still, if we suppose that there is a Cynic there, I see no reason why he should not marry and have children. His wife will be wise, like him, and like her father; and their children will grow up to be the same.

[69] But with things as they are – in a virtual crisis – it's better, perhaps, that the Cynic not be distracted by domestic duties. He needs to focus on his sacred ministry, and be free to move around – not be tied down by personal obligations that he cannot very well ignore, but which, if he honours, will detract from his role as messenger, scout and herald of the gods. [70] Consider the responsibilities he owes to his father-in-law and his wife's other relations, to his wife as well; in the end, he is reduced to the role of nurse and provider. [71] To give just a few examples: he has to find a pot to heat water for the baby, and a tub to bathe it in; wool for his wife after she's given birth, together with oil, a cot, a drinking cup – the list of accessories is already long. [72] And he has other duties and distractions. In the end, what's left of that king devoted to the commons – the king *who has the people in his care, and so many concerns?*[24] Where is the king whose duty it is to watch over others who have married and got children, to see which of them is treating his wife well, which badly, who is quarrelling, which households are prospering, which are in decline?

In effect, he makes rounds like a doctor, taking his patients' pulse, alternately saying, [73] 'You have a fever, you have a headache, you have gout; you should fast, you should eat, you should not bathe; you need an operation, you have to be cauterized.' [74] How is someone encumbered by private duties going to find time for this? And he has to put little coats on his children's backs, and send them off to school with little notebooks and little pens, and make up a little bed for them at night; because, after all, his children will not be Cynics straight out of the womb.[25] If he does not do all this for them, he would have done better to expose them at birth, rather than kill them by long neglect. [75] Now look at the condition we've reduced our Cynic to – he's more a butler than a king.

[76] 'Yes, but Crates had a wife.'[26] You are talking about a circumstance that arose out of love, and a wife who was Crates' virtual twin. We, on the other hand, are discussing normal marriages, not special circumstances; and our analysis has not discovered, in our present state, that marriage is advisable for the Cynic.

[77] 'Then how will he help the community carry on?'

For God's sake, who benefits society more, people who produce two or three brats with runny noses to survive them or those who supervise in each person's life what they care about, or mistakenly neglect? [78] Who benefited the Thebans more – those who gave them children, or Epaminondas, who died childless? Did Priam, with his fifty worthless sons, or Danaus, or Aeolus, contribute more to society than Homer?[27] [79] Their contribution to society as poet, or general, is considered more than fair return for their failure to marry or have children; should not the kingdom of the Cynic be reckoned reasonable exchange as well?

[80] I fear we don't appreciate its grandeur, nor do we have a fair idea of Diogenes' character. We are influenced by the sad spectacle of today's Cynics, these *dogs who beg at table and hang about the gate*[28] who have nothing in common with the Cynics of old except maybe for farting in public, not much else. [81] Because, if we did, we would not be surprised or disappointed if a Cynic does not marry or procreate. My friend, he fathers everyone: every man is his son, every woman his daughter. That is how he regards everyone, and how much he cares for them. [82] Don't think he hectors strangers in a spirit of impudence; he is acting like a father, or a brother – like the vicar of God, the father of everyone.

[83] Now go on, ask me whether he will take part in public life. [84] Look, is any form of public life superior to his? Why

should he stoop to preparing speeches about income and expenditures for the Athenians, say, when he is called upon to address everyone – Athenians, Corinthians, Romans – and not about debits and credits, or war and peace, but about happiness and unhappiness, success and misfortune, freedom and slavery? [85] You are asking me if someone will take part in politics when they are already engaged in politics on a major scale. Ask me further if he will hold office, and again I will say to you, 'Fool, what office is superior to the one he has?'

[86] Furthermore, the Cynic's body should be in good shape, since his philosophy will not carry as much conviction coming from someone pale and sickly. [87] He not only needs to show his qualities of soul in order to convince ordinary people that it is possible to be a gentleman without the material goods they usually admire, he also has to prove, with his physique, that his simple, frugal life outdoors is wholesome. [88] 'What I testify to, my body testifies to as well.' Which is what Diogenes did: he went about with a healthy glow on his face, and his body alone was enough to win the common people over. [89] A Cynic who excites pity is taken for a beggar; everyone is disgusted and walks around him. The Cynic shouldn't be so filthy that he drives people away; his very ruggedness should be of a clean and pleasant kind.

[90] The Cynic ought to be naturally sharp and witty, too (otherwise he's just a boring windbag), to be equal to every occasion that calls for a quick reply – [91] the way Diogenes responded to the man who greeted him with, 'So Diogenes, you don't believe the gods exist?' with 'How can you say that, when I know that *you* are headed for hell?' [92] Or again, when Alexander the Great stood over him while he was resting, and recited: *A man charged with making decisions shouldn't sleep the night away*, Diogenes, still half-asleep, replied: *Who has the people in his care, and so many concerns.*[29]

[93] Above all, though, his mind should be purer than the sun, because anyone guilty of wrongdoing who presumes to lecture others can only be considered slick and unscrupulous. [94] For you see how it is: the kings and tyrants of this world, even if they are corrupt, can reprimand and punish offenders

by virtue of their arms and soldiers; instead of weapons and bodyguards, his conscience gives the Cynic the same authority. [95] For he works overtime on his fellow man's behalf; what sleep he gets only leaves him purer than when he first lay down;[30] his thoughts are never unworthy of a friend and minister of the gods, and he shares in Zeus' administration. '*Lead me, Zeus, lead me, Destiny*' is always on his lips, as well as 'If it pleases the gods, so be it.' [96] Conscious of all this, why shouldn't he venture to speak truth to his own brothers, his own children – his own relations, in a word?

[97] A person of his conscience is neither bossy nor officious; he is not poking into other people's business when he looks after the common welfare, he is tending to his own. If you disagree, then by your lights a general who inspects, drills and oversees his troops, punishing those who get out of line, is intrusive too.

[98] If, however, you reprimand others with a bit of cake under your arm, I will say, Wouldn't you rather go and wolf down in secret what you've stolen there? [99] What are other people's affairs to *you*? Who are you – are you the bull, or the queen of the hive? Show me proof of your authority, such as the queen is endowed with by nature. If you are a drone disputing control over the bees, expect your fellow citizens to get rid of you, just as worker bees get rid of the drones.

[100] The Cynic's powers of endurance should be such that he appears to most people insensible, a veritable block of wood. As far as he's concerned, nobody insults or hits or hurts him. He has personally surrendered his body to be used or abused however anyone likes. [101] He knows that whatever is inferior, in that respect in which it *is* inferior, must yield to what is superior; and that his body is inferior to the crowd – what's physically weaker, in other words, is inferior to what is physically stronger. [102] So he never condescends to compete with them on their level. He has completely renounced things outside himself and makes no claim to things that are by nature enslaved.

[103] But when it comes to matters of the will and the use of impressions, then you'll see how many eyes he has – enough to

make Argus seem blind by comparison.[31] [104] With him there is no premature assent, mistaken impulse, frustrated desire, unsuccessful aversion or unrealized purpose; hence no blame, envy or humiliation. [105] All his effort and energy go into this. As for the rest, he yawns away, in a state of perfect indifference. Of free will there can be neither thief nor tyrant; [106] of the body, however, yes. Of material things? Yes. Of honours and offices – yes. Which is why he is not interested in them. When someone tries using these things to affect him, he says, 'Go look for children to intimidate; masks are meant to frighten them; I know there's nothing behind them.'

[107] This, then, is the nature of Cynicism. You consider undertaking it; then please take some time to judge your aptitude. [108] And remember what Hector said to Andromache:

No, go inside, and see to your weaving instead. Men will see to war; men, and me in particular.[32] [109] He sensed both his own endowment, you see, and his wife's incapacity.

III 23 *On rhetorical display*

[1] First, tell yourself what you want to be, then act your part accordingly. This, after all, is what we find to be the rule in just about every other field. [2] Athletes decide first what they want to be, then proceed to do what is necessary. If they decide to be a distance runner, it means one particular diet, racecourse, workout and mode of physical therapy. If they want to be sprinters, those factors are different. And if it's a pentathlete they want to be, they vary again. [3] You will find the same thing true of the crafts. If you want to be a carpenter, you will have one kind of training, if you want to be a sculptor, quite another. All our efforts must be directed towards an end, or we will act in vain. If it is not the right end, we will fail utterly.

[4] Now, there are two standards of reference, one general and one particular. To begin with, then, we must act like a human being, which means, not like a sheep, however gentle, nor violently like a wild beast. The particular standard relates

to the skill and the end to which it is put. The musician should
act like a musician, the carpenter like a carpenter, the philosopher like a philosopher, the orator like an orator. Therefore,
when you say, [6] 'Come and hear me lecture,' be sure you have
a purpose in lecturing. When you find your direction, check to
make sure that it is the right one. [7] Is your goal to educate or
be praised?

Right away the answer comes back, 'What do I care for the
praise of the vulgar masses?' And those are fine words. The
musician too, *qua* musician, does not care about praise, any
more than praise matters to a mathematician.

[8] So you aim to educate, you say. But for what purpose?
Tell us, so we will go running to the auditorium too. Can
anyone educate others, though, if they have not first been educated themselves? No – any more than a person who is not a
carpenter can give lessons in carpentry, or someone who is not
a cobbler can give lessons in making shoes. [9] Do you want to
know if *you* are educated? Show us your values, philosopher.
What is the goal of the faculty of desire? 'Not to fail in desire.'
[10] Of aversion? 'Not to get what it doesn't want.' Well – are
we meeting these goals? Tell me the truth; because if you lie, I
will say to you, 'The other day your audience greeted you rather
coolly* and didn't applaud – and you left dejected. [11] Another
day, having been acclaimed, you went around and said to
everyone, 'How do you think I did?'

'Splendidly, sir, on my word.'

'How did that one part come off?'

'Which?'

'The one where I described Pan and the Nymphs.'[33]

[12] 'It was marvellous!'

'Then you try to tell me that with regard to desire and aversion you are behaving in line with nature? Get lost, try telling
it to somebody else. [13] Didn't you praise someone just the
other day in defiance of your true opinion? Weren't you sucking
up to some officer? How would you like it if your children
acted that way?'

---

* Reading σοι for the σου after ψυχρότερον.

[14] 'God forbid.'

'Then why were you praising and extolling him so?'

'He's a clever young man and a fan of rhetoric.'

'How do you know?'

'He praises *me*.'

Oh, well, that proves it, of course. Look, what do you think is really going on? Don't these same people secretly despise you? [15] I mean, if someone hears himself described by a philosopher as 'a great talent, ingenuous and unspoiled' when he's well aware that he hasn't done the man any good or even wished him well, what must he be thinking except, 'He must want me for some favour or another.' [16] If that's wrong, then tell me, what sign of great talent has he displayed? I mean, he's been with you for some time, he's heard you engage in dialogue, he's heard you lecture on philosophy – has he gained self-control, has he taken himself in hand, has he come to a realization of his faults? [17] Has he shed his presumption, and begun looking for a teacher?

'He has.'

One who will teach him how to live? No, fool – one who will teach him how to turn a phrase instead; because that is precisely what he admires you for. Just listen to what he says: 'This person writes with great sophistication, much better than Dio.'[34] [18] It's a whole other matter. He *doesn't* say, 'The man is civil, he is constant, he is calm.' And even if he *had* said it, I would have asked, 'Since this man is constant, what characteristics does the constant man have?'[35] And if he could not say, I would have added, 'Understand what words you use first, *then* use them.' [19] So in your sorry state – eager for admirers, counting the number of audience members – do you intend to come to *others'* assistance?

'Today I had a much bigger audience.'

'There certainly was a crowd.'

'I put the turnout at around five hundred.'

'Nonsense, it was a thousand at least.'

'That many never showed up to hear Dio.'

'Him? Never.'

'And it was a sophisticated audience, too, where their taste in rhetoric was concerned.'

'Sir, beauty can even move a stone.'

[20] There are the words of a philosopher for you, and the character of a man bound to benefit humanity! There's one who has listened to reason, certainly, and read the Socratic discourses as coming from Socrates, not from Lysias or Isocrates.[36]

'I often wondered by what sort of arguments . . .'[37]

'Stop right there: ". . . by what sort of *argument*" reads better.'

[21] You read them as if they were pretty poems. If you read them properly, you wouldn't care about that, you would attend more to this: 'Anytus and Meletus can kill me, but they cannot harm me.'[38] 'I've always been the sort to attend to the argument that seems best to me upon inspection, even to the detriment of my own affairs.'[39] [22] Which is why no one ever heard him say, 'I know something and I teach it.'[40]

[23] No, I suppose you think he would say to his companion, 'Come listen to me speak today at the house of Codratus.'

Why should I hear you speak? You want to show me that you arrange words elegantly? So you do; but what do you gain by it?

'You're supposed to praise me.'

[24] 'What do you mean, "praise me"?

'Shout "bravo!" and "marvellous!"'

Fine, I'll shout it. But if praise is one of those things that philosophers categorize as 'good', then how can I praise you? Teach me that it is good to be eloquent, and I will praise you.

[25] Should listening to speeches be an experience totally devoid of pleasure, then? Of course not. I take pleasure in listening to lyre players, too. But is that good enough reason for me to get up and play the lyre? Listen to what Socrates says: 'It would not suit me at my age, gentlemen, to come before you formulating phrases like a callow youth.'[41] [26] It is an exquisite little art, this choosing up words, joining them together, then appearing in public to give them an artistic reading. And how

delightful if during the recital someone shouts out, 'Not many people can appreciate *this*, by God!'*

[27] Does a philosopher solicit an audience? As the sun draws sustenance to itself, that is how a true philosopher attracts people who stand in need of help.[42] What sort of doctor is it that invites patients to be treated by him? And yet I hear that in Rome now even the doctors advertise for patients. In my day it was the other way around. [28] 'I invite you to come and hear how unwell you are. How you care for everything except what counts. How you don't know good from evil. That you are unhappy and unsuccessful.' What a charming invitation! And yet if the philosopher does not make such an impression with his speech, it's dead, and the speaker might as well be too. [29] Rufus[43] used to say, 'If you have nothing better to do than praise me for it, then my speech was a failure.' He used to address us in such a way as to make everyone sitting there suppose that someone had informed on them – that's how well he intuited the truth, and how vividly he evoked for each one of us our private faults.

[30] Friends, the school of a philosopher is a hospital. When you leave, you should have suffered, not enjoyed yourself. Because you enter, not in a state of health, but with a dislocated shoulder, it may be, or an abscess, a fistula, or head pain. [31] So am I supposed to sit down alongside you and recite clever thoughts and phrases, so that patients applaud and leave with their shoulder in the same condition as when they were admitted, their head, their abscess, their fistula the same? [32] Is it for this that young people should travel abroad, leaving behind their parents, friends, relations and possessions – all so that they can say 'Bravo!' when you deliver your clever phrases? Is this what Socrates, Zeno or Cleanthes did?

[33] 'Well, isn't there the protreptic style of discourse?' Naturally – as there are the elenctic and didactic styles. But whoever included the epideictic style in the curriculum as a fourth subject?[44] [34] The hortatory style purports to expose to all the conflict in which they are embroiled, and how they are

* Reading εἴ τινα for εἰπεῖν.

interested in everything except what they want. Because what people want is what conduces to happiness; but they look for it in the wrong place. [35] If this is to happen, do we really need a thousand chairs set up, invitations sent out and the speaker turned out in a fancy robe or gown, astride a podium, narrating the death of Achilles? For gods' sake, do your best to honour such famous names and deeds by forbearing to name them.

[36] There is nothing more inspiring than a speaker who makes clear to his audience that he has need of them. [37] Tell me – has anyone who has ever heard you read or discourse felt self-remorse as a result, or experienced self-realization, or afterwards left thinking, 'The philosopher touched a nerve there; I can't go on acting as I have'?

[38] No; if you perform really well, one says to another, 'He put the bit about Xerxes nicely, I thought,' and another says, 'I liked his description of the battle of Thermopylae better.'

Does that sound like the lecture of a philosopher?

BOOK IV

IV 1 *On freedom*

[1] Free is the person who lives as he wishes and cannot be coerced, impeded or compelled, whose impulses cannot be thwarted, who always gets what he desires and never has to experience what he would rather avoid.

Now, who would want to go through life ignorant of how to achieve this?

'No one.'

[2] Who wants to live with delusion and prejudice, being unjust, undisciplined, mean and ungrateful?

'No one.'

[3] No bad person, then, lives the way he wants, and no bad man is free. [4] Who wants to live life experiencing sadness, envy and pity, being frustrated in their desires and liable to experience what they want to avoid?

'No one.'

[5] So, can we find any bad person who is without sadness, fear, frustration or misfortune?

'No.'

No more, then, can we find one who is free.

[6] Now, a two-term consul will tolerate such talk only on condition that you add, 'But you know that already; it hardly applies to *you*.' If you tell him the truth and say, [7] 'You're just as much enslaved as someone sold into captivity three times over,' don't expect anything but a punch in the nose. 'How am *I* a slave?' he wants to know. [8] 'My father is free, my mother is free, and there is no deed of sale for *me*. Add to which I'm a

senator, I'm a personal friend of Caesar, I've been a consul and I own many slaves personally.' [9] In the first place, Senator, sir, your father could have been slavish in the same respect as you, along with your mother, your grandfather and all your ancestors down the line. [10] And even if they were as free as free can be, what does that have to do with you? Suppose that they were noble, and you are depraved? Or that they were courageous, whereas you are a coward? Or that they were disciplined, while you are dissolute?

[11] 'What's that got to do with being a slave?'

Doesn't it seem to you that acting against one's will, under protest and compulsion, is tantamount to being a slave?

[12] 'Maybe, but who has power to compel me except Caesar, who rules over everyone?'

[13] So you admit that you have at least one master. And don't let the fact that Caesar rules over everyone, as you say, console you: it only means that you're a slave in a very large household. [14] You remind me of the citizens of Nicopolis, who are forever proclaiming, 'By the grace of Caesar, we are free.'[1]

[15] If you like, however, for the moment we'll leave Caesar out of account. Just tell me this: haven't you ever been in love with someone, be they man or woman, slave or free?

[16] 'How does that affect whether I am slave or free?'

[17] Weren't you ever commanded by your sweetheart to do something you didn't want to do? Did you never flatter your pet slave, and even kiss her feet? And yet if someone were to force you to kiss Caesar's feet, you'd regard it as hubris and the height of tyranny.

[18] If your lovesick condition isn't slavery, then what is? Didn't you ever risk going out at night where you didn't want to go, spend more money than you had intended, say things in the course of the evening in accents of misery and woe, put up with being mocked, and finally locked out? [19] If you're too embarrassed to share your own experience, though, just consider the words and actions of Thrasonides, who fought more campaigns, perhaps, than you.[2] To begin with, he went out at a time of night that even his slave wouldn't dare do, or if forced to, only with much moaning and groaning about his bitter

condition. [20] And what does Thrasonides say? 'A pretty woman has made of me a perfect slave, something not even my fiercest enemies could accomplish.' [21] Poor guy, to be enslaved to a whore, and a cheap one at that! What right do you still have to call yourself free? What point is there in boasting about your military victories?

[22] Then the man calls for a sword to end it all, yells at the slave who refuses to give him one out of compassion, sends gifts to his girl – who still despises him – begs and implores her and rejoices when he meets with the least success. [23] But until he succeeds in suppressing his lust and anxiety, how is he really free?

[24] Consider how we apply the idea of freedom to animals. [25] There are tame lions that people cage, raise, feed and take with them wherever they go. Yet who will call such a lion free? The easier its life, the more slavish it is. No lion endowed with reason and discretion would choose to be one of these pet specimens.

[26] The birds above us, when they are caught and raised in a cage, will try anything for the sake of escape. Some starve to death rather than endure their condition. [27] Those that survive – barely, grudgingly, wasting away – fly off in an instant when they find the least little opening to squeeze through, so great is their need for their native freedom, so strong the desire to be independent and unconfined. [28] 'Well, what's wrong with you here in your cage?' 'You can ask? I was born to fly wherever I like, to live in the open air, to sing whenever I want. You take all this away from me and then say, "What's wrong with you?"'

[29] For this reason we will only call those animals free that refuse to tolerate captivity and escape instead by dying as soon as they are caught. [30] Apropos of which, Diogenes says somewhere that one way to guarantee freedom is to be ready to die. To the Persian king he wrote, 'You can no more make slaves of the Athenians than you can make slaves of the fish of the sea.' [31] 'Why? Can't Athenians be captured?' 'Capture them, and straight away they'll give you the slip and be gone, like fish, which die directly they are caught and taken on board.

And if the Athenians die when taken captive, what good in the end is all your military might?' [32] There's the word of a free man who has given the subject of freedom considerable thought and, sure enough, discovered the real meaning of the word. If you continue to look for it in the wrong place, however, don't be surprised if you never find it.

[33] The slave urgently prays to be emancipated. Why? Do you suppose it's because he can't wait to pay the tax collector the five per cent tax?[3] No, it's because he imagines that, lacking liberty, he's been thwarted and unhappy all his life up to then. [34] 'Once I'm set free,' he says, 'everything will be roses right away. I won't have to wait on anybody, I can talk to everyone as an equal and a peer, travel wherever I like, come and go as I please.'

[35] Then he is liberated, but now, lacking a place to eat, he looks around for someone to sweet-talk and dine with. Next he resorts to prostitution and, if he gets a sugar daddy, he suffers the most degrading fate of all, having now fallen into a far more abject slavery than the one he escaped. [36] Even if he succeeds on his own, his low breeding makes him fall in love with a common prostitute. When she refuses him he falls apart and longs to be a slave again.

[37] 'What did I lack then, anyway? Another person supplied me with clothes, shoes and food and took care of me when I was sick; and I had little enough to do by way of service in return. Now I go through hell catering to many people instead of just the one. [38] Still – if I can only manage to get a ring on my finger, then finally my life will be blissful and complete.'[4] Well, to get it he has to endure the usual humiliations; and once he has it, it's the same old story again.

[39] So then he thinks: 'If I serve a stint in the military all my troubles will be over.' Consequently he joins the army, suffers everything a rank-and-file soldier has to suffer, and enlists for a second and then a third tour of duty.[5] [40] Finally, when he crowns it off by becoming a senator, then he becomes a slave in fine company, then he experiences the poshest and most prestigious form of enslavement.

[41] No more foolishness. The man has to learn 'what each

specific thing means', as Socrates often said, and stop casually applying preconceptions to individual cases. [42] This is the cause of everyone's troubles, the inability to apply common preconceptions to particulars.[6] Instead the opinions of men as to what is bad diverge.* [43] One thinks that he is unwell, when it's nothing of the kind; the problem is that he is not adapting preconceptions correctly. One imagines that he is poor, another that he has a difficult mother or father, still another that Caesar is not disposed in his favour. This is all caused by one and the same thing, namely, ignorance of how to apply one's preconceptions.

[44] Who, after all, does not have a preconception of 'bad', to the effect that it is harmful, that it should be avoided, and that we should use every means to get rid of it? One preconception does not conflict with another, [45] conflict arises when it comes to their application. What is this 'bad', then, which is also harmful and needs to be avoided? One says it's not being Caesar's friend:[7] he's off the mark, he's not applying preconceptions properly, and is distressed because he's stuck on something that doesn't meet the definition. Because if he succeeds in securing Caesar's friendship he still hasn't got what he wants – [46] the same thing, really, that we all want: to live in peace, to be happy, to do as we like and never be foiled or forced to act against our wishes.

When a man gains Caesar's friendship, does he stop being hindered or constrained, does he live in peace and happiness? Whom should we ask? Well, who is more to be trusted than the person who has actually gained his confidence? [47] So step up, sir, and tell us, when did you sleep more soundly, now or before you became intimate with Caesar? 'By the gods, stop mocking my condition. You don't know what agonies I endure. I can't even fall off to sleep before someone comes and announces, "The emperor is up already, and about to make his appearance," and then I'm harassed by one worry and crisis after another.'

[48] Well, and when did you dine with greater contentment,

* Reading ἄλλοι ἄλλα κακά.

now or earlier? Hear him testify to this, too. He says that if he's not invited to dine with Caesar, he's an emotional wreck; and if he is invited, he behaves like a slave asked to sit beside his master, anxious the whole time lest he say or do something gauche. But is he afraid that, like a slave, he'll get whipped? He should be so lucky. As befits a personage as lofty as a friend of Caesar, he's afraid his head will be chopped off.

[49] When did you bathe with more ease, when were you more relaxed at your exercise – in a word, which life would you prefer, the present or the previous one? [50] I could swear that there is no one so crude or forgetful that they don't actually regret their fortune in precise proportion to how close to Caesar they've become.

[51] Well, if neither kings, so-called, nor their companions live as they please, who is left that can be considered free? Look and you will find: nature has endowed you with resources to discover the truth. And if you can't infer the answer yourself using only these resources, [52] listen to what those who have explored the question have to say:

'Do you think freedom is something good?'

'The greatest good of all.'

'Can anyone in possession of the greatest good be unhappy or unfortunate?'

'No.'

'Anyone you see who is unhappy, then, malcontent or disheartened, you can confidently characterize as not being free?'

'Yes.'

[53] Now we have surely advanced beyond consideration of buying, selling and other such mundane transactions.[8] Because if you were right to agree to what we said above, then if he is unhappy the Great King himself cannot be free, nor can any prince, consul or two-term consul.

'Granted.'

[54] Well, then, answer me something else: do you think freedom is grand and glorious, a thing of some significance?

'Of course.'

And can anyone possessed of something so grand, glorious and important feel inferior?

'Impossible.'

[55] Then whenever you see someone grovel before another, or flatter them insincerely, you can safely assume that that person is not free – and not just if a meal is at stake, but even when they abase themselves for the sake of a governorship or consulship. In fact, you can call the people who behave that way for small gains petty slaves, while the latter deserve to be called slaves on a grand scale.

[56] 'I would have to agree with that too.'

And do you think of freedom as something autonomous and self-sufficient?

'Yes.'

Then whoever is liable to be hindered or compelled by someone else is assuredly not free. [57] And please don't research the status of their grandfather and great-grandfather, or inquire into whether they were bought or sold. If you hear someone say 'Master' sincerely and with feeling, call him a slave no matter if twelve bodyguards[9] march ahead of him. Or if you hear, 'God, the things I put up with!', call the person a slave. If you just see him disconsolate, angry or out of sorts, call him a slave – albeit a slave in a purple toga.

[58] Even if he does none of these things, don't call him free just yet, acquaint yourself with his judgements, in case they show any sign of constraint, disappointment or disaffection. And if you find him so disposed, call him a slave on holiday at the Saturnalia.[10] Say that his master is away; when he returns, the man's true condition will be made plain to you.

[59] 'When who returns?'

Whoever has the means to give or take away any of the things he values.

'Do we have that many masters?'

We do. Because over and above the rest we have masters in the form of circumstances, which are legion. And anyone who controls any one of them controls us as well. [60] No one, you realize, fears Caesar himself, it is death, exile, dispossession, jail and disenfranchisement that they are afraid of. Nor is Caesar loved, unless by chance he is personally deserving; we love money, a tribuneship, a military command or consulship.

But when we love, hate or fear such things, then the people who administer them are bound to become our masters. [61] As a result we even honour them as gods, because we associate godhead with whatever has the capacity to confer most benefit. Then we posit a false minor premise: *this* man has the power to confer the most benefit. And the conclusion that follows from these premises is necessarily false as well.[11]

[62] What is it then that renders a person free and independent? Money is not the answer, nor is a governorship, a consulship, or even a kingdom. [63] Something else needs to be found. Well, what makes for freedom and fluency in the practice of writing? Knowledge of how to write. The same goes for the practice of playing an instrument. It follows that, in the conduct of life, there must be a science to living well. [64] Now, you have heard this stated as a general principle, consider how it is borne out in particular cases. Take someone in want of something under the control of people other than himself; is it possible for him to be unrestricted or unrestrained?

'No.'

[65] Consequently he cannot be free either. Now consider: is there nothing that is under our control, is *everything* under our control – or are there some things we control, and others that we don't?

'What do you mean?'

[66] Is it within your power to have your body perform perfectly whenever you want?

'No.'

Or be in good health?

'No.'

Or attractive?

'Again, no.'

Well, then, the body isn't yours, and is subject to everything physically stronger.

'Granted.'

[67] What about land – can you have as much as you want, for as long as you want, in the condition you prefer?

'No.'

And what about slaves?

'No again.'

Clothing?

'No.'

Your house?

'No.'

Your horses?

'No to all of the above.'

And if more than anything else you want your children to live, or your wife, your brother, or your friends, is this within your power to effect?

'No, that isn't either.'

[68] Is there nothing that is under your authority, that you have exclusive control over – does anything of the kind exist?

'I don't know.'

[69] Well, look at it this way. Can anyone make you assent to a false proposition?

'No, no one can.'

So in the field of assent you cannot be hindered or obstructed.

'Evidently.'

[70] And can anyone force you to choose something to which you're opposed?

'They can: when they threaten me with death or imprisonment, they compel my choice.'

But what if you despise death and imprisonment – are you still in that person's thrall?

'No.'

[71] Is your attitude towards death your affair, then?

'It is.'

Therefore your will is your own business too.

'I grant it.'

And that goes for being opposed to something, also.

[72] 'But suppose I choose to walk, and someone obstructs me?'

What part of you will they obstruct? Certainly not your power of assent?

'No, my body.'

Your body, yes – as they might obstruct a rock.

'Perhaps; but the upshot is, now I'm not allowed to walk.'

[73] Whoever told you, 'Walking is your irrevocable privilege'? I said only that the will to walk could not be obstructed. Where use of the body and its cooperation are concerned, you've long been told that that isn't your responsibility.

[74] 'Very well.'

And can you be forced by anyone to desire something against your will?

'No.'

Or to plan for, or project – or, in a word, regard outside impressions in any one way at all?

[75] 'No again. But when I've already conceived a wish for something, they can stop me from getting it.'

If you wish for something that is under your authority and cannot be obstructed, how will they stop you?

'They can't.'

And who says if you desire something outside your authority that you cannot be obstructed?

[76] 'Well, should I not desire health, then?'

No – nor, for that matter, anything else outside the limits of your authority; [77] and whatever you cannot produce or preserve at will lies outside your range. Don't let your hands go near it, much less your desire. Otherwise you've consigned yourself to slavery and submitted your neck to the yoke, as you do whenever you prize something not yours to command, or grow attached to something like health that's contingent on God's will and variable, unstable, unpredictable and unreliable by nature.

[78] 'So my arm isn't mine either?'

It's a part of you, but by nature it is dirt, subject to restraint and main force, a slave to anything physically stronger. [79] And why single the arm out? For as long as its time lasts the whole body should be treated like a loaded donkey. If a donkey is requisitioned and seized by a soldier, let it go: don't resist or complain, or you'll be beaten, and lose the animal all the same. [80] And if this is how you should treat the body, what treatment should be reserved for the things that serve the body? If it's a donkey, then they are the donkey's bridle, pack saddle, shoes, barley and feed. Let them go too, give them up with even more speed and good grace than you did the animal.

[81] When you're thus practised and prepared to discriminate between what belongs to you and what doesn't, what is subject to hindrance and what is not, and are ready to regard the latter as important to you and the former as irrelevant, then is there anyone, any more, you need be frightened of?

'No.'

[82] No; because what would you fear them *for*? Not the things that are your own, that constitute the essence of what is good and bad, because no one has power over them but you. You can no more be blocked or deprived of them than can God.* [83] Perhaps you fear for the body and material possessions – things that lie outside your scope of responsibility and have no meaning for you. But what else have you been doing from the start except distinguishing between what you own and what you don't, between what is in your power and what is not, between what is subject to hindrance and what isn't? Why else have you been frequenting philosophers? So that you could be as lost and unhappy as you were before? [84] In that case you will never be free of fear or anxiety – or sorrow, which does you no credit either, seeing as fear for future evils turns to sorrow when they turn up.

Nor should you feel irrational desire any more. You have a fixed and measured desire for the goods of the soul, since they are within your power and accessible. You disdain external goods, so that no opening exists for that irrational, intemperate and impulsive form of desire. [85] With such an attitude toward things, you can no longer be intimidated by anyone. What can one human being find strange or frightful in a fellow human's appearance, conversation or companionship generally? Nothing – any more than one horse, or dog, or bee is frightening to another of its kind. People find particular things, however, frightening; and it's when someone is able to threaten or entice us with those that the man himself becomes frightening.

[86] How is a fortress demolished?[12] Not with weapons or fire – with judgements. We can capture the physical fortress, the one in the city, but our judgements about illness, or about

* Reading τίς σ' ἀφελέσθαι for τίς ἀφελέσθαι.

attractive women, remain to be dislodged from the fortress inside us, together with the tyrants whom we host every day, though their identities change over time. [87] It's here that we need to start attacking the fortress and driving the tyrants out. Surrender the body and its members, physical faculties, property, reputation, office, honours, children, siblings – repudiate them all. [88] And if the tyrants are expelled from it, the fortress itself will not have to be destroyed, not, at least as far as I'm concerned. For it does me no harm while it stands.

The tyrants' bodyguards, too, can stay, for how can they affect me? Their sticks, their spears and their knives are meant for other people. [89] I, personally, was never kept from something I wanted, nor had forced upon me something I was opposed to. How did I manage it? I submitted my will to God. He wants me to be sick – well, then, so do I. He wants me to choose something. Then I choose it. He wants me to desire something, I desire it. He wants me to get something, I want the same; or he doesn't want me to get it, and I concur. [90] Thus I even assent to death and torture. Now no one can make me, or keep me, from acting in line with my inclination, any more than they can similarly manipulate God.

[91] This is the way circumspect travellers act. Word reaches them that the road is beset with highwaymen. A solitary traveller doesn't like the odds, he waits in order to attach himself to an ambassador, quaestor[13] or provincial governor and only travels securely once he's part of their entourage. [92] Which is how a prudent person proceeds along life's road. He thinks, 'There are countless thieves and bandits, many storms, and many chances to get lost or relieved of one's belongings. [93] How are we to evade them and come through without being attacked? [94] What party should we wait to join, with whom should we enlist, to ensure safe passage? With this man, perhaps – the person who is rich and influential? No, not much to be gained there; he's liable to lose his position, break down and prove of no use to me at all. And suppose my travel companion himself betrays and robs me?

[95] 'Well, then, I'll become a friend of Caesar – no one will try to take advantage of me as long as I am Caesar's friend. But

in the first place, what will I need to suffer or sacrifice in order to get close to him? How much money will I have to spend, on how many people? [96] And if I do manage it – well, after all, the emperor is mortal too. Add to which, if by some mischance he becomes my enemy, I suppose I will have no recourse except to flee and take refuge in the wilderness. [97] But what about illness – I can't escape that in the wilderness. So what remains? Is no travel companion dependable, honest and above suspicion?'

[98] By a process of logical elimination, the conclusion emerges that we will come through safely only by allying ourselves with God.

[99] 'What do you mean, "allying ourselves"?'

Acting in such a way that, whatever God wants, we want too; and by inversion whatever he does *not* want, this we do not want either. [100] How can we do this? By paying attention to the pattern of God's purpose and design. To start with, then, what has he given me as mine outright, and what has he reserved to himself? He has conferred on me the functions of the will, made them mine and made them proof against resistance or obstruction. But the body, which is made of clay – how could he make that unconstrained? So he assigned it its place in the cosmic cycle – the same as other material things like my furniture, my house, my wife and children.

[101] So don't go up against God by hoping for what is unattainable, namely to keep forever what doesn't really belong to you. Keep them in the spirit they were given, for as long as possible. If he gives he also takes away. So why try and resist him? It would be stupid to oppose one who is stronger than I, but more importantly, it would be wrong. [102] For how did I come by these belongings in the first place? From my father – who got them from his. Who created the sun, though, the fruits of the earth, and the seasons? Who engineered mankind's mutual attraction, and the social order?

[103] When everything you have has been given you, including your very existence, you proceed to turn on your benefactor and fault him for taking things back. [104] Who are you, and how did you get here? It was God brought you into the world,

who showed you the light, gave you the people who support you, gave you reason and perception. And he brought you into the world as a mortal, to pass your time on earth with a little endowment of flesh, to witness his design and share for a short time in his feast and celebration. [105] So why not enjoy the feast and pageant while it's given you to do so; then, when he ushers you out, go with thanks and reverence for what you were privileged for a time to see and hear.

'No, I want to keep celebrating.'

[106] Yes, just as initiates want the mysteries to continue, or crowds at the Olympic Games want to see more contestants. But the festival is over; leave and move on, grateful for what you've seen, with your self-respect intact. Make room for other people, it's their turn to be born, just as you were born, and once born they need a place to live, along with the other necessities of life. If the first people won't step aside, what's going to happen? Don't be so greedy. Aren't you ever satisfied? Are you determined to make the world more crowded still?

[107] 'All right; but I'd like my wife and children to remain with me.'

Why? Are they yours? They belong to the one who gave them to you, the same one who created you. Don't presume to take what isn't yours, or oppose one who is your better.

[108] 'Why did he bring me into the world on these conditions?'

If the conditions don't suit you, leave. He doesn't need a heckler in the audience. He wants people keen to participate in the dance and revels – people, that is, who would sooner applaud and favour the festival with their praise and acclamation. [109] As for those who are grumpy and dour, he won't be sad to see them excluded. Even when they are invited, they don't act as if they are on holiday, or play an appropriate part; instead they whine, they curse their fate, their luck and their company. They don't appreciate what they have, including moral resources given to them for the opposite purpose – generosity of spirit, high-mindedness, courage and that very freedom we are now exploring.

[110] 'What did I get externals for, then?'

To use.

'For how long?'

For as long as the one who gave them decides.

'And if I can't live without them?'

Don't get attached to them and they won't be. Don't tell yourself that they're indispensable and they aren't.

[111] Those are the reflections you should recur to morning and night. Start with things that are least valuable and most liable to be lost – things such as a jug or a glass – and proceed to apply the same ideas to clothes, pets, livestock, property; then to yourself, your body, the body's parts, your children, your siblings and your wife. [112] Look on every side and mentally discard them. Purify your thoughts, in case of an attachment or devotion to something that doesn't belong to you and will hurt to have wrenched away. [113] And as you exercise daily, as you do at the gym, do not say that you are philosophizing (admittedly a pretentious claim), but that you are a slave presenting your emancipator;[14] because this is genuine freedom that you cultivate.

[114] This is the kind of freedom Diogenes got from Antisthenes, saying he could never again be enslaved by anyone. [115] Which explains his behaviour toward the pirates when they took him captive.[15] Did he call any of them 'master'? No. And I don't mean the word; it's not the word I'm concerned with, but the attitude behind it. [116] He yelled at them for not feeding their captives better. And when he was sold, it was not a master he looked to get, but a slave of his own.

And how did he act toward his new owner? He at once began to criticize him, saying that he shouldn't dress this way, shouldn't cut his hair that way – besides advising him on how his sons should be brought up. [117] And why not? If the owner had bought a personal trainer, he would have acknowledged the trainer to be his superior, not his slave, so far as exercise is concerned. The same goes if he had bought a doctor or architect. In any field you care to name, the person with experience should command the one without. [118] So whoever is possessed of knowledge about how to live should naturally take precedence there. For who else is master of a ship except the captain? Why? Just because whoever disobeys him is punished?

[119] 'But so-and-so can have me whipped.'

Not with impunity, however.

'Well, so I believed too.'

And because he does not act with impunity, he does not act with authority; no one can get away with injustice.

[120] 'And what punishment do you foresee for the master who puts his own slave in chains?'

The act itself of putting him in chains – an idea even you will accept if you have any wish to honour the principle that human beings are civilized animals, not beasts. [121] A plant or animal fares poorly when it acts contrary to its nature; [122] and a human being is no different. Well, then, biting, kicking, wanton imprisonment and beheading – is that what our nature entails? No; rather, acts of kindness, cooperation and good will. And so, whether you like it or not, a person fares poorly whenever he acts like an insensitive brute.

[123] 'So you're saying that Socrates did not fare poorly?'

That's right – the jurors and his accusers did instead.

'Nor Helvidius at Rome?'

No – but the person who killed him did.

'How do you reckon that?'

[124] Well, you don't call a fighting cock that's bloodied but victorious unfortunate, but rather one who lost without receiving a scratch. And you don't yell 'Good dog!' at one that doesn't hunt or work; you do it when you see one panting, labouring, exhausted from the chase. [125] What's odd in asserting that what's bad for anything is what runs contrary to its nature? You say it for everything else, why make humanity the sole exception?

[126] Well, but we assert that in their nature human beings are gentle, honest and cooperative – that's pretty ridiculous, is it not? No, that isn't either – [127] which is why no one suffers harm even if they are flogged, jailed or beheaded. The victim may be majestic in suffering, you see, and come through a better, more fortunate person; while the one who really comes to harm, who suffers the most and the most pitifully, is the

person who is transformed from human being to wolf, snake or hornet.

[128] All right then, let us go over the points we are agreed on. The unhindered person is free, that is, the person who has ready access to things in the condition he prefers. Whoever can be thwarted, however, or coerced, frustrated or forced into a situation against their will – that person is a slave. [129] The person who renounces externals cannot be hindered, as externals are things that are not within our power either to have or not to have – or to have in the condition we might like. [130] Externals include the body and its members, as well as material goods. If you grow attached to any of them as if they were your own, you will incur the penalties prescribed for a thief.

[131] This is the road that leads to liberty, the only road that delivers us from slavery: finally to be able to say, with meaning:

Lead me, Zeus, lead me, Destiny,

to the goal I was long ago assigned

[132] What about you, philosopher? The tyrant is going to call on you to bear false witness. Tell us: do you play along or not?

'Let me think it over.'

Think it over *now*? What were you thinking over in school? Didn't you rehearse which things are good, which are bad, and which are neither?

[133] 'I did.'

And what did you decide?

'That justice and fairness are good, vice and injustice bad.'

Is life a good?

'No.'

Is dying bad?

'No.'

Or jail?

'No.'

And what about slanderous and dishonest talk, betraying a friend, and trying to ingratiate yourself with a tyrant – how exactly did you characterize those?

[134] 'As bad.'

Well, it's obvious that you aren't thinking it over, and you

never did think it over in the past. I mean, how much thought
is really required to decide whether you should exercise your
power to get the greatest goods and avoid the greatest evils? A
fit subject for thought, no doubt, calling for a great deal of
deliberation. Who are you kidding? No such inquiry ever took
place. [135] If you really did believe that vice alone is bad and
everything else indifferent, you never would have needed time
to 'think it over' – far from it. You'd be able to make a decision
immediately, using your faculty of reason as readily as sight.
[136] I mean, when do you have to 'think over' whether black
things are white, or light things heavy? No, the clear evidence
of the senses is enough. So why say now that you have to 'think
over' whether indifferents are more to be avoided than evils?
[137] The fact is, this is not what you really believe: you don't
think that death and jail, etc. are indifferent, you count them
among the greatest evils; and you don't regard false witness,
etc. as evil, but matters of indifference.

[138] You've developed this habit from the beginning.
'Where am I? In school. And who is my audience? I'm conversing with philosophers. But now that I've left school, away with
those pedantic and naive doctrines.' And thus a philosopher
comes to traduce a friend, [139] thus a philosopher turns in-
former and prostitutes his principles, thus a member of the
Senate comes to betray his beliefs. Inside, his real opinion cries
out to be heard – [140] no faint or timid idea, based on casual
reasoning and hanging, as it were, by a thread, but a strong
and vital conviction rooted in practical experience.

[141] Be careful how you take the news – I won't say that
your child died, because you couldn't possibly tolerate that –
but that your cruet of oil fell over. Or that someone drank up
all your wine. [142] Anyone finding you in despair might well
say, simply, 'Philosopher, you sang a different tune in school.
Don't try to deceive us, or pretend that you are a human being
when you're no more than a worm.' [143] I'd like to come
upon one of them having sex, just to see how much they exert
themselves and what kind of sounds they make; whether they
remember who they are or recall any of the sentiments which
they hear and preach and read.

[144] What has any of this to do with freedom? On the contrary, nothing *except* this relates to freedom, whether rich people such as you choose to believe it or not.

[145] 'What proof do you have of that?'

Only you yourselves, with your abject reverence for your great master, the emperor, whose every nod and gesture you live by. You faint if he even squints at you, and toady before the old men and women of the court, saying, 'I can't possibly do that, I'm not allowed.' [146] And why can't you? Weren't you just arguing with me that you were free? 'But Aprulla won't let me.' Tell the truth, slave – don't run away from your masters or refuse to acknowledge them, don't dare to invoke an emancipator when proofs of your servitude are so manifest.

[147] I mean, someone constrained by love to act against their better judgement, who sees the right thing to do but is powerless to act on it, might be considered the more deserving of compassion inasmuch as they are in the grip of a violent and, in some ways, a supernatural force. [148] But what sympathy can you expect with your passion for old men and women, as you wipe their nose and wash their face, ply them with presents and nurse them when they're sick as if you are their slave – all the while praying for their death and pestering their doctors to find out if they are terminal yet or not. Or when you kiss the hands of other people's slaves, making yourself the slave of slaves, all for the sake of these great and glorious honours and offices – what can you expect then?

[149] So don't parade before me in your pride because you are a consul or a praetor – I know how you came by these offices, and who presented them to you. [150] Speaking for myself, I would rather be dead than owe my living to Felicio, having to put up with his airs and his typical slave's impertinence. I know what a slave is like who has acquired influence and self-importance.

[151] 'Are *you* free, then?'

By God I wish I were, and I pray to be; but I still can't face my masters, I continue to value my poor body, I attach great importance to keeping healthy – though it isn't healthy at all.[16]

[152] But I *can* show you a free man, to satisfy your desire for an exemplar. Diogenes[17] – he was free. Why? Not because his parents were free (they weren't), but because he himself was. He had eliminated any means to capture him, there was no opening to attack or seize him in order to make him a slave. [153] Everything he owned was disposable, and only temporarily attached. If you had seized any of his possessions, he would have surrendered it to you sooner than be pulled along behind it. If you had grabbed him by the leg, he would have given up the leg; if you had seized his entire body, the entire body would have been sacrificed. The same with family, friends and country: he knew where they had come from, from whom, and on what terms.

[154] His true parents, the gods – these he never would have dared sacrifice; nor his real country, the world at large. He yielded to no one in his zeal to serve and obey the gods, and there is no one who would have sooner died for his country. [155] He did not care for the mere appearance of acting on the world's behalf; he constantly bore in mind that events all have their source there and happen for the sake of that universal homeland by the command of God, who governs it. Observe, therefore, what he personally says and writes: [156] 'Here's why, Diogenes, you are at liberty to speak your mind to the Persian king as well as to Archidamus, king of the Spartans.'[18] [157] Is it because he was of freeborn parentage? Sure, and I suppose the reason all the citizens of Athens, Sparta and Corinth could *not* address them as they pleased, but feared and flattered them instead, was that their parents all were slaves. [158] So why did he enjoy this licence? 'Because I don't consider the body to be my own, because I lack for nothing, and because the law[19] is the only thing I esteem, nothing else.' That's what enabled him to be free.

[159] And just so you don't think I choose as my exemplar of freedom someone unencumbered by wife, children, friends, relatives and the demands of citizenship, factors that could make one bend and compromise, take for consideration Socrates, who had both wife and children, but as if they were

on loan. He had a country, to the degree and in the manner called for; he had friends and relatives – but all these were subordinate to the law and the need to obey it.[20]

[160] And so, when he was drafted to serve, he was the first one to leave home, and once on the line fought without any regard for his life. Ordered by the tyrants to arrest Leon, he did not give a thought to obeying, because he thought the act unlawful, even knowing there was a chance he might die if he refused. [161] He didn't care; it was not his skin he wanted to save, but the man of honour and integrity. These things are not open to compromise or negotiation.

[162] Later, when he had to defend himself at risk of his life, he did not comport himself like someone with a wife and children, but as someone alone and unattached. And how did he behave when it was time to drink the poison? [163] Given the opportunity to save himself, with Crito urging him to go into exile for his children's sake, did he look upon this as the lucky pretext he needed to stay alive? Hardly. He reflected on the right thing to do, with no thought or regard for anything else. In his own words, he didn't want to save the body, he wanted to preserve the element that grows and thrives with every act of justice, the element that is diminished and dies by injustice.[21] [164] Socrates does not save his life at the cost of dishonour – Socrates, who resisted the Athenians' call to bring an illegal motion to a vote,[22] defied the tyrants, and spoke so memorably on the subject of virtue and character. Such a man is not saved with dishonour; [165] an honourable death, not flight, is his salvation. A good actor preserves his reputation not by speaking lines out of turn but by knowing when to talk – and when to keep quiet.

[166] So what will become of his children? 'If I had run off to Thessaly, you would have cared for them. If I go to Hades, will no one be there to look after them?' Note how he makes light of death, and sports with the idea of it. [167] If it had been you or I, we quickly would have rationalized our behaviour thus: 'People who wrong us should be paid back in kind,' not failing to add, 'If my life is spared I will help many people, but dead I'm of no use to anyone.' If we had to squeeze

through a mousehole to escape, we would have done it. [168] But how could we then have helped anyone, with our friends still back in Athens?* If we had been helpful alive, wouldn't we have done people much more good by accepting death in the appropriate time and manner? [169] Even now, long after Socrates' death, the memory of what he did and said benefits humanity as much as or more than ever.

[170] Study this – these principles, these arguments – and contemplate these models of behaviour, if you want to be free, and your desire corresponds to the goal's importance. [171] Don't be surprised if so great a goal costs you many a sacrifice. For love of what they considered freedom men have hanged themselves, have thrown themselves over cliffs – and whole cities have occasionally been destroyed. [172] For true, inviolable, unassailable freedom, yield to God when he asks for something back that he earlier gave you. Prepare yourself, as Plato says,[23] not just for death, but for torture, exile, flogging – and the loss of everything not belonging to you. [173] You will be a slave among slaves otherwise; even if you are a consul ten thousand times over, even if you make your residence on the Palatine,[24] you will be a slave none the less.

And you'll realize, as Cleanthes used to say, that what philosophers say may be contrary to expectation, but not to reason. [174] For you will learn by experience that it's true: the things that men admire and work so hard to get prove useless to them once they're theirs. Meanwhile people to whom such things are still denied come to imagine that everything good will be theirs if only they could acquire them. Then they get them: and their longing is unchanged, their anxiety is unchanged, their disgust is no less, and they still long for whatever is lacking. [175] Freedom is not achieved by satisfying desire, but by eliminating it. [176] Assure yourself of this by expending as much effort on these new ambitions as you did on those illusive goals: work day and night to attain a liberated frame of mind. [177] Instead of a rich old man, cultivate the company of a philosopher, be seen hanging around *his* door for a change. There's no shame

---

* The text of this sentence is corrupt, the translation partly conjectural.

in the association, and you won't go away unedified or empty-handed, provided you go with the right attitude. Try at least; there is no shame in making an honest effort.

IV 2 *On social intercourse*

[1] You should be especially careful when associating with one of your former friends or acquaintances not to sink to their level; otherwise you will lose yourself. [2] If you are troubled by the idea that 'He'll think I'm boring and won't treat me the way he used to,' remember that everything comes at a price. It isn't possible to change your behaviour and still be the same person you were before.

[3] So choose: either regain the love of your old friends by reverting to your former self or remain better than you once were and forfeit their affection. [4] And if you choose the latter, stick to it from here on out. Don't give in to second thoughts, because no one who wavers will make progress. And if you are committed to making progress and ready to devote yourself to the effort, then give up everything else. [5] Otherwise your ambivalence will only ensure that you don't make progress, and you won't even get to revisit the pleasures of the past.

[6] Formerly, when you were devoted to worthless pursuits, your friends found you congenial company. [7] But you can't be a hit in both roles. To the extent you cultivate one you will fall short in the other. You can't seem as affable to your old cronies if you don't go out drinking with them as of old. So choose whether you want to be a charming drunk in their company, or dull and sober on your own. You can't expect the same reception from the group you used to associate with if you don't go carousing with them regularly any more.

So again you have a choice: [8] if you value dignity and restraint over being called a 'sport' by your old mates, then forget other considerations, renounce them, walk away and have nothing more to do with that crowd. [9] If you don't like that, then commit to the opposite course with all your heart.

Join the louche set, become one of the degenerates – do as they do and indulge your every impulse and desire. Jump around and yell at a musical performance, what's to stop you now?

[10] Such different roles don't mix. You can't play the part of both Thersites and Agamemnon. If you want to be Thersites, you should be bald and crippled. Agamemnon needs to be tall and handsome, and a leader with a genuine love for the people under his command.

IV 3 *What to aim for in exchange for what*

[1] If you forfeit an external possession, make sure to notice what you get in return. If it is something more valuable, never say, 'I have suffered a loss.' [2] It is no loss if you get a horse in return for an ass, cattle for sheep, a kind act for a little money, real peace in place of idle chatter, decency in exchange for vulgarity.

[3] Bear this in mind and you will everywhere preserve your proper character; forget it and I assure you that your time here will be a waste, and whatever care you are now expending on yourself will all go down the drain. [4] Very little is needed for everything to be upset and ruined, only a slight lapse in reason. [5] It's much easier for a mariner to wreck his ship than it is for him to keep it sailing safely; all he has to do is head a little more upwind and disaster is instantaneous. In fact, he does not have to do anything: a momentary loss of attention will produce the same result.

[6] It's much the same in our case. If you doze off, all your progress up to that point will be negated. [7] So keep a sharp eye on your impressions, and never fall asleep. It is no small thing that is being watched over, it equates with honesty, trustworthiness and stability. It is freedom from passion, grief, fear and consternation – it is freedom itself.

[8] What are you going to get when you trade your freedom away? Check to see what your proud new possessions will be worth.

'But I won't be getting anything like it in return.'

If you go ahead and get it anyway, consider again what you are getting for it. [9] 'I have self-control, he has a tribuneship; he has a generalship, I have my honour. I don't scream and yell when to do so would be rude; and I won't jump up out of my seat where such behaviour would be out of place. I am free and a friend of God, whom I obey willingly. [10] I do not claim possession over anything that does not belong to me, not the body, not possessions, not power, not fame – nothing. Because God does not want me competing for such things. Had he wished it, he would have made them good for me. But he has not done that. And I must not ignore his orders.'

[11] Guard what is good for you always; make wise use of material things for as long as they are granted you to enjoy, and be content with virtue exclusively. Otherwise you will meet with bad luck, disappointment and frustration at every turn.

[12] These are the laws that have been sent to us from God, the directives you should be trying to learn – not the statutes of Cassius and Masurius.[25]

IV 4 *To those intent on living quietly*

[1] Remember, it isn't just desire for power and money that makes a man humble and deferential towards others, but also desire for the opposite – for a life of peace and quiet, of travel and scholarship. It is a general rule that externals of any kind, if we attach importance to them, make us subject to somebody. [2] It makes no difference whether we wish to be a senator, or wish *not* to be one; whether we desire to have office, or to avoid it; whether we say, 'I can't do anything, unfortunately, I'm tied to my books like a stiff,' or, 'Sadly, I have no leisure for study.' [3] A book is an external, just like office or public honours. [4] Why do you want to read anyway – for the sake of amusement or mere erudition? Those are poor, fatuous pretexts. Reading should serve the goal of attaining peace; if it doesn't make you peaceful, what good is it?

[5] 'But it does help with that – which is exactly why I regret being deprived of it.'

What kind of peace is this that is so easily shattered – not by the emperor or even by a friend of the emperor, but by a crow, a street musician, a cold, or a thousand other annoyances? True peace is characterized by nothing so much as steadiness and imperturbability.

[6] Now I am being called upon for some purpose. I answer the call determined to observe the right limits; to act with restraint, but also with confidence, devoid of desire or aversion towards externals. [7] At the same time I observe other people's words and actions – not maliciously, in order to judge or ridicule them, but to better assess whether I engage in any of the same behaviour. 'How should I stop, then?' 'Once I was liable to the same mistakes, but, thanks to God, no longer . . .'*

[8] Well, isn't it just as worthwhile to have devoted and applied yourself to this goal as to have read or written fifty pages? After all, when you are eating, you don't wish you were reading, you are content to be eating in a manner consistent with the principles you learned from your reading; likewise when you bathe or exercise. [9] So be consistent in other respects – when you meet Caesar, or when you meet some random passer-by. If you keep yourself calm, poised and dignified, [10] if you observe rather than are observed, if you don't envy people with greater success, don't let externals disconcert you – if you do all this, what more do you need? [11] Books? Yes, but how, or for what purpose?

'Isn't reading a kind of preparation for life?'

But life is composed of things other than books. It is as if an athlete, on entering the stadium, were to complain that he's not outside exercising. [12] This was the goal of your exercise, of your weights, your practice ring and your training partners. You want them now that the time to exploit them has arrived? [13] Or it's as if, in the matter of assent, when faced with impressions, instead of distinguishing which ones are convincing

* The text here is doubtful.

and which are not, we prefer to read a book entitled *On Comprehensive Impressions*.

[14] So what accounts for such behaviour? The fact that our reading and our writing have never aimed at using in conformity with nature the impressions that we encounter in real life. Instead, it is enough for us to learn what is written on the topic and be able to explicate it before someone else; it is enough if we can analyse an argument or develop a hypothesis.

[15] Consequently, there is bound to be frustration when you exert yourself. You desire what is not in your control: fine, but be prepared to be refused, to be frustrated, to come up empty-handed. [16] If, on the other hand, we read books entitled *On Impulse* not just out of idle curiosity, but in order to exercise impulse correctly; books entitled *On Desire* and *On Aversion* so as not to fail to get what we desire or fall victim to what we would rather avoid; and books entitled *On Moral Obligation* in order to honour our relationships and never do anything that clashes or conflicts with this principle; [17] then we wouldn't get frustrated and grow impatient with our reading. Instead we would be satisfied to act accordingly. And rather than reckon, as we are used to doing, [18] 'How many lines I read, or wrote, today,' we would pass in review how 'I applied impulse today the way the philosophers recommend, how I desisted from desire, and practised aversion only on matters that are under my control. I wasn't flustered by *A* or angered by *B*; I was patient, restrained and cooperative.' That way we will be able to thank God for things that we truly should be grateful for.

[19] As it is, though, we fail to realize how little we differ from the mass of men, the only difference being that they are afraid they will not hold office, while you are afraid you will. Don't act that way; [20] if you must laugh at someone who is anxious that he won't hold office, then laugh at yourself as well. Someone suffering from rabies and afraid of water is no better off than someone suffering from fever and ready to drain the ocean dry. [21] If you would dictate to circumstance, how can you emulate Socrates, who said, 'If it pleases the gods, so be it'?

Do you think Socrates would have been as ready to serve on so many campaigns if he had longed to linger in the Academy or the Lyceum every day, conversing with young men? No, he would have groused and grumbled, 'Hell, here I am in misery when I might be back in the Lyceum sunning myself.' Is that your job, sunning yourself? [22] Isn't it rather to be happy, unflappable and equal to every occasion? How could he have remained Socrates, had he yielded to disaffection? How would he have been the same man who wrote hymns of praise behind prison walls?[26]

[23] Just keep in mind: the more we value things outside our control, the less control we have. And among things outside our control is not only access to, but relief from, public office; not just work, but leisure too.

[24] 'So now I have to live my life among the mob?'

The mob? You mean crowds? What's wrong with crowds? Imagine you're at Olympia, in the middle of the festival, where you will likewise find some people shouting while others conduct business on the side, and everywhere people are jostling one another. The baths, too, are a madhouse. Yet which of us does not enjoy the party, and regret when it's time to leave? [25] Don't grow peevish about trivialities. 'The vinegar is bad, it's sharp; the honey's bad, it upsets my constitution; I didn't like the vegetables.'

[26] Similarly, someone says, 'I don't like leisure, it's boring; I don't like crowds, they're a nuisance.' But if events ordain that you spend time either alone or with just a few other people, look upon it as tranquillity and play along with it for the duration. Talk to yourself, train your thoughts and shape your preconceptions. If, on the contrary, you happen upon a crowd, call it a sporting event, a festival or celebration, [27] and try to keep holiday with the people. What could better please a person who loves his fellow man than the sight of them in numbers? We like to see herds of cows or horses, we delight in the sight of a fleet of boats; why hate the sight of a gathering of human beings?

[28] 'But they deafen me with their shouting.'

So your hearing is offended; what does it have to do with

you? Your power of using impressions isn't diminished, is it? Who can keep you from using desire and aversion, or choice and refusal, in conformity with nature? No mob is big enough for that.

[29] Just keep in mind the central questions: 'What is mine, what is not mine? What has been given to me? What does God want me to do, or not do, now?' [30] It wasn't long ago he wanted you to take time off, to commune with yourself, to read, write and attend classes on these subjects – all by way of preparation, because you had the time available. Now, however, he's saying to you, 'It's high time you were tested. Show us what you've learned, show us how well you've trained. How long do you plan on working out alone? We want to know whether you are champion material or a touring professional pushover. [31] So don't make difficulties, no public match is devoid of commotion. There have to be trainers, supporters, many judges and many people in the stands.'

[32] 'But I was hoping to lead a peaceful life.'

Well, then, mope and be miserable, as you should be. What greater punishment do you deserve for ignoring and defying God's will than to be sad, disgruntled and malcontent – unhappy, in short, and ill-fated? Don't you want to be free of all that?

[33] 'But how can I do it?'

You've often heard how – you need to suspend desire completely, and train aversion only on things within your power. You should dissociate yourself from everything outside yourself – the body, possessions, reputation, books, applause, as well as office or lack of office. Because a preference for any of them immediately makes you a slave, a subordinate, and prone to disappointment. [34] Keep Cleanthes' verse handy:

Lead me, Zeus, lead me, Destiny.

Do I have to go to Rome? Then I go to Rome. To Gyara? All right, I go to Gyara instead. To Athens? Then Athens it is. To jail? Well then I go to jail. [35] But if you ever think, 'When do we get to go to Athens?' you are already lost. Either you're going to be depressed when your wish is not realized or foolishly pleased with yourself if it is, overjoyed for the wrong reasons.

And next time, if you're not so lucky, you'll grow disconsolate when events are not so much to your liking. [36] Give them all up.

'But Athens is lovely.'

It would be lovelier still if you could secure happiness, free of emotion, poised and dependent on no one except yourself.

'And Rome is all crowds and sycophancy.'

[37] But the reward for enduring such inconveniences is peace. So if this is the time for them, why not conquer your aversion? Why endure them like a donkey hit by sticks? [38] Otherwise, look, you will always have to serve the person who is able to secure your release, or the person who can block your way. You will have to serve him the way you would an evil deity.

[39] There is one road to peace and happiness (keep the thought near by morning, noon and night): renunciation of externals; regarding nothing as your own; handing over everything to fortune and the deity. Leave those things in the care of the same people God appointed to govern them, [40] while you devote yourself to the one thing that is truly yours and that no one can obstruct; make *that* the focus of all your reading, your writing and your lecture attendance.

[41] I cannot call somebody 'hard-working' knowing only that they read and write. Even if 'all night long' is added, I cannot say it — not until I know the focus of all this energy. You don't call someone 'hard-working' who stays up nights with their girlfriend. No more do I. [42] If the goal is glory, I call them ambitious; if it's money, I call them avaricious. [43] If, however, their efforts aim at improving the mind, then – and only then – do I call them hard-working. [44] Never praise or blame people on common grounds; look to their judgements exclusively. Because that is the determining factor, which makes everyone's actions either good or bad.

[45] Bearing all this in mind, welcome present circumstances and accept the things whose time has arrived. [46] Be happy when you find that doctrines you have learned and analysed are being tested by real events. If you've succeeded in removing or reducing the tendency to be mean and critical, or thoughtless,

or foul-mouthed, or careless, or nonchalant; if old interests no longer engage you, at least not to the same extent; then every day can be a feast day – today because you acquitted yourself well in one set of circumstances, tomorrow because of another.

[47] How much better cause is this to celebrate than becoming consul or governor; because you have yourself to thank, and the gods. Remember, then, who is responsible for the gift, to whom it was given, and for what reason. [48] With these thoughts, can you doubt where your future happiness lies, or how you will best please God? Is it not the same distance to God everywhere? Are not events equally visible from every vantage point?

IV 13 *To those who lightly share personal information*

[1] Whenever we think that someone has spoken frankly about their personal affairs, somehow or other we are impelled to share our secrets with them too and think this is being honest; [2] in the first place, because it seems unfair that we should hear news from our neighbour, and not share with them some news of our own; and secondly, because we imagine that we won't make a forthright impression if we keep our personal affairs confidential. [3] People often say, in fact, 'I have told you everything about myself, while you won't share with me anything about *your* life; why?' [4] Additionally, we believe that it is safe to confide in someone who has already entrusted us with private information, on the assumption that they would never betray our secrets lest we betray theirs – [5] which is just how incautious people are entrapped by soldiers in the capital. A soldier in civilian dress sits down beside you and begins to criticize the emperor. Then you, encouraged to trust them by the fact that they initiated the conversation, open up on this score too. Next thing you know you are being hauled off to prison in chains.[27]

[6] Something similar happens in our everyday life. We keep one person's secrets, and likewise share our own with whomever. [7] But I don't divulge what I've been told in confidence (if, indeed, I am so honourable), whereas the other person goes off and blabs to all and sundry. Now, if I am like him, after finding out what's happened I want to get even and proceed to spill his secrets, hurting him and myself in the process. [8] If, on the other hand, I remind myself that one person cannot harm another, but it is rather our own actions that help or harm each of us, then I refrain from acting similarly. My own thoughtlessness was the cause of the trouble to begin with.

[9] 'Yes, but it's unfair to receive the confidences of your neighbour and not share anything of your own with him.'

[10] Did I invite your confidences, sir? Did you open up to me solely on condition that you would get to hear my secrets? [11] Just because you are so stupid as to suppose that everyone you meet is your friend, why expect me to do likewise? You were right to trust me with your secrets, whereas you cannot well be trusted with mine; should I then be indiscreet? [12] It's as though I owned a watertight jug, while you had one with a hole in it, and you came and left your wine with me to store in my jug, and then got angry because I didn't deposit my wine with you – in your leaky jug, that is.

[13] So how can an exchange between us still be considered fair? You made a deposit with someone trustworthy and high-minded, someone who only regards his personal actions, not externals, as good or bad. [14] Do you want me to make a deposit with you – you who don't value your character, but only want to earn money, or an office, or advancement at court – even if you have to sacrifice your children to get it, like Medea? [15] What's fair about that? Just prove to me that you are trustworthy, high-minded and reliable, and that your intentions are benign – prove to me that your jar doesn't have a hole in it – and you'll find that I won't even wait for you to open your heart to me, I'll be the first to implore you to lend an ear to my own affairs. [16] Who, after all, wouldn't want to make use of a sound vessel, who doesn't welcome a friendly and reliable counsellor, who wouldn't gladly invite someone to

share his problems as he would share his burden, and lighten it by the very act of sharing?

[17] 'Fine. But I have faith in you, and you don't have faith in me.'

First of all, the reason you can't keep anything to yourself is that you're a born loudmouth. If you really do trust me, show it by confiding in me alone. [18] As it is, however, you pull up a seat alongside whoever is free and proceed to accost them. 'Brother, I have no one nearer or dearer to me than you, please listen to my story.' You say this to people whom you have barely known a week.

[19] Let's suppose you do trust me. It must be because you think I'm trustworthy and discreet – not because I've already shared with you my private life. [20] So allow me to entertain the same opinion of you. Show me that, if someone discloses his secrets to another, he is therefore personally discreet and reliable. Well, if that were so, I would go around telling everyone my story – if that would really improve my character. But such is not the case; what we need are judgements of a particular kind. [21] At any rate, if you see someone fond of externals, someone who values them over their own moral integrity, you can be sure that he is vulnerable to thousands of people who can frustrate or coerce him. [22] There's no need of pitch or the wheel to force him to say what he knows; a mere nod from a young woman is enough to get him to talk, a token of favour from a partisan of Caesar, a longing for office, the hope of an inheritance – a thousand other such things in addition.

[23] In general, remember that sharing intimate details calls for people of faithfulness and sound principles; [24] and how easy is it to find people of that description today? Just point out to me, please, someone with the moral fibre to say, 'I'm only interested in my own business, in what is inalienable, what is by nature free. This, the essence of the good, I hold secure; as for the rest, let it be as it is, it makes no difference to me.'

FRAGMENTS

The 'fragments' are mostly brief quotations of passages not found elsewhere in Epictetus' extant writings. Fragment 9 purports to be taken from 'the fifth book of Discourses', *which indicates that at least one whole book has been lost, since only four survive. It is likely that some of the other fragments also derive from this source – or perhaps from other books of* Discourses *that have disappeared. Most of these fragments ('excerpts' might be a better word) are preserved in an anthology of writings, mainly on ethical topics, compiled in the fifth century AD by Johannes Stobaeus for the education of his son. Those with a different provenance are indicated below by naming the alternative source.*

For the text (and selection of fragments) I follow the Loeb edition (Epictetus: The Discourses as Reported by Arrian, the Manual, and Fragments, *ed. W. A. Oldfather, 2 vols., London and Cambridge, Mass., 1925–8), which is based in turn on the edition of Schenkl (Epicteti:* Dissertationes ab Arriano Digestae, *ed. H. Schenkl, 2nd edn, Leipzig, 1916) with an additional fragment (28b).*

1. What do I care whether matter is made up of atoms, indivisibles, or fire and earth? Isn't it enough to know the nature of good and evil, the limits of desire and aversion, and of choice and refusal, and to use these as virtual guidelines for how to live? Questions beyond our ken we should ignore, since the human mind may be unable to grasp them. However easily one assumes they can be understood, what's to be gained by understanding them in any case? It must be said, I think, that

those who make such matters an essential part of a philosopher's knowledge are creating unwanted difficulties.

And what of the commandment at Delphi, to 'know yourself'
– is that redundant too? No, not that, certainly. Well, what
does it mean? If someone said to a chorus member 'Know
yourself,' the command would mean that he should give attention to the other chorus members and their collective harmony.
Similarly with a soldier or sailor. So do you infer that man is
an animal created to live on his own, or in a community?

'A community.'

Created by whom?

'By nature.'

What nature is and how it governs everything, whether it is
knowable or not – are these additional questions superfluous?*

2. Whoever chafes at the conditions dealt by fate is unskilled in
the art of life; whoever bears with them nobly and makes wise
use of the results is a man who deserves to be considered good.

3. Everything obeys and serves the universe[1] – the land and sea,
the sun and other stars, as well as the world's plants and
animals. Our body also obeys it in both sickness and health
(whichever it dictates), in youth and old age, and in the course
of the body's other changes. So it is unreasonable that our will,
which is in our power, be the only thing to try to resist it. It is
stronger than we are and very powerful indeed; besides, it has
planned for us better than we could ourselves by including us
in its grand design. Resistance is vain in any case; it only leads
to useless struggle while inviting grief and sorrow.

4. Of things that are, God has put some under our control,
some not. The best and most important thing is under our
control and the basis of God's own well-being – the use of
external impressions. Rightly used, this leads to freedom, ser-

---

* Comparing I 20, 16, the last sentence has been translated as a (rhetorical)
question; and 'knowable' has been added *exempli gratia* to supply the evident
loss of an adjective from the text, which would otherwise read '. . . whether
[nature] exists or not'.

enity, happiness and satisfaction; it is also the source of justice, law, restraint and virtue in general. He did not put anything else under our control. So we should support God by making the same distinction and doing everything to lay claim to what is in our control, while surrendering what is not to the care of the universe. Whether it asks for our children, our homeland, our body or anything else, resign it gracefully.

5. Which one of you does not admire what Lycurgus the Spartan[2] said? He was blinded in one eye by a young citizen of Sparta, who was then handed over to Lycurgus to punish as he saw fit. Lycurgus not only declined to exact revenge, he gave the youth an education and made a good man of him. He then publicly introduced him at the theatre. The Spartans were indignant, but Lycurgus said, 'The person you gave me was violent and aggressive; I'm returning him to you civilized and refined.'

6. Above all, nature demands that we conform and adapt our will to our idea of what's right and useful.

7. To imagine that we will be despised by others unless we use every means to inflict harm, especially on our enemies, is typical of very mean and ignorant people. We say that worthless people are recognized by, among other things, their inability to do harm; it would be much better to say that they're recognized by their inability to do anyone good.

8. The nature of the universe was, is and always will be the same, and things cannot happen any differently than they do now. It's not just mankind and the other animals on earth that share in the cycle of change, but also the heavens and even the four basic elements: up and down they change and alternate, earth becoming water, water air, and air in turn becoming fire – with an analogous change from above downwards.[3] If we try to adapt our mind to the regular sequence of changes and accept the inevitable with good grace, our life will proceed quite smoothly and harmoniously.

*

9. [*from* Aulus Gellius, *Attic Nights*[4] XIX 1, 14–21] A renowned Stoic philosopher drew from his satchel Book Five of the *Discourses* of Epictetus, edited by Arrian, writings that undoubtedly agree with those of Zeno and Chrysippus. There (translated from the Greek) we find a passage to this effect:

Impressions (which philosophers call φαντασίαι), striking a person's mind as soon as he perceives something within range of his senses, are not voluntary or subject to his will, they impose themselves on people's attention almost with a will of their own. But the act of assent (which they call συγκατάθεσις) which endorses these impressions *is* voluntary and a function of the human will. Consequently, when a frightening noise comes from heaven or in consequence of some accident, if an abrupt alarm threatens danger, or if anything else of the kind happens, the mind even of a wise man is inevitably shaken a little, blanches and recoils – not from any preconceived idea that something bad is about to happen, but because certain irrational reflexes forestall the action of the rational mind.

Instead of automatically assenting to these impressions (i.e. these frightening mental images), however (that is, οὐ συγκατα-τίθεται οὐδὲ προσεπιδοξάζει), our wise man spurns and rejects them, because there is nothing there that need cause *him* any fear.[5] And this, they say, is how the mind of the wise man differs from the fool's: the latter believes that impressions apparently portending pain and hardship when they strike his mind really are as they seem, so he approves (προσεπιδοξάζει: the word the Stoics use when discussing this matter) them and accepts that he should fear them as if this were self-evident. But the wise man, soon regaining his colour and composure, οὐ συγκα-τατίθεται (does not assent), reaffirms his support of the view he's always had about such impressions – that they are not in the least to be feared, but are only superficially and speciously frightening.

10. [*from* Aulus Gellius, *Attic Nights* XVII 19] According to Favorinus,[6] Epictetus said that most apparent philosophers were philosophers 'not in their actions, only their words'. A

more incisive form of the idea was committed to writing in the books that Arrian composed based on Epictetus' lectures: 'Whenever,' Arrian writes, 'Epictetus noticed a person with no sense of shame but plenty of misplaced energy, vicious in character but possessed of a ready tongue, concerned with everything to the exclusion of his soul, whenever (he says) he saw such a character apply himself to any of various philosophical disciplines – taking up physics, studying logic, exploring various abstract topics of this sort – he'd be moved to cry out, invoking both gods and men, and in the course of his appeal would address these remarks to the person: "Friend, where are you storing all this erudition? Consider whether the receptacle is clean. If it's being added to the vessel of vague opinion, it's as good as lost. And if it spoils, it will turn into urine, vinegar or something even worse."'

There is absolutely nothing truer than these words, or more important; the greatest of philosophers thus implies that the writings and teachings of philosophy, when emptied into someone vicious and a fake – as into a foul and filthy vessel – become spoiled, degraded, and debased, turning into urine (as he says, in rather Cynic style) or, if it's possible, something even more disgusting.

According to Favorinus, Epictetus would also say that there were two vices much blacker and more serious than the rest: lack of persistence and lack of self-control. The former means we cannot bear or endure hardships that we have to endure, the latter means that we cannot resist pleasures or other things we ought to resist. 'Two words,' he says, 'should be committed to memory and obeyed by alternately exhorting and restraining ourselves, words that will ensure we lead a mainly blameless and untroubled life.' These two words, he used to say, were 'persist *and* resist'.

10a. [*from* Arnobius, *Against the Pagans*[7] II 78] When the health of our soul and our self-respect is at stake, even irrational measures are justified, as Arrian quotes Epictetus saying, with approval.

*

11. Archelaus[8] invited Socrates to his court with the promise of wealth. But Socrates reported back that 'In Athens four quarts of barley meal can be bought for a penny, and there are plenty of springs of fresh water. If my means are slight, still I can manage on them, which makes them adequate for my purposes.' Can't you see that Polus performed Oedipus as a king no more pleasingly or eloquently than he played Oedipus as a beggar and wanderer?[9] Then won't the good man make as fine a showing as Polus by performing well in every costume in which destiny dresses him? Shouldn't he imitate Odysseus, who was no less dignified wearing rags than in his royal purple robe?[10]

12. There are some quietly temperamental people who coldly and calmly act the same way as people wholly carried away by anger. Their vice should be avoided too as it is much worse than being boiling mad; people of the latter sort soon get their satisfaction, whereas the former hold on to their anger like patients with a low-grade fever.

13. 'But,' someone objects, 'I see good people dying of cold and hunger.'

Well, don't you see wicked people dying of luxury, pride and excess?

'Yes, but it's demeaning to depend on others for one's living.'[11]

Who is really self-sufficient, fool – apart from the universe itself? In any case, to object to providence on the grounds that the wicked go unpunished since they are rich and powerful is like saying that, if they lost their sight, they escaped punishment since they still had their fingernails intact. Personally, I say that virtue is more valuable than wealth to the same degree that eyes are more valuable than fingernails.

14. Let's question those gloomy philosophers[12] who say that pleasure is not itself in agreement with nature but a mere by-product of the things in agreement with nature, like justice, self-control and freedom. Why, then, does the soul delight and 'find content', as Epicurus says, in the goods of the body,

which are supposed to be inferior, but not take pleasure in its own (supposedly superior) goods? Well, nature has also endowed me with a sense of shame, and I blush deeply whenever I catch myself saying anything disgraceful. It's this reflex that will not allow me to propose pleasure as the good and the goal of life.

15. Women in Rome thumb Plato's *Republic* because it advocates for the community of women. They attend only to the letter, not the spirit, which was not to encourage one man and one woman to marry and move in together – with the idea that women would then be shared – but to do away with that sort of marriage and introduce a different kind. People in general love to cite authority as a pretext to indulge their vices – when we know that philosophy says we should not even extend a finger without good reason.[13]

16. We should realize that an opinion is not easily formed unless a person says and hears the same things every day and practises them in real life.

17. When we are guests at a dinner party, we content ourselves with the food on offer; if anyone were to tell the host to put out fish or cake, he would seem rude. In real life, however, we ask the gods for what they do not give, and this though they have provided us with plenty.

18. It is just charming how people boast about qualities beyond their control. For instance, 'I am better than you because I have many estates, while you are practically starving'; or, 'I'm a consul,' 'I'm a governor,' or 'I have fine curly hair.' One horse doesn't say to another, 'I'm better than you because I have lots of hay and barley, my reins are of gold, and my saddle is embroidered,' but 'I'm better because I'm faster than you.' Every animal is judged better or worse based on its particular virtue or defect. Is man the only creature lacking a virtue, that we have to take account of his hair, his clothes, or his ancestry?

*

19. People who are physically ill are unhappy with a doctor who doesn't give them advice, because they think he has given up on them. Shouldn't we feel the same towards a philosopher – and assume that he has given up hope of our ever becoming rational – if he will no longer tell us what we need (but may not like) to hear?

20. People with a strong physical constitution can tolerate extremes of hot and cold; people of strong mental health can handle anger, grief, joy and the other emotions.

21. It is only right to praise Agrippinus, who never praised himself, although he was a man of the highest character. If he was praised by anyone else, he only became embarrassed. He was more inclined to praise every difficulty he faced: if he had a fever, he composed a paean to fever, if he faced exile or disgrace he would celebrate those. Once, when he was preparing for lunch, a messenger arrived from Rome announcing that Nero had sentenced him to exile. Unflustered he replied, 'Then why don't we just move our lunch to Aricia.'[14]

22. When he was governor, Agrippinus tried to convince the people whom he sentenced that it was for their own good to be sentenced. 'I don't at all condemn them in a spirit of malice,' he said, 'much less with an eye to seizing their property. I act in a spirit of concern and good will, like a doctor who comforts the patient whom he plans to cut open, and cajoles him into submitting to the operation.'

23. Nature is amazing and 'on the side of life', as Xenophon says.[15] Take the body – the nastiest and least pleasant thing of all – which we nevertheless love and look after. If we had to look after our neighbour's body, we'd be sick of it inside of a week. Imagine what it would be like to rise at dawn and brush someone else's teeth, or wipe their private parts after they've answered nature's call. Really, it's amazing that we can love something that on a daily basis requires so much of our attention.

I stuff this paunch, then empty it; and what could be more tedious? But God must be obeyed, and so I live on and put up with washing, feeding and housing my miserable body. When I was younger it asked something else of me, and I put up with that too. So why can't you tolerate it, when nature, which gave you this body, asks for it back?

'But I love it.'

Wasn't it nature, as I just finished saying, that made you love it? It's nature, too, that tells you it's time to let it go, so that you won't have to fuss over it any more.

24. Whenever someone dies young, they blame the gods *because they are being taken before their time; an old man who does not die also blames the gods** for his ailments, because by now he ought to have reached his resting place. Nevertheless, when death approaches he wants to live and sends for the doctor, begging him to spare nothing of his skill and energy. People are strange, Epictetus said: they neither wish to live nor die.

25. Whenever you set about attacking someone with violent threats, remember to give them fair warning, because you are not a savage animal. And if you refrain from savage behaviour, in the end you will have nothing to regret or explain.

26. [*from* Marcus Aurelius, *The Meditations*[16] IV 41] You are a bit of soul carrying around a dead body, as Epictetus used to say.

27. [*from* Marcus Aurelius, *The Meditations* XI 37] Epictetus said that we must find a method for managing assent. In the field of assent we have to be careful to use it with reservation, with restraint and in the service of society. Drop desire altogether and apply aversion to nothing that is not under our control.

*

* The words in italics have been supplied *exempli gratia* to mend an evident lacuna in the text.

28. [*from* Marcus Aurelius, *The Meditations* XI 38] It is nothing trivial at stake here, Epictetus said, but a question of sanity or insanity.

28a. [*from* Marcus Aurelius, *The Meditations* XI 39] Socrates would say, 'What do you want? To have the souls of rational or irrational animals?'

'Rational.'

'Healthy or unhealthy rational animals?'

'Healthy'

'Then why don't you work at it?'

'Because we have them already.'

'Then why are you fighting and quarrelling with one another?'

28b. [*from* Marcus Aurelius, *The Meditations* IV 49, 2–6] 'Poor me, because this happened to me.' No, say rather, 'Lucky me, because though this happened to me I'm still happy, neither broken by present circumstance nor afraid for the future.' Because the same thing could have happened to anyone, but not everyone could have remained content. So why is the former a misfortune any more than the latter is a blessing? Do you actually call anything a human misfortune that isn't a perversion of human nature? And don't you think a perversion of human nature must run counter to nature's will? Well, you understand its will. So does this misfortune prevent you in any way from being just, generous, sober, reasonable, careful, free from error, courteous, free, etc. – all of which together make human nature complete?

Remember from now on whenever something tends to make you unhappy, draw on this principle: 'This is no misfortune; but bearing with it bravely is a blessing.'

ENCHIRIDION

Chapter 1

[1] We are responsible for some things, while there are others for which we cannot be held responsible. The former include our judgement, our impulse, our desire, aversion and our mental faculties in general; the latter include the body, material possessions, our reputation, status – in a word, anything not in our power to control. [2] The former are naturally free, unconstrained and unimpeded, while the latter are frail, inferior, subject to restraint – and none of our affair.

[3] Remember that if you mistake what is naturally inferior for what is sovereign and free, and what is not your business for your own, you'll meet with disappointment, grief and worry and be at odds with God and man. But if you have the right idea about what really belongs to you and what does not, you will never be subject to force or hindrance, you will never blame or criticize anyone, and everything you do will be done willingly. You won't have a single rival, no one to hurt you, because you will be proof against harm of any kind.

[4] With rewards this substantial, be aware that a casual effort is not sufficient. Other ambitions will have to be sacrificed, altogether or at least for now. If you want these rewards at the same time that you are striving for power and riches, chances are you will not get to be rich and powerful while you aim for the other goal; and the rewards of freedom and happiness will elude you altogether.

[5] So make a practice at once of saying to every strong impression: 'An impression is all you are, not the source of the

impression.' Then test and assess it with your criteria, but one
primarily: ask, 'Is this something that is, or is not, in my control?' And if it's not one of the things that you control, be ready
with the reaction, 'Then it's none of my concern.'

Chapter 2

[1] The faculty of desire purports to aim at securing what you
want, while aversion purports to shield you from what you don't.
If you fail in your desire, you are unfortunate, if you experience
what you would rather avoid you are unhappy. So direct
aversion only towards things that are under your control and
alien to your nature, and you will not fall victim to any of the
things that you dislike. But if your resentment is directed at
illness, death or poverty, you are headed for disappointment.

[2] Remove it from anything not in our power to control,
and direct it instead toward things contrary to our nature that
we do control. As for desire, suspend it completely for now.
Because if you desire something outside your control, you are
bound to be disappointed; and even things we do control, which
under other circumstances would be deserving of our desire,
are not yet within our power to attain. Restrict yourself to
choice and refusal; and exercise them carefully, with discipline
and detachment.[1]

Chapter 3

In the case of particular things that delight you, or benefit you,
or to which you have grown attached, remind yourself of what
they are. Start with things of little value. If it is china you like,
for instance, say, 'I am fond of a piece of china.' When it breaks,
then you won't be as disconcerted. When giving your wife or
child a kiss, repeat to yourself, 'I am kissing a mortal.' Then
you won't be so distraught if they are taken from you.

Chapter 4

Whenever planning an action, mentally rehearse what the plan entails. If you are heading out to bathe, picture to yourself the typical scene at the bathhouse – people splashing, pushing, yelling and pinching your clothes. You will complete the act with more composure if you say at the outset, 'I want a bath, but at the same time I want to keep my will aligned with nature.' Do it with every act. That way if something occurs to spoil your bath, you will have ready the thought, 'Well, this was not my only intention, I also meant to keep my will in line with nature – which is impossible if I go all to pieces whenever anything bad happens.'

Chapter 5

It is not events that disturb people, it is their judgements concerning them. Death, for example, is nothing frightening, otherwise it would have frightened Socrates. But the judgement that death is frightening – now, that is something to be afraid of. So when we are frustrated, angry or unhappy, never hold anyone except ourselves – that is, our judgements – accountable. An ignorant person is inclined to blame others for his own misfortune. To blame oneself is proof of progress. But the wise man never has to blame another *or* himself.

Chapter 6

Don't pride yourself on any assets but your own. We could put up with a horse if it bragged of its beauty. But don't you see that when *you* boast of having a beautiful horse, you are taking credit for the horse's traits? What quality belongs to you? The intelligent use of impressions. If you use impressions as nature prescribes, go ahead and indulge your pride, because then you will be celebrating a quality distinctly your own.

Chapter 7

If you are a sailor on board a ship that makes port, you may decide to go ashore to bring back water. Along the way you may stop to collect shellfish, or pick greens. But you always have to remember the ship and listen for the captain's signal to return. When he calls, you have to drop everything, otherwise you could be bound and thrown on board like the livestock.

So it is in life. If, instead of greens and shellfish, you have taken on a wife and child, so much the better. But when the captain calls, you must be prepared to leave them behind, and not give them another thought. If you are advanced in years, don't wander too far, or you won't make it back in time when the summons reaches you.

Chapter 8

Don't hope that events will turn out the way you want, welcome events in whichever way they happen: this is the path to peace.

Chapter 9

Sickness is a problem for the body, not the mind – unless the mind decides that it is a problem. Lameness, too, is the body's problem, not the mind's. Say this to yourself whatever the circumstance and you will find without fail that the problem pertains to something else, not to you.

Chapter 10

For every challenge, remember the resources you have within you to cope with it. Provoked by the sight of a handsome man or a beautiful woman, you will discover within you the contrary power of self-restraint. Faced with pain, you will discover the power of endurance. If you are insulted, you will discover patience. In time, you will grow to be confident that there is not a single impression that you will not have the moral means to tolerate.

Chapter 11

Under no circumstances ever say 'I have lost something,' only 'I returned it.' Did a child of yours die? No, it was returned. Your wife died? No, *she* was returned. 'My land was confiscated.' No, it too was returned.

'But the person who took it was a thief.'

Why concern yourself with the means by which the original giver effects its return? As long as he entrusts it to you, look after it as something yours to enjoy only for a time – the way a traveller regards a hotel.

Chapter 12

[1] If you want to make progress, drop reflections like: 'I will end up destitute if I don't take better care of my affairs,' or, 'Unless I discipline my slave, he'll wind up good for nothing.' It is better to die of hunger free of grief and apprehension than to live affluent and uneasy. Better that your slave should be bad than that you should be unhappy.

[2] For that reason, starting with things of little value – a bit of spilled oil, a little stolen wine – repeat to yourself: 'For such

a small price I buy tranquillity and peace of mind.' But nothing is completely free. So when you call your slave, be prepared for the possibility that he might ignore you, or if he does answer, that he won't do what he's told. He is not worth entrusting with your peace of mind.

Chapter 13

If you want to make progress, put up with being perceived as ignorant or naive in worldly matters, don't aspire to a reputation for sagacity. If you do impress others as somebody, don't altogether believe it. You have to realize, it isn't easy to keep your will in agreement with nature, as well as externals. Caring about the one inevitably means you are going to shortchange the other.

Chapter 14

[1] You are a fool to want your children, wife or friends to be immortal; it calls for powers beyond you, and gifts not yours to either own or give. It is equally naive to ask that your slave be honest; it amounts to asking that vice be not vice but something different.[2] You can, however, avoid meeting with disappointment in your desires; focus on this, then, since it is in the scope of your capacities. [2] We are at the mercy of whoever wields authority over the things we either desire or detest. If you would be free, then, do not wish to have, or avoid, things that other people control, because then you must serve as their slave.

Chapter 15

Remember to act always as if you were at a symposium. When the food or drink comes around, reach out and take some politely; if it passes you by don't try pulling it back. And if it has not reached you yet, don't let your desire run ahead of you, be patient until your turn comes. Adopt a similar attitude with regard to children, wife, wealth and status, and in time, you will be entitled to dine with the gods. Go further and decline these goods even when they are on offer and you will have a share in the gods' power as well as their company. That is how Diogenes, Heraclitus[3] and philosophers like them came to be called, and considered, divine.

Chapter 16

Whenever you see someone in tears, distraught because they are parted from a child, or have met with some material loss, be careful lest the impression move you to believe that their circumstances are truly bad. Have ready the reflection that they are not upset by what happened – because other people are not upset when the same thing happens to them – but by their own view of the matter. Nevertheless, you should not disdain to sympathize with them, at least with comforting words, or even to the extent of sharing outwardly in their grief. But do not commiserate with your whole heart and soul.

Chapter 17

Remember that you are an actor in a play, the nature of which is up to the director to decide. If he wants the play to be short, it will be short, if he wants it long, it will be long. And if he casts you as one of the poor, or as a cripple, as a king or as a commoner – whatever role is assigned, the accomplished actor will accept and perform it with impartial skill. But the assignment of roles belongs to another.[4]

Chapter 18

If you hear a raven croak inauspiciously,[5] do not be alarmed by the impression. Make a mental distinction at once, and say, 'These omens hold no significance for me; they only pertain to my body, property, family, or reputation. For *me* every sign is auspicious, if I want it to be, because, whatever happens, I can derive some benefit from it.'

Chapter 19

[1] You will never have to experience defeat if you avoid contests whose outcome is outside your control. [2] Don't let outward appearances mislead you into thinking that someone with more prestige, power or some other distinction must on that account be happy. If the essence of the good lies within us, then there is no place for jealousy or envy, and you will not care about being a general, a senator or a consul – only about being free. And the way to be free is to look down on externals.

Chapter 20

Remember, it is not enough to be hit or insulted to be harmed, you must believe that you are being harmed. If someone succeeds in provoking you, realize that your mind is complicit in the provocation. Which is why it is essential that we not respond impulsively to impressions; take a moment before reacting, and you will find it is easier to maintain control.

Chapter 21

Keep the prospect of death, exile and all such apparent tragedies before you every day – especially death – and you will never have an abject thought, or desire anything to excess.

Chapter 22

If you commit to philosophy, be prepared at once to be laughed at and made the butt of many snide remarks, like, 'Suddenly there's a philosopher among us!' and 'What makes him so pretentious now?' Only *don't* be pretentious: just stick to your principles as if God had made you accept the role of philosopher. And rest assured that, if you remain true to them, the same people who made fun of you will come to admire you in time; whereas, if you let these people dissuade you from your choice, you will earn their derision twice over.

Chapter 23

If you are ever tempted to look for outside approval, realize that you have compromised your integrity. So be satisfied just being a philosopher, and if you need a witness in addition, be your own; and you will be all the witness you could desire.

Chapter 24

[1] Don't let thoughts like the following disturb you: 'I am going to live a life of no distinction, a nobody in complete obscurity.' Is lack of distinction bad?* Because if it is, other people cannot be the cause of it, any more than they can be the cause of another's disgrace. Is it solely at your discretion that you are elevated to office, or invited to a party? No; so it cannot be a dishonour if you are not. And how can you be 'a nobody in obscurity' when you only have to be somebody in the areas you control – the areas, that is, where you have the ability to shine?

[2] But your friends, you say, will be helpless. If by 'helpless' you mean that they won't get money from you, and you won't be able to make them Roman citizens – well, whoever told you that responsibility for such things belongs to us? Besides, who can give another what he does not have himself? 'Make money,' someone says, 'so that we can all share in it.' [3] If I can make money while remaining honest, trustworthy and dignified, show me how and I will do it. But if you expect me to sacrifice my own values, just so you can get your hands on things that aren't even good – well, you can see yourself how thoughtless and unfair you're being. Which would you rather have, anyway – money, or a worthy and faithful friend? So why not support me to that end, rather than asking me to engage in behaviour that involves the loss of these qualities?

[4] 'But my community will be helpless – to the extent that I can help.' Again, what kind of help do you have in mind? You can't give it buildings or baths, true, but so what? The blacksmith can't give it shoes, nor can the cobbler supply it with arms. It's enough if everyone plays their respective part. I mean, wouldn't you benefit your community by adding another lawful and loyal citizen to its rolls?

'Yes.'

---

* Reading ἢ γάρ for εἰ γάρ.

Then evidently you have it in you to benefit it all on your own.

'Well, what will my profession in the community be?'

Whatever position you are equipped to fill, so long as you preserve the man of trust and integrity. [5] If you lose that in your zeal to be a public benefactor, what use in the end will you be to the community once you have been rendered shameless and corrupt?

Chapter 25

[1] Someone was preferred above you at a formal dinner or awards banquet, and their advice was solicited before yours. If such marks of esteem are good, you should be pleased for the other person; if they are not, don't chafe because you did not get them. And remember, if you do not engage in the same acts as others with a view to gaining such honours, you cannot expect the same results. [2] A person who will not stoop to flattery does not get to have the flatterer's advantages. One who dances attendance on a superior is rewarded differently from someone who sits out. Refuse to praise someone and you cannot expect the same compensation as a flatterer. It would be unfair and greedy on your part, then, to decline to pay the price that these privileges entail and hope to get them free.

[3] How much is a head of lettuce worth? One obol, perhaps? Now if someone pays an obol and gets the head of lettuce, while you will not pay this much and therefore go without, don't imagine that you necessarily come off second best. As he has the lettuce, you still have the money. [4] And it's much the same in our case. You were not invited to someone's party, because you wouldn't pay the host the price of admission, namely paying her court and singing her praises. So pay the bill, if you expect to gain by it, and give no further thought to the expense. But if you won't pay the bill and still want the benefits, you are not only greedy but a fool. [5] If you forgo the meal, however, must it mean that you leave empty-handed?

You have the advantage of not having to praise the host, which you find disagreeable (and won't have to put up with the insolence of his slaves).

Chapter 26

We can familiarize ourselves with the will of nature by calling to mind our common experiences. When a friend breaks a glass, we are quick to say, 'Oh, bad luck.' It's only reasonable, then, that when a glass of your own breaks, you accept it in the same patient spirit. Moving on to graver things: when somebody's wife or child dies, to a man we all routinely say, 'Well, that's part of life.' But if one of our own family is involved, then right away it's 'Poor, poor me!' We would do better to remember how we react when a similar loss afflicts others.

Chapter 27

Just as a target is not set up in order to be missed, so evil is no natural part of the world's design.

Chapter 28

If your body was turned over to just anyone, you would doubtless take exception. Why aren't you ashamed that you have made your mind vulnerable to anyone who happens to criticize you, so that it automatically becomes confused and upset?

Chapter 29

[1] Reflect on what every project entails in both its initial and subsequent stages before taking it up. Otherwise you will likely tackle it enthusiastically at first, since you haven't given thought to what comes next; but when things get difficult you'll wind up quitting the project in disgrace. [2] You want to win at the Olympics? So do I – who doesn't? It's a glorious achievement; but reflect on what's entailed both now and later on before committing to it. You have to submit to discipline, maintain a strict diet, abstain from rich foods, exercise under compulsion at set times in weather hot and cold, refrain from drinking water or wine whenever you want – in short, you have to hand yourself over to your trainer as if he were your doctor. And then there are digging contests to endure, and times when you will dislocate your wrist, turn your ankle, swallow quantities of sand, be whipped – and end up losing all the same.

[3] Consider all this, and if you still want to, then give athletics a go. If you don't pause to think, though, you'll end up doing what children do, playing at wrestler one minute, then gladiator, then actor, then musician. And you – you're an athlete now, next a gladiator, an orator, a philosopher – but nothing with all your heart. You're like a monkey who imitates whatever it happens to see, infatuated with one thing after another. You haven't approached anything attentively, or thought things through; your approach to projects is casual and capricious.

[4] Some people, likewise, see a philosopher or hear someone like Euphrates lecture (only, who can lecture like him?) and get it in their heads to become philosophers too. [5] Listen, friend, research the role, then assess your capacity to fill it, just as you assess your arms, thighs and back if you hope to be a wrestler or pentathlete. [6] We are not all cut out for the same thing. Do you think that as a philosopher you can eat and drink, or exercise desire and aversion, as you do at present? You have to stay up nights, put up with pain, leave your family, be looked

down on by slaves, suffer ridicule from strangers, be outdone in status, in power, in legal matters – get the worst of it, in other words, down to the last little thing. [7] Ponder whether you're prepared to pay this price for serenity, freedom and calm. If not, then don't go near it – don't, like children, be a philosopher now, a tax officer later, then an orator or politician. These roles don't mix; you have to be one person, good or bad. You have to care either for your mind or for material things; specialize in what is within you or without – which is to say, you have to stick to the role of philosopher or layman.

Chapter 30

Duties are broadly defined by social roles. This man is your father: the relationship demands from you support, constant deference and tolerance for his verbal, even his physical, abuse.

'But he's a bad father.'

Look, nature has endeared you to a father, not necessarily a *good* one.

'My brother is unfair to me.'

Well then, keep up your side of the relationship; don't concern yourself with his behaviour, only with what *you* must do to keep your will in tune with nature. Another person will not hurt you without your cooperation; you are hurt the moment you believe yourself to be.

The titles of neighbour, citizen and general will likewise suggest to you what functions they entail, once you begin to give social relationships their due in your daily deliberations.

Chapter 31

[1] Realize that the chief duty we owe the gods is to hold the correct beliefs about them: that they exist, that they govern the

world justly and well, and that they have put you here* for one purpose – to obey them and welcome whatever happens, in the conviction that it is a product of the highest intelligence. This way you won't ever blame the gods or charge them with neglect. [2] And this cannot happen unless you stop applying 'good' and 'bad' to externals and only describe things under our control that way. Because, if you regard any external as good or bad, and fail to get what you want or get what you don't want instead, you will blame the gods and inevitably hate them for being the cause of your trouble.

[3] Every living thing by nature shrinks and turns away from whatever it considers harmful or malicious, just as it loves and gravitates toward what is helpful and sympathetic. Anyone who imagines that they are being wronged can no more love the offender than the offence. [4] And so we find even fathers being blamed by their children, when they fail to give them what the child regards as good. It is the same reason Polyneices and Eteocles became enemies – the idea each had that it would be better to rule alone. It is why farmers curse the gods; why sailors, traders and men who have lost wives or children curse them too. Piety cannot exist apart from self-interest. The upshot is, when you practise using desire and aversion correctly, you practise being pious.

[5] At the same time, it is never wrong to make sacrifice, pour libations, or offer first fruits in the traditional manner, as long as it is done attentively and not carelessly or by rote, and you neither offer too little nor spend beyond your means.

Chapter 32

[1] In your approach to divination, bear in mind that you don't know what will happen, you go in order to learn it from the prophet. A philosopher, however, arrives already knowing the value of what's to come. If it's anything outside his sphere of

---

* Adopting the emendation κατατεταχότων for κατατεταχέναι.

influence, he knows it can be neither good nor bad. [2] So if you consult a prophet, leave desire, fear, and aversion behind, in the assurance that the future, *per se*, is indifferent, and nothing to you. You can make use of it, whatever it is, and there's not a soul who can stop you. Approach the gods with a dignified attitude, think of them as your advisers. But once their advice has been given, remember the source and consider who you would be slighting if you were to set that advice aside.

[3] Make use of divination the way Socrates thought it should be used,[6] i.e. solely when it's a matter of learning the future – not when there's a problem that can be resolved by the application of reason (another human resource). Don't, for example, resort to divination if you are duty-bound to come to the defence of your country or share in some danger threatening a friend. Suppose the seer declares the omens unfavourable – which, in cases like this, could spell exile for you, physical injury, even death. And still reason demands that you stick by your friend, or help defend your country. On that score we have only to consult the greatest prophet of all, Apollo: he refused to let someone enter his temple who had once ignored cries for help from a friend under assault from robbers.

Chapter 33

[1] Settle on the type of person you want to be and stick to it, whether alone or in company.

[2] Let silence be your goal for the most part; say only what is necessary, and be brief about it. On the rare occasions when you're called upon to speak, then speak, but never about banalities like gladiators, horses, sports, food and drink – commonplace stuff. Above all don't gossip about people, praising, blaming or comparing them. [3] Try to influence your friends to speak appropriately by your example. If you find yourself in unfamiliar company, however, keep quiet.

[4] Keep laughter to a minimum; do not laugh too often or too loud.

[5] If possible, refuse altogether to take an oath; resist, in any case, as far as circumstances will permit.

[6] Avoid fraternizing with non-philosophers. If you must, though, be careful not to sink to their level; because, you know, if a companion is dirty, his friends cannot help but get a little dirty too, no matter how clean they started out.

[7] Where the body is concerned, take only what is strictly necessary in the way of food, drink, clothing, shelter and household slaves. Cut out luxury and ostentation altogether.

[8] Concerning sex, stay as chaste as you can before marriage. If you do indulge, engage only in licit liaisons. Don't be harsh or judgemental towards others who have sex; if you are celibate yourself, don't advertise the fact.

[9] If you learn that someone is speaking ill of you, don't try to defend yourself against the rumours; respond instead with, 'Yes, and he doesn't know the half of it, because he could have said more.'

[10] There is no call to be a regular at the public games. But if the occasion should arise and you go, don't be seen siding with anyone except yourself; which is to say, hope only for what happens to happen, and for the actual winner to win; then you won't be unhappy. Yelling, jeering and excessive agitation should be avoided completely. Don't talk much about the event afterwards, or any more than is necessary to get it out of your system. Otherwise it becomes obvious that the experience captivated you.

[11] Don't too soon, or too lightly, attend other people's lectures; when you do go remain serious and reserved, without being disagreeable.

[12] When you are going to meet someone, especially someone deemed important, imagine to yourself what Socrates or Zeno would have done in the situation and you won't fail to get on, whatever happens. [13] When you are going to the house of someone influential, tell yourself that you won't find them in, that you will be locked out, that the door will be slammed in your face, that they won't give you the time of day. And, despite that, if it's the right thing to go, then go and face the consequences. Don't say to yourself later, 'It wasn't worth

it.' That's the mark of a conventional person at odds with life.

[14] In your conversation, don't dwell at excessive length on your own deeds or adventures. Just because you enjoy recounting your exploits doesn't mean that others derive the same pleasure from hearing about them.

[15] And avoid trying to be funny. That way vulgarity lies, and at the same time it's likely to lower you in your friends' estimation.

[16] It is also not a good idea to venture on profanity. If it happens, and you aren't out of line, you may even criticize a person who indulges in it. Otherwise, signal your dislike of his language by falling silent, showing unease or giving him a sharp look.

Chapter 34

As with impressions generally, if you get an impression of something pleasurable, watch yourself so that you are not carried away by it. Take a minute and let the matter wait on you. Then reflect on both intervals of time: the time you will have to experience the pleasure, and the time after its enjoyment that you will beat yourself up over it. Contrast that with how happy and pleased you'll be if you abstain. If the chance to do the deed presents itself, take extra care that you are not overcome by its seductiveness, pleasure and allure. Counter temptation by remembering how much better will be the knowledge that you resisted.

Chapter 35

If you decide to do something, don't shrink from being seen doing it, even if the majority of people disapprove. If you're wrong to do it, then you should shrink from doing it altogether; but if you're right, then why worry how people will judge you?

Chapter 36

Just as the propositions 'It is day' and 'It is night' together contribute much to disjunctive propositions, but nothing to conjunctive ones,[7] so, even allowing that taking the largest portion of a dish contributes to the health of the body, it contributes nothing to the communal spirit that a dinner party should typify. So when you dine in company, remember not only to consider what the food on offer can do for your health, have some consideration for your host's good health too.

Chapter 37

If you undertake a role beyond your means, you will not only embarrass yourself in that, you miss the chance of a role that you might have filled successfully.

Chapter 38

As you are careful when you walk not to step on a nail or turn your ankle, so you should take care not to do any injury to your character at the same time.[8] Exercise such caution whenever we act, and we will perform the act with less risk of injury.

Chapter 39

Each man's body defines the limit of his material needs, as, on a small scale, the foot does with regard to shoes. Observe this principle, and you will never be in any confusion as to what those limits are. Exceed them, and you inevitably fall off a virtual cliff. As with shoes – if you don't limit yourself to what the foot needs, you wind up with gold heels, purple pumps or even embroidered slippers. There's no end once the natural limit has been exceeded.

Chapter 40

At the age of fourteen girls begin to be addressed by men as 'ladies'. From this they infer that the world honours them for nothing so much as their potential as sexual partners. Consequently, they become preoccupied with their appearance to the exclusion of everything else. They must be made to realize that they are entitled to be called 'ladies' only insofar as they cultivate modesty and self-respect.

Chapter 41

It shows a lack of refinement to spend a lot of time exercising, eating, drinking, defecating or copulating. Tending to the body's needs should be done incidentally, as it were; the mind and its functions require the bulk of our attention.

Chapter 42

Whenever anyone criticizes or wrongs you, remember that they are only doing or saying what they think is right. They cannot be guided by your views, only their own; so if their views are wrong, they are the ones who suffer insofar as they are misguided. I mean, if someone declares a true conjunctive proposition to be false, the proposition is unaffected, it is they who come off worse for having their ignorance exposed. With this in mind you will treat your critic with more compassion. Say to yourself each time, 'He did what he believed was right.'

Chapter 43

Every circumstance comes with two handles, with one of which you can hold it, while with the other conditions are insupportable. If your brother mistreats you, don't try to come to grips with it by dwelling on the wrong he's done (because that approach makes it unbearable); remind yourself that he's your brother, that you two grew up together; then you'll find that you can bear it.

Chapter 44

The following are non-sequiturs: 'I am richer, therefore superior to you'; or 'I am a better speaker, therefore a better person, than you.' These statements, on the other hand, are cogent: 'I am richer than you, therefore my wealth is superior to yours'; and 'I am a better speaker, therefore my diction is better than yours.' But *you* are neither wealth nor diction.

Chapter 45

Someone bathes in haste; don't say he bathes badly, but in haste. Someone drinks a lot of wine; don't say he drinks badly, but a lot. Until you know their reasons, how do you know that their actions are vicious? This will save you from perceiving one thing clearly, but then assenting to something different.

Chapter 46

[1] Never identify yourself as a philosopher or speak much to non-philosophers about your principles; act in line with those

principles. At a dinner party, for instance, don't tell people the right way to eat, just eat the right way. Remember how Socrates so effaced himself that people used to approach him seeking an introduction to philosophers, and he would graciously escort them; that's how careless he was of the slight. [2] If conversation turns to a philosophical topic, keep silent for the most part, since you run the risk of spewing forth a lot of ill-digested information. If your silence is taken for ignorance, but it doesn't upset you – well, that's the real sign that you have begun to be a philosopher. Sheep don't bring their owners grass to prove to them how much they've eaten, they digest it inwardly and outwardly bring forth milk and wool. So don't make a show of your philosophical learning to the uninitiated, show them by your actions what you have absorbed.

Chapter 47

When your body gets used to simple living, don't preen over it; if you're a water drinker, don't take every opportunity to announce it. If you want to train for physical austerities, do it for yourself, not for outsiders. Don't embrace marble statues;[9] but if you happen to be very thirsty, try taking some cold water in your mouth and spitting it out – and don't tell anyone.

Chapter 48

[1] The mark and attitude of the ordinary man: never look for help or harm from yourself, only from outsiders. The mark and attitude of the philosopher: look for help and harm exclusively from yourself.

[2] And the signs of a person making progress: he never criticizes, praises, blames or points the finger, or represents himself as knowing or amounting to anything. If he experiences frustration or disappointment, he points the finger at himself.

If he's praised, he's more amused than elated. And if he's criticized, he won't bother to respond. He walks around as if he were an invalid, careful not to move a healing limb before it's at full strength. [3] He has expunged all desire, and made the things that are contrary to nature and in his control the sole target of his aversion. Impulse he only uses with detachment. He does not care if he comes across as stupid or naive. In a word, he keeps an eye on himself as if he were his own enemy lying in ambush.

Chapter 49

Whenever someone prides himself on being able to understand and comment on Chrysippus' books, think to yourself, 'If Chrysippus had written more clearly, this person would have nothing to be proud of.' As for me, I care only about understanding nature, and following its leads. So I look for someone to interpret nature for me, and after hearing that Chrysippus can, I turn to him. So far, I have no cause for conceit. When I find that Chrysippus really can interpret nature, it still remains for me to act on his suggestions – which is the only thing one can be proud of. If I admire the interpretation, I have turned into a literary critic instead of a philosopher, the only difference being that, instead of Homer, I'm interpreting Chrysippus. But whenever people ask me to interpret Chrysippus for them, I only feel shame that my actions don't meet or measure up to what he says.

Chapter 50

Whatever your mission, stick by it as if it were a law and you would be committing sacrilege to betray it. Pay no attention to whatever people might say; this no longer should influence you.

Chapter 51

[1] How long will you wait before you demand the best of yourself, and trust reason to determine what is best? You have been introduced to the essential doctrines, and claim to understand them. So what kind of teacher are you waiting for that you delay putting these principles into practice until he comes? You're a grown man already, not a child any more. If you remain careless and lazy, making excuse after excuse, fixing one day after another when you will finally take yourself in hand, your lack of progress will go unnoticed, and in the end you will have lived and died unenlightened.

[2] Finally decide that you are an adult who is going to devote the rest of your life to making progress. Abide by what seems best as if it were an inviolable law. When faced with anything painful or pleasurable, anything bringing glory or disrepute, realize that the crisis is now, that the Olympics have started, and waiting is no longer an option; that the chance for progress, to keep or lose, turns on the events of a single day. [3] That's how Socrates got to be the person he was, by depending on reason to meet his every challenge. You're not yet Socrates, but you can still live as if you want to be him.

Chapter 52

[1] The first and most important field of philosophy is the application of principles such as 'Do not lie.' Next come the proofs, such as why we should not lie. The third field supports and articulates the proofs, by asking, for example, 'How does this prove it? What exactly is a proof, what is logical inference, what is contradiction, what is truth, what is falsehood?' [2] Thus, the third field is necessary because of the second, and the second because of the first. The most important, though, the one that should occupy most of our time, is the first. But we do just the opposite. We are preoccupied with the third field and

give that all our attention, passing the first by altogether. The result is that we lie – but have no difficulty proving why we shouldn't.

Chapter 53

[1] In every circumstance we should have the following sentiments handy:

Lead me, Zeus, lead me, Destiny,
To the goal I was long ago assigned
And I will follow without hesitation. Even should I resist,
In a spirit of perversity, I will have to follow nonetheless.
[2] *Whoever yields to necessity graciously*
We account wise in God's ways.[10]
[3] 'Dear Crito if it pleases the gods, so be it.'
[4] 'Anytus and Meletus can kill me, but they cannot harm me.'

Glossary of Names

(Note: Most names that appear only once are glossed in the notes and not included here in the glossary.)

Academy and Academics. *See* Plato, Sceptics.

Achilles. Main character in Homer's *Iliad*, reputed the best fighter on the Greek side.

Admetus. Character in Euripides' play *Alcestis*, who is released from impending death on condition he can find someone to take his place.

Aeolus. Greek god in control of the winds.

Agamemnon. Character in Homer's *Iliad*, commander-in-chief of the Greek forces in the Trojan War.

Agrippinus. Quintus Paconius Agrippinus, Roman senator, joined the Pisonian conspiracy against Nero in 66 AD; convicted and sentenced to exile.

Alexander the Great, 356–323 BC. Macedonian prince who at the age of twenty initiated military campaigns of unprecedented ambition, acquiring an empire that eventually included Greece, Egypt and Asia as far as western India.

Antipater of Sidon, fl. first century BC. Stoic philosopher.

Antipater of Tarsus. Stoic philosopher and head of the Stoic school in Athens *c.*152–*c.*129 BC.

Antisthenes of Athens, *c.*445–360 BC. Follower of Socrates; credited with helping to inspire the Cynicism of Diogenes and described by Plato as 'Socrates gone mad'.

Anytus. Along with Meletus, one of Socrates' chief accusers on the charges of impiety and corrupting the youth of Athens that resulted in his death.

Apollodorus of Seleucia. Stoic philosopher of the late second century BC.

Archedemus. Stoic philosopher active in the second century BC.

Asclepius. Greek god of healing.

Augustus, 63 BC–14 AD, born Gaius Octavius, adoptive son of Julius Caesar and emperor of Rome (27 BC–14 AD). Founder of Epictetus' hometown of Nicopolis; after his death worshipped as a god in Nicopolis and throughout the Empire.

Boreas. In Greek mythology, name of the north wind.

Caesar. Title of the emperor of Rome from Augustus to Hadrian.

Chryseis. A character in Homer's *Iliad*, the name of Agamemnon's captive 'prize' whom he replaces with Achilles, leading to a quarrel, and Achilles' decision to withdraw from the fighting.

Chrysippus of Soli (Cilicia), *c.*280–208 BC. The third head of the Stoic school in Athens, and its acknowledged authority in most doctrinal matters.

Cleanthes of Assos, *c.*331–232 BC. The second head of the Stoic school in Athens, author of a *Hymn to Zeus* that Epictetus often quotes.

Crates of Thebes, fl. late fourth–early third century BC. Cynic pupil of Diogenes of Sinope, teacher of the Stoic Zeno of Citium.

Crinis. Stoic philosopher of the late second century BC, noted mainly for his definitions.

Croesus, fl. sixth century BC. King of Lydia, proverbial for great wealth, defeated in an ill-considered war of aggression against Cyrus of Persia.

Demeter. Greek god of agriculture, mother of Triptolemus.

Diodorus Cronus, d. *c.*284 BC. Leader of the Dialectical school of philosophy, teacher of Zeno of Citium and author of the Master Argument (II 19, 1–9).

Diogenes of Babylon. Head of the Stoic school in early to mid-second century BC.

Diogenes Laertius, fl. *c.* 200 AD. Author of the *Lives of the Philosophers*, a major source for Epicurean and early Stoic doctrine.

Diogenes of Sinope, fl. mid-fourth century BC. Founder of Cynicism; second only to Socrates in the number of times he is cited as a model in the *Discourses*.

Domitian. Emperor of Rome (81–96 AD). His rule, especially in its last years, was notoriously oppressive.

Epaphroditus. Greek freedman who served the emperor Nero as his secretary in charge of petitions; Epictetus' master when he was still a slave.

Epicurus of Athens, 341–271 BC. Founder of an important contemporary school of philosophy in rivalry with Stoicism. His physics revived the atomism of the fifth-century BC Greek philosopher

Democritus, denying any element of design or divine involvement in the world's composition; in ethics he was a principled hedonist, identifying pleasure as the goal of life.

Eteocles. *See* Polyneices.

Euphrates of Tyre, died *c.*120 AD. Stoic philosopher; like Epictetus, a former student of Musonius Rufus. He was known for his powers of oratory.

Eurystheus. In Greek mythology Eurystheus was king of Tiryns in the Peloponnese. Partly out of fear for Heracles' strength he devised and imposed on him the twelve famous labours.

Favorinus, fl. late first–early second centuries AD. Academic philosopher and contemporary of Epictetus.

Gratilla. Wife of a Roman senator exiled by Domitian; also mentioned in III.11 of Pliny the Younger's *Letters*.

Gyara (or Gyaros). A barren island in the Aegean that served as a place of exile during the early Principate.

Hector. In Homer's *Iliad* a prince of Troy and the chief Trojan warrior.

Helvidius Priscus. Roman senator and Stoic, son-in-law of Thrasea Paetus, executed by the emperor Vespasian in 75 AD for challenging the power of the Principate.

Heracles. Most famous of the Greek heroes of legend; completed twelve labours at the behest of King Eurystheus; adopted by the Cynics and Stoics as a model of manly virtue.

Heraclitus, fl. *c.*500–480 BC. Major Presocratic philosopher, acknowledged to be a major influence on the Stoics, with whom he shared a belief in the periodicity of time and other doctrines.

Lateranus. Platius Lateranus, Roman senator and consul designate in 65 AD, member of the Pisonian conspiracy to replace the emperor Nero; condemned with the rest and executed.

Meletus. One of the Athenians who in 399 BC brought charges against Socrates leading to his execution.

Milo. Name of a famous ancient Greek athlete.

Musonius Rufus. Stoic philosopher, and Epictetus' teacher at Rome.

Nero. Emperor of Rome (54–68 AD), the very type of the 'tyrant.' Epictetus resided at his court when he was slave to Epaphroditus in Rome.

Panthoides, fl. early third century BC. Member of the Dialectical school, a contributor to the debate on the Master Argument.

Paris. In Greek mythology Paris was a prince of Troy. Tradition has it that he ran off with Helen, wife of his then host, Menelaus, the king of Sparta. As Homer relates it in the *Iliad*, this blatant breach of hospitality precipitated the Trojan War.

Patroclus. In Homer's *Iliad* Patroclus is a Greek warrior close to Achilles; when he dies at Hector's hands Achilles indulges in a dramatic and protracted bout of grief.

Peripatetic School and Peripatetics. Name given to the school founded in Athens by Aristotle in the fourth century BC, and its adherents.

Phidias, fifth century BC. Greek sculptor, best known for his gold-and-ivory statues of Zeus at Olympia, and of Athena in the Parthenon at Athens.

Philip II. King of Macedon (359–336 BC) and father of Alexander the Great.

Plato of Athens, 427–347 BC. Student of Socrates, founder of the Academy, author of the *Apology*, *Gorgias* and other dialogues that are frequently quoted in the *Discourses* with approval. In Epictetus' day, the Academy had become, along with Pyrrhonism, one of the two main Sceptical schools of philosophy.

Polyneices and Eteocles. In Greek mythology, brothers who fight each other for control of Thebes after their father, Oedipus, went into self-exile.

Posidonius of Apamea, *c*.135–*c*.50 BC. Major Stoic philosopher, noted for his scientific researches and historical writings.

Pyrrho of Elis, *c*.365–270 BC. Semi-legendary founder of the Sceptical movement in philosophy, figurehead of the revived Pyrrhonism (so-called) of Epictetus' day.

Pythia (or Pythian priestess). The mouthpiece of Apollo's oracles delivered in Delphi.

Rufus. *See* Musonius Rufus.

Saturnalia. Major Roman holiday, lasting five days, marked by inversion rituals such as releasing slaves from their duties and allowing them certain privileges usually reserved to their masters.

Sceptics. Generic title for the Academics and Pyrrhonists, philosophers committed to the doctrine, *contra* the Stoics, that nothing can be known with absolute certainty.

Socrates, 470–399 BC. Philosopher and dialectician. Native of Athens. Served honourably in the Peloponnesian War against Sparta. Convicted on politically motivated charges of impiety and corrupting the youth and executed. Plato's *Apology* purports to transmit his defence speech at the trial. Socrates continues as main speaker in most of Plato's dialogues.

Syrians. Generic name for the non-Jewish Semitic peoples of the Near East.

Thermopylae. Narrow pass in Greece, site of a desperate stand made by the Spartans in 480 BC against a far larger invading troop from Persia.

Thersites. In Greek mythology Thersites was a low-ranking soldier in the Greek army during the Trojan War. He is described as ugly inside and out: bow-legged, hunched, bald – also vulgar and rude to his superior officers.

Thrasea Paetus. Roman senator and Stoic, father-in-law of Helvidius Priscus; committed suicide in 66 AD after being implicated in the Pisonian conspiracy against Nero.

Trajan. Emperor of Rome (98–117 AD), the pattern of the 'good emperor', as Nero represented the typical tyrant for Epictetus and his generation.

Vespasian. Emperor of Rome (69–79 AD), restored order and dignity to the imperial office after Nero's disastrous reign, but still had to contend with republican sentiment among certain senators, including the Stoic Helvidius Priscus, who was put to death by the emperor in 75 AD.

Xanthippe. Wife of Socrates, a proverbial nag.

Xenophon of Athens, c.430–c.355 BC. Follower of Socrates, author of the *Memorabilia*, considered inferior only to Plato's dialogues as a primary source for our knowledge of Socrates' life and teachings.

Zeno of Citium (Cyprus), 334–262 BC. Founder of the Stoa at Athens, c.300 BC.

Zephyrus (Zephyr). In Greek mythology, name of the west wind.

Notes

THE DISCOURSES

BOOK 1

1. *when Epaphroditus ... to your master*: The meaning of the anecdote in §20 is obscure.

2. *I would sooner be killed ... tomorrow*: Thrasea was a Roman senator with Republican sympathies. He literally regarded exile as a fate worse than death; 'tomorrow' stands for any date in the future.

3. *the purple stripe*: A toga with a purple stripe was the uniform of a Roman senator.

4. *five denarii*: A sum that might buy a modestly priced book.

5. *Dear Crito ... so be it*: A quotation of Socrates from Plato's *Crito* 43d. It is cited again at I 29, 18; IV 4, 21; and *Enchiridion* 53, 3. 'Prison' and 'hemlock' allude to the circumstances of Socrates' death.

6. *A benefactor ... has shown us the way*: The reference is to Chrysippus.

7. *Triptolemus*: In Greek mythology, Triptolemus was inventor of the plough and the first person to sow grain.

8. *Against the Sceptics*: The Sceptics maintained that nothing could be known for certain. In Epictetus' day, Sceptics were represented by two schools: the Academics and the Pyrrhonists. This essay seems directed not only against these philosophers but against the common human frailty of 'a foolish consistency'.

9. *two kinds of petrifaction*: Actually, three forms of petrifaction are described in this section. Two generic forms of petrifaction, that of the body, and that of the soul, are recognized. Then within the soul two species of petrifaction are distinguished, of the intellect, and of the sense of honour.

10. *add and subtract impressions . . . related*: Epictetus alludes first to the formation of such concepts as a pygmy (by picking a concept formed by a sense impression – e.g. a man – then 'subtracting'), or a giant (by 'adding'), or a centaur (by 'combining'), or a painting of a man (by analogy, i.e. by 'passing from certain things to others in some way connected'). Compare I 14, 7–8.

11. *If not, it's left to us . . . on their own*: Epictetus indirectly opposes the Epicurean explanation of nature as the product of 'accident and chance'.

12. *God needed animals . . . their use*: Epictetus means that the beasts use their impressions, and so do we; but what distinguishes us from them is that we regard impressions critically, refer them to a standard and consider them within a larger context.

13. *You eagerly travel . . . sight*: The colossal gold-and-ivory statue of Zeus inside his temple at Olympia was designed by Phidias in the fifth century BC; it was numbered among the Seven Wonders of the Ancient World.

14. *So what should I do . . . premises*: This paragraph alludes to the subject of changing arguments, mentioned above in §1. In Stoicism changing arguments contain a temporal component and involve the element of 'truth-at-a-time'. Sextus Empiricus (*Outlines of Pyrrhonism* II 229) gives an example: 'It is not the case both that I have already presented you with a proposition and that it is not the case that the stars are even in number. But I have presented you with a proposition. Therefore the number of the stars is even.' The truth-value of the first premise – 'I have already presented you with a proposition' – changes in the course of the argument, indeed during the time the premise itself is propounded; or, as Epictetus puts it (§20), 'in the very process of questioning, answering, [or] drawing conclusions'. The argument as a whole is fallacious, insofar as it leads to the conclusion that the stars are not even in number when the argument begins, but odd by the time the argument ends. Moreover, it is fallacious on purpose – a sophism of the kind Epictetus says 'cause[s] the untutored to become confused when confronted with the conclusions' – since the number of the stars was the standard example of something that could not be certainly decided one way or another. The first premise, however, does change its truth-value in the course of being articulated, if we conceive of the argument literally as a sequence of words, articulated aloud, in real time, in a prearranged order.

15. *I will make you accept . . . impossible*: On hypothetical argu-

ments in general cf. I 25, 11–12; for an example of an 'impossible'
proposition in Stoic logic, cf. Alexander of Aphrodisias, *On
Aristotle's Prior Analytics* 177. 27–30: 'Chrysippus ... says that
in the conditional "If John is dead, this one is dead," which is
true when John is being demonstratively referred to, the ante-
cedent "John is dead" is possible, since it can one day become
true that John is dead; but "This one is dead" is impossible.
For when John has died the proposition "This one is dead" is
destroyed, the object of the demonstrative reference no longer
existing.'

16. *But wasn't Plato a philosopher?*: The objection is based on the
stylistic elegance of Plato's dialogues.

17. *if I were a philosopher ... lame as well?*: Epictetus was lame –
and of course a philosopher also, but he modestly disclaims this
title.

18. *Can Jews ... for example?*: The Jews were well known for their
elaborate dietary laws, and peculiarities of diet are duly noted
by ancient authors in the case of the Syrians and Egyptians as
well; like the Jews, for instance, Egyptian priests were forbidden
to eat pork. The line of questioning in this passage assumes that
the races are not just different in this respect, but actually either
'right' or 'wrong', the reason being that the basis of their dietary
laws was assumed to be religious (cf. I 22, 4); and the Stoics had
very definite views about the gods, as the next discourse (I 12)
shows, and confidence that they were right (and other schools of
philosophy wrong).

19. *On the subject of the gods ... God's notice*: These five groups
can be roughly identified. The atheists of the first group include
Diagoras of Melos and Critias of Athens. The second group,
those who say 'that God exists ... and does not pay attention
to anything', are the Epicureans. The third group represents
Aristotle and his followers. The view that God looks after the
greater good, and 'doesn't sweat the details' (as a contemporary
expression has it) is widely attested, even for some Stoics. The
fifth group presents the orthodox Stoic view; it was also attributed to Socrates. The quotation, 'I cannot make a move ...' is
from the *Iliad* 10. 279–280, where Odysseus addresses his patron
deity, Athena.

20. *follow the gods*: A Stoic and Platonic motto.

21. *He arranged for there to be ... family and friends*: The form of
theodicy outlined here, which seeks to show that good cannot
exist without evil, was argued by Chrysippus: 'Nothing is more

foolish than to maintain that there could have been goods without the coexistence of evils. For since goods are opposite to
evils, the two must necessarily exist in opposition to each other,
supported by a kind of opposed interdependence. And there is
no such quality without its matching opposite. For how could
there be perception of justice if there were no injustice? What
else is justice, if not the removal of injustice? . . . Goods and evils,
fortune and misfortune, pain and pleasure, are tied to each other
in polar opposition' (Aulus Gellius, *Attic Nights* VII 1,1). The
idea of 'opposed interdependence' is similar to what Epictetus
calls 'the harmony of the whole'. The last clause – 'and he gave
us each a body . . . and associates' – anticipates another defence
of Stoic providence found below (§18), and elsewhere (e.g. I 1,
8–9) motivated by the problems entailed in having a body, and
living in a community, with people not all of whom, unfortunately, were Stoics.

22. *Conversely, Socrates . . . chose to be there*: In Plato's *Phaedo*
(98e–99b), Socrates is shown making light of his imprisonment,
and in the *Crito* he gives reasons for declining a hypothetical
offer of escape.

23. *the small shadow that the earth casts*: This is what astronomers
call the 'umbra' and what the rest of us call 'night', i.e. the
darkness that covers a hemisphere of the earth at any one time.

24. *Who says so? . . . I mean?*: In other words, it was not just
Stoics (like Chrysippus, Zeno and Cleanthes), other notable philosophers also gave priority to the definition of terms – and
(according to the Stoics), definition of terms was part of logic.
Antisthenes was a Cynic philosopher; the position ascribed to
him here is supported by Diogenes Laertius, *Lives of the Philosophers* VI 17. Socrates' interest in definition motivates many of
the dialogues of Plato in which he participates. The reference to
Xenophon is apparently to his *Memorabilia* I 1, 16.

25. *we always err unwillingly*: The famous Socratic 'paradox', which
the Stoics bravely defended. Here 'unwillingly' means 'unwit-
tingly', i.e. because we do not know better.

26. *what if he's drunk? . . . Or dreaming?*: 'Really delusive impressions may come in sleep, or under the influence of wine, or
insanity' (Cicero, *Academica* II 51).

27. *the Altar of Fever at Rome*: Fever, or *Febris* in Latin, actually
had three temples in Rome, the principal one on the Palatine.
The cult was apotropaic, i.e. people prayed and sacrificed to it
to keep it at bay.

28. *The sun moves across the sky for its own ends*: Stoics, in a departure from traditional Greek religion, held that the sun, the moon and the stars were full-fledged divinities; these celestial objects led a nomadic life in search of sustenance from the rivers, lakes and oceans below, explaining (the Stoics believed) their steady motion across the sky.

29. *appropriation*: This is one of several possible translations for the Greek word *oikeiôsis*, a key concept of Stoic ethics. The principle of 'appropriation' views animal and human development in terms of a creature's growing self-awareness of its own mental and physical faculties. The egoism or 'selfishness' that Epictetus describes and defends in this section he ties to 'appropriation' by way of the correlative view that, as a creature comes to appreciate its natural gifts, it wants nothing more than to protect and develop them to their fullest extent. Here Epictetus argues that in the case of man and the gods reason brings with it the realization that self-interest and altruism are compatible.

30. *Felicio*: A common name for a slave or (as here) a freedman.

31. *priesthood of Augustus*: Augustus, the first Roman emperor, received divine honours in his lifetime and continued to have his own cult in Rome and elsewhere after his death. As Nicopolis had been founded by Augustus himself after his victory over Antony, his cult was especially prominent in Epictetus' home-town, and the priesthood of Augustus was an important public office. The priest had to lay out his own money to perform the essential functions of sacrifice, etc.

32. *once he has identified our good with the shell*: Cf. I 20, 17.

33. *we who supposedly ... our children?*: Epicurus (341–271 BC) maintained that pleasure, especially bodily pleasure, was humanity's chief good and denied that there was any natural affection between parents and children.

34. *Mouse*: (*Mus* in Greek), the pet name of one of Epicurus' household slaves, liberated by the terms of his will (Diogenes Laertius, *Lives of the Philosophers* X 10 and 21).

35. *exposed*: A euphemism for the ancient practice of infanticide.

36. *Diogenes*: This is Diogenes the Cynic.

37. *I'll wear the ordinary toga now*: The broad hem distinguished the senator's toga, the narrow hem was reserved to the class of knights (*equites*) at Rome, and the unadorned toga was what the common person (or *pleb*) wore, so that this sequence of commands outlines a gradual loss in rank.

38. *'Deck the palace halls ... receive me'*: The first citation is from

a choral ode of an unknown play; the second is line 1390 of
Sophocles' *Oedipus the King*.

39. *The chief thing . . . the door is open*: Cf. I 25, 18.

40. *At the Saturnalia . . . convention*: Play-acting, including the naming of a mock king to preside over the festivities, was a defining
feature of the Roman holiday of Saturnalia.

41. *The way we handle . . . behaviour*: Cf. I 29, 39–41.

42. *there is another who won't let me*: Cf. I 30, 1.

43. *Gyara*: (Or Gyaros), a barren island in the Aegean Sea that during
the early Principate served as a place of penal exile.

44. *the Pyrrhonists and the Academics*: Cf. I 5; the Pyrrhonists and
Academics of Epictetus' day were Sceptic philosophers who
argued that it was impossible for anything to be known with
absolute certainty.

45. *'I will go . . . to gain it'*: A paraphrase of Homer, *Iliad* 12. 322–8.

46. *convention*: 'Convention' (*sunêtheia*) in this context means normal (complacent) reliance on the senses as a guide to everyday
behaviour.

47. *'Every Soul is deprived . . . will'*: Plato, *Sophist* 228c.

48. *I know that the acts . . . children safe*: The lines are from Euripides' *Medea*, lines 1078–9. In order to get back at her unfaithful
husband, Jason, Medea kills the children they had together. The
lines quoted were standard in discussions of what the Greeks
called *akrasia*, 'lack of control', the inability to do what one
knows is right – or to refrain from doing what one knows is
wrong – for being subject to a contrary emotion or desire. Epictetus tries to show that the two lines can be reconciled with the
law of psychological determinism expressed in §6. So in §7 he
gives an intellectualist account of Medea's motivation, implying
that 'But anger is master of my intentions' need not be taken to
mean that she is forced to sin under the pressure of passion; it is
merely a poetic way of expressing her value system – she places
revenge above her children's welfare. As for her confession that
'I know that the acts I intend to do are wrong', this amounts to
no more than an admission that she knows the murders she is
contemplating are criminal; but the fact that she goes forward
with them demonstrates that she considers herself above the
traditional laws of human society.

49. *The Phoenix . . . Hippolytus*: The *Phoenix* and the *Hippolytus*
are plays by Euripides. The *Hippolytus* still survives.

50. *'Anytus . . . harm me'*: Plato, *Apology* 30c.

51. *This is how I came to lose my lamp*: Cf. I 18, 15.

52. *But what if someone in authority . . . atheistic?*: Epictetus evokes the circumstances of Socrates' execution on grounds of impiety.

BOOK II

1. *When deer . . . hunters' nets*: 'The beaters use to frighten deer into the nets by stretching a cord, with brightly coloured feathers on it, across the safe openings in the woods' (W. A. Oldfather (ed.), Epictetus, *The Discourses as Reported by Arrian, the Manual, and Fragments*, 2 vols., London and Cambridge, Mass., 1925–8, vol. 1, p. 214).

2. *Socrates used to call such fears 'hobgoblins'*: Plato, *Phaedo* 77e.

3. *The door needs to stay open . . . disappear*: Suicide should remain an option of last resort in intolerable material circumstances.

4. *But wasn't Socrates . . . at that?*: Socrates is generally thought not to have written anything, so this passage is a puzzle.

5. *I mean, do you think . . . different result?*: The quotation is from Plato's *Apology* 30c. Epictetus implies that this and other statements in the *Apology* further antagonized Anytus and Meletus, Socrates' accusers, and that his defiant attitude not only showed his indifference to worldly fortune but actually contributed to his condemnation, even though, strictly speaking, his fate at this point lay in the hands of a jury, not Anytus and Meletus, the men who originally brought the accusation. But in the sentencing portion of the trial, after the jury had found him guilty, Socrates suggests that his 'punishment' should consist of free meals for the rest of his life at public expense, words that – if Plato reports them accurately – would have incited the jury members and may even have influenced some to vote for death. Epictetus may allude to this additional piece of provocation on Socrates' part in the next sentence.

6. *Heraclitus*: Not, of course, Heraclitus the famous philosopher referred to at *Enchiridion* 15, but a contemporary of Epictetus otherwise unknown.

7. *it is stupid to say, 'Tell me what to do!'*: 'Stupid' because one has to decide for oneself what to do depending on circumstance, as the preceding section showed.

8. *this general principle*: The principle established in the opening paragraph of this chapter, concerning the importance of 'protecting one's own'.

9. *Diogenes*: Diogenes the Cynic philosopher, as at I 24, 6. Diogenes

rejected the polite conventions of society, including, as we learn
here, reliance on letters of recommendation.

10. *analytic*: The exact meaning of *analyticon*, which I have translated – or transliterated – as 'analytic' is a matter of conjecture.

11. *doesn't nature intend women to be shared?*: Zeno, the founder
of Stoicism, advocated the community of wives in his book *The
Republic*, just as Plato had done, to a limited extent, in his
own *Republic*; cf. Fragment 15. This radical social doctrine was
something of an embarrassment to later, Roman Stoics, as this
section suggests.

12. *like Socrates' fellow diners in the Symposium*: The reference is
to works by Plato and Xenophon both entitled *Symposium*,
featuring Socrates at a party with other cultured guests; the
comparison, of course, is sarcastic.

13. *how to strike a balance ... on the other*: The contrast is analogous to the contrast between 'confidence' and 'caution' drawn in
II 1, and their respective objects are the same, although the
terminology is different.

14. *The chips ... my responsibility begins*: The text says dice, not
cards, and 'counters' instead of chips; but since most modern
dice games don't have counters I have ventured on a different
analogy. Strictly speaking, Epictetus exaggerates in saying that
the fall of the dice (or deal of the cards) does not matter: some
rolls (or hands) are clearly better than others. But ultimately it is
what you do with what chance hands you that matters; a skilled
player will know how to turn defeat into victory.

15. *It isn't easy ... would be impossible*: Cf. Diogenes Laertius, *The
Lives of the Philosophers* VII 104: '[The Stoics] call "indifferent"
things that contribute neither to happiness nor unhappiness, like
wealth, reputation, health, strength and so on. For it is possible
to be happy without these, although how they are used determines one's happiness or unhappiness.' Thus Epictetus says that
we should be indifferent toward external things or circumstances
such as wealth, reputation, etc., because they too are 'indifferent'
in a moral sense, i.e. neither good nor bad in themselves. Only
virtue is good, and it consists in proper use of these external
things – thus the call to be careful as well as indifferent at the
same time.

16. *You will find that skilled ballplayers ... sporting match*: The
player who is unsure of himself is too focused on catching the
ball, or throwing it, to get into the flow of the game; to the expert
player the ball is only the means used to execute the essential

tasks of throwing and catching – and he doesn't freeze when it comes his way, or need coaching by the other players as to what his next move is.

17. *'Well, if someone acknowledged . . . produced them?'*: A paraphrase of Plato, *Apology* 26e sq.

18. *Then how are some externals . . . nature?*: Cf. Stobaeus II 79,18 sq.: '[According to the Stoics] some indifferent things are in accordance with nature, others are contrary to nature . . . The following are in accordance with nature: health, strength, well-functioning sense organs, and the like . . . and these are preferable.' Stoics acknowledged a value difference among externals, i.e. 'indifferents', between health and sickness, for instance, though the right thing to do in some cases is to reject the 'things in accordance with nature', as Socrates did. The point of the question, then, is why do the Stoics recognize such a distinction between indifferents and call the 'things in accordance with nature' preferable, if we don't always choose them? Epictetus answers by invoking the 'universal perspective' that he alludes to in §13 above and cites more explicitly at II 6, 10 and II 10, 5.

19. *On 'indifference'*: This discourse is in some ways a continuation of the preceding one, II 5; see the notes there for the philosophical background relevant to certain sections.

20. *The conjunctive argument*: See note 7 to *Enchiridion*, below.

21. *life and the like*: The reference is to the Stoic 'indifferents', i.e. life, health, wealth, etc. and their opposites, sickness, etc.; see note 15 above.

22. *Look at Chrysantas . . . welfare*: The story of Chrysantas appears in Xenophon's *Cyropedia* IV 1, 3; by pausing mid-stroke he consciously left himself open to his intended victim's counterstroke.

23. *'All roads to Hades are of equal length'*: A saying attributed to Diogenes the Cynic among others.

24. *his Zeus or his Athena*: The fifth-century BC sculptor Phidias made the cult statue of Zeus at Olympia (mentioned also at I 6, 23) and of Athena in the Parthenon at Athens. The latter supported a winged figure representing Victory in her right hand.

25. *'My word is true and irrevocable'*: Zeus is quoted from the *Iliad* 1. 526.

26. *look at what wrongdoing is . . . philosophers*: The 'philosophers' here are not just Stoics but also Socrates in Plato's *Gorgias*, who argues against doing harm, even in retaliation, on the grounds that it does the agent more harm than it does the victim.

27. *lead someone to the truth . . . follow*: This confidence in every-one's capacity to arrive at the truth with help from an able guide derives from Socrates; cf. the episode with the slave boy in Plato's *Meno* 82b–85b.

28. *No one's vote counts . . . dialogue*: A paraphrase of Plato, *Gorg-ias* 474a.

29. *Is a man racked . . . Obviously not*: This snatch of dialogue appears to be based on Xenophon, *Memorabilia* III 9, 8, where Socrates argues that people can help their friends in difficulty and still be ready to envy them when they are successful; but that passage is not in dialogue form, so citing it here seems to miss much of the point.

30. *He could cut short . . . his diplomacy*: Hesiod, *Theogony* 87.

31. *'this constant fretting and shifting from foot to foot'*: Epictetus quotes a line from the *Iliad* 13. 281.

32. *Zeno . . . Antigonus*: Zeno was founder of the Stoic school; Antigonus Gonatas was one of the Macedonian rulers of Greece in the third century BC; their meeting is reported in Diogenes Laertius, *The Lives of the Philosophers* VII 6.

33. *Syllogisms and changing arguments*: On 'changing arguments', see note 14 to Book I, above.

34. *Socrates must have practised . . . in jail*: The Thirty Tyrants were an oligarchic faction that controlled Athens in 404–403 BC; Socrates refused to involve himself in their violence against other Athenians. A version of his defence against the charge of impiety and corrupting youth is given in Plato's *Apology*, his conver-sations before and after trial are reported in Plato's *Crito* and *Phaedo*.

35. *Diogenes . . . Alexander, Philip . . . slave*: Diogenes is Diogenes the Cynic; Alexander is Alexander the Great, the Macedonian king and conqueror; Philip is Alexander's father. The ease and honesty with which Diogenes addressed them were characteristic of Cynics generally; he exhibited the same fearlessness before pirates and the man to whom he was sold when his boat was seized on one occasion. The incidents are reported in Diogenes Laertius, *The Lives of the Philosophers* VI 38, 43 and 74.

36. *To Naso*: Naso is presumably the name of the man from Rome to whom Epictetus addresses much of the discourse. He may be the Julius Naso several times mentioned by Pliny the Younger (*Letters* IV 6; V 21; VI 6 and 9).

37. *Our condition can be compared to a festival*: The famous com-parison of life to an Olympic festival originated with the fourth-

century BC philosopher Heraclides of Pontus, who distinguished among three classes of people: the athletes, who equate with the segment of humanity devoted to the pursuit of glory and public honours; the merchants, who represent people devoted to making money and acquiring wealth; and the spectators, who stand for the philosophers, motivated purely by curiosity and a wish to see and learn as much as they can of the world around them. Epictetus in his version of the metaphor also distinguishes three classes of attendees at the festival, but not the same three; and the way he departs from his model catches the reader off guard, as he ends up offering a rather sardonic twist on the theme.

38. *if it is the right decision ... passage*: The Stoics, Epictetus included (cf. II 1, 19, etc.), condoned suicide in desperate material circumstances; Seneca, Thrasea Paetus and Marcus Cato were notable Stoic suicides.

39. *the big one and the small*: The big city is the cosmic community of god and man; cf. II 5, 26.

40. *the water of Dirce*: The fountain of Dirce was located in Thebes.

41. *Ah, for Nero's baths, and the water of Marcia*: A parody of Euripides' *Phoenissae* 368: 'The gymnasia in which I was reared and the water of Dirce' (Polyneices speaking). The Marcian aqueduct brought water to the city of Rome.

42. *Diogenes*: This is Diogenes the Cynic.

43. *Whoever can exit the party ... until death*: In other words, he would sooner die ('leave the party') than live in uncongenial circumstances.

44. *Eurystheus*: The cowardly king who dispatched Heracles on twelve labours from the safety of his palace.

45. *you are not even Theseus ... troubles*: Theseus was Athens' hometown hero, whose exploits were modelled on Heracles', but confined to the area around Athens called Attica.

46. *Procrustes or Sciron*: Two robbers killed by Heracles.

47. *the orator Theopompus ... every little thing*: Epictetus refers to Theopompus, the fourth-century BC historian, as an 'orator' because his writing reflects the training in rhetoric he received at the feet of Isocrates, from whom he also absorbed his bias against Plato; Isocrates' philosophical differences with Plato are laid out in his speech *Against the Sophists*.

48. *impulse ... appropriate acts*: Cf. I 4, 11–12.

49. *It is just this that Medea ... dashed*: The brilliant psychological handling of the Medea legend in Euripides' play was invoked by later philosophers in support of their own theories of moral

misguidance; Epictetus treats her case in greater detail at I 28, 7. The following monologue is loosely based on lines 790ff. of the play.

50. *Give me one student . . . delirious*: Cf. I 18, 23 for the putative perfectibility of the mind implied in Epictetus' third field of study, which correlates with the traditional description of the Stoic sage.

51. *the Liar*: One of the most notorious of the 'logic problems' alluded to above in §3. Cf. Cicero, *Academica* II 92–6: 'If you say that you are lying, and say so truly, are you lying or telling the truth? . . . If you say that you are lying, and you say so truly, you are lying. But you say that you are lying, and you say so truly. Therefore you are lying.' Epictetus references the Liar paradox again at II 18, 18 and II 21, 17.

52. *Antisthenes*: On Antisthenes, one of the foundational figures of Cynicism, cf. I 17, 12.

53. *Antipater*: This is Antipater of Tarsus.

54. *the Master Argument itself*: On the Master Argument, cf. II 19, 1–9.

55. *the Quiescent*: Cf. Sextus Empiricus, *Against the Professors* VII 416: 'Since in the sorites the last cognitive impression is adjacent to the first non-cognitive impression and virtually indistinguishable from it, the school of Chrysippus say that in the case of impressions which differ so little the wise man will stop and become quiescent.'

56. *It will even do . . . the past*: Cf. Plato, *Laws* 854b.

57. *how he lay . . . youthful beauty*: The reference is to Plato's *Symposium* 218d sq.

58. *an Olympic-sized victory . . . Heracles*: Heracles was the mythical founder of, and first victor in, the Olympic games.

59. *pancratiasts*: The pancration was an Olympic contest that combined elements of both boxing and wrestling.

60. *the Dioscuri*: The Dioscuri, Castor and Pollux, were patron deities of sailors and seafarers generally.

61. *Hesiod's verse . . . ever after*: Hesiod was a seventh-century Greek poet; the quotation is from his poem *Works and Days*, line 413.

62. *The Master Argument*: This is the primary surviving reference to what Diodorus Cronus (for reasons unknown) named the 'Master Argument'. It owes something to the discussion of 'The Sea Battle' in chapter 9 of Aristotle's *De Interpretatione*. Stoics (and their opponents) explored the implications of the argument for free will and personal responsibility, and their place (if any)

within a determinist system like the Stoics' own. This probably also explains Epictetus' interest in it.

First, a précis of Aristotle's 'Sea Battle'. Either there will be a sea battle tomorrow, or there will not be. Only one of these statements can be true, the other must be false. But if it is now true that there will not be a sea battle tomorrow, then one might be led to infer that there is nothing one could do between now and tomorrow to bring about a sea battle – even supposing that one were king of the country, say, or either of the fleet commanders.

Diodorus' 'Master Argument' seems to have drawn on or developed this paradox insofar as it also engages the question of the truth value of statements about the future, and the deterministic implications of that question. But what Epictetus gives us is not Diodorus' argument – or any argument, for that matter, in the sense of a set of premises yielding a conclusion – but instead three propositions that he declares to be irreconcilable. His decision to present the Master Argument in this form has complicated efforts to reconstruct Diodorus' original, and distinguish it from rival counter-arguments. It would take us too far afield to analyse the Master Argument and its new modal language of possibility and necessity by adducing sources that complement Epictetus here. A tentative reconstruction of the Master Argument along the following lines, however, drawing on the present passage and continuing to use Aristotle's example of the sea battle, may be useful for readers interested in pursuing the subject further.

If a sea battle will not be fought tomorrow, then it was also true in the past that it would not be fought. And since (by principle 1 in Epictetus' text) everything past that is true is necessary, it was necessarily the case in the past that the battle would not take place, and necessarily false that it would take place. Thus, it was impossible that the sea battle would take place. And since (by principle 2) an impossibility cannot follow a possibility, it was impossible from the first moment of time (or from eternity) that the sea battle would take place. Therefore, if something will not be the case, it is never possible for it to be the case. And thus principle 3 in the text is proven false, and shown to be logically incompatible with the other two propositions. The conclusion that remains is that nothing, in fact, is possible which is not either true, or going to be true.

63. *Antipater*: This is Antipater of Tarsus.

64. *Look, I wasn't born ... subject*: The sequel shows that these replies are meant as satire and that Epictetus disapproves of the purely scholastic interest in the controversy that they evince.

65. *Hellanicus*: (*c.*480–395 BC), a writer on history, myth and ethnography.

66. *you will tell us all about ... ever will*: Epictetus plays on the terms of the third principle in the Master Argument, above.

67. '*The wind ... Ciconians*': Homer, *Odyssey* IX 39.

68. *Diogenes*: This is Diogenes of Babylon, head of the Stoic school in the early to mid-second century BC.

69. *Peripatetics*: The Peripatetics were the followers of Aristotle. Unlike the Stoics, Aristotle and his school taught that some portion of what Epictetus calls 'externals' or 'indifferents' (such as health or social status) were indispensable for happiness.

70. *you cannot be certain of anything*: On the Sceptic philosophy of the Academics see I 5, and further below.

71. *Epicurus is the same way ... distinction*: This passage tries to convict Epicurus of self-refutation, as the preceding passage aimed to do for the Sceptic philosophy of the New Academy. The claim that scepticism is internally incoherent made along the lines laid out in §§1–5, was not new; Aristotle already cites and discusses the problem in *Metaphysics* III 5. A different kind of self-refutation argument, also aimed at the Academics, is used below, in §§28–29: the Sceptics refute their doctrines in the process of performing life's most basic tasks. This resembles the argument levelled at Epicurus here, in that he is shown negating his doctrines by the way he acts – indeed, by the act of writing and publishing his doctrines. The close relation of the things that are supposed to be mutually incompatible brings the argument close in kind to the first one made against the Academics; accusations of self-refutation in this form were supposed to have particular force.

A simpler form of the argument in §§6–11 is used in I 23. This one is more involved, and requires some explanation. In the view of Epictetus, Epicurus' social philosophy amounts to a kind of nihilism which, if enforced, would loose a free-for-all in which his followers would be as much at risk as the rest; so that, (Epictetus facetiously implies) if Epicurus were intelligent he would have allowed the mass of men to be neutralized by exposure to the social teachings of the Stoics, and only shared the truth with his disciples, who would then be better prepared for the state of war that naturally prevails among men, and therefore be in a better position to impose their will on the 'sheep', who are ready to be 'shorn and milked'.

Epictetus is not entirely unfair to Epicurus in representing his philosophy this way; as another Epicurean philosopher put it, '[Without sound government] we would live a life of beasts, and one man on meeting another would all but devour him' (Colotes, third-century BC, in Plutarch, *Against Colotes* 1124D). By deliberately omitting any reference to 'sound government', however, i.e. to the Epicurean social contract, he might be charged with only giving half the story. Be that as it may, Epictetus does correctly imply, in the last section (§14), that, according to Epicurus again, men historically have been selective in who they make peace with, i.e. social relations are made on an *ad hoc* basis and for motives of self-interest – or, as Epictetus puts it, they 'make . . . a distinction': 'sociability should be extended to some, but not others'.

72. *We hear of Orestes . . . irresistible*: The myth involving Orestes' murder of his mother, and subsequent persecution by the allegorized figures of Furies and Avengers, is best known from Aeschylus' dramatic trilogy, *The Oresteia*. Cybele was an agricultural deity whose priests in their drunken frenzy went so far as to castrate themselves. Epictetus implies that Epicurus' doctrines amount to sanctioning murder of the worst sort, such as Orestes' matricide, and encouraging drunken abandon, as represented by the behaviour of Cybele's priests.

73. *here come the refutations*: The following passage is meant to illustrate the Academics' ability to argue either side of any argument, a practice that played an integral part in their Sceptic attitude, 'in order to show that their [opponents] had no certain or firm arguments about [any subject]' (Lactantius, *Divine Institutes* V 14, 5).

74. *slavery is no more bad than good . . . quit their city?*: Thermopylae was the site of one of the battles in the Persian War, which was also the occasion for the Athenians' twice evacuating their city (490–479 BC). 'No more this than that' was a formula of Sceptic epistemology, which Epictetus mimics above, and again in §30 below.

75. *a Demeter, a Persephone, or a Pluto*: Demeter was the Greek goddess of agriculture generally, and of grain in particular; Persephone was her daughter, Pluto (= Hades) was Persephone's husband. Academics argued from the doubtful deity of minor gods

like Persephone to challenge belief in the existence of major gods like Demeter. Epictetus suggests that, since bread was the staff of life, and in traditional Greek religion was the gift of Demeter, the Sceptics' agnosticism is proof of ingratitude as well as deliberate obtuseness.

76. *most will allow that they are liable to feel pity*: Stoics stigmatized pity (like most emotions) as a fault of character; but I 28, 9 shows that exceptions were allowed.

77. *'You want to see the light . . . father does too?'*: From a passage in Euripides' *Alcestis* (line 691) where Admetus is roundly refused his request of his elderly father, Pheres, that he die in his place.

78. *Anyone seeing them . . . views on friendship*: The reference is probably to the Epicureans, who held that pleasure is the foundation of friendship, and that friends are not chosen for themselves, but for the benefits they bring; cf. Epicurus, *Vatican Sayings* 23: 'All friendship is an intrinsic virtue, but it originates from benefiting.' In light of what is argued in §§15–21 below, however, conceivably it could include Epictetus' own views.

79. *'Where before the tower . . . same desire'*: From the *Phoenissae* of Euripides, lines 621–2. Eteocles and Polyneices battle for control of Thebes after their father, Oedipus, blinds himself.

80. *his beloved*: Hephaestion, often described as Alexander's 'alter ego', who died on campaign with him in 324 BC.

81. *'Honour is nothing . . . approved'*: Possibly an allusion to the statement of Epicurus that 'I spit on honour if it does not involve pleasure' (H. Usener, *Epicurea*, Leipzig, 1887, p. 512).

82. *And Eriphyle . . . came between them*: Eriphyle was induced by the bribe of a necklace to get her husband to join Polyneices in his war on Eteocles for control of Thebes.

83. *'Every soul . . . will'*: A paraphrase of Plato's *Sophist*, 228c, quoted again at I 28, 4.

84. *endowed them with breath . . . their shape*: The Stoics explained vision as an active rather than a passive process, whereby the 'breath' (*pneuma*) of which the soul is composed exits the eyes and apprehends objects by essentially modelling them.

85. *Which part let your beard grow long?*: A long beard was the badge of a philosopher.

86. *Your goal was different . . . citizen yourself*: A Greek citizen traditionally served a term in the army ('help insure the safety of the citizenry') before settling down to civilian life. In urging his students to return to their native cities after studying under him, and deprecating the study of rhetoric, Epictetus evidently wanted

to discourage his students from adopting the life of a travelling sophist, which was fashionable in his day (the movement collectively known as the 'Second Sophistic').

87. *'Lead me, Zeus ... Destiny'*: From Cleanthes' 'Hymn to Zeus'; cf. III 22, 95 and *Enchiridion* 53.

88. *Demosthenes*: A famous Athenian orator of the fourth century BC.

BOOK III

1. *another from within*: An allusion to God, as at I 25, 13.

2. *breath*: 'Breath' translates *pneuma*, one of the elements in Stoic physics and the substance of the human soul. Epictetus alludes to *pneuma* again, at II 23, 3.

3. *The soul ... normal also*: This last paragraph is irrelevant here and probably displaced from its original context. We find other fragments of this kind appended to the end of III 8, 7.

4. *Nemean, Pythian, Isthmian and Olympic Games conjointly*: A list of the four Panhellenic festivals.

5. *One person ... self-improvement*: A paraphrase of Xenophon, *Memorabilia* I 6, 8 sq., or Plato, *Protagoras* 318a.

6. *These are the things ... Protagoras or Hippias*: Protagoras and Hippias were prominent teachers of rhetoric, or 'Sophists', contemporaneous with Socrates in Athens. This passage is influenced by two traditions concerning Socrates: 1) that he was the first philosopher devoted primarily to the pursuit of knowledge about ethical as opposed to physical questions; and 2) that he simultaneously claimed to know nothing except that he knew nothing. He can be found escorting young men to Protagoras and Hippias, respectively, at Plato, *Protagoras* 310e and *Theaetetus* 151b.

7. *cognitive impression*: (*Phantasia katalêptikê*), the centrepiece of Stoic epistemology: an impression so clear and accurate that there could be no doubt as to its veracity.

8. *If you care to know ... like him*: That the Romans had a low opinion of philosophers, and believed philosophy was a waste of time at best, at worst a brand of charlatanry, is a well-known half-truth; but as the otherwise unknown Italicus is described as 'one of [Rome's] finest philosophers', his remark is unlikely to reflect that attitude. Clearly he intends no compliment, however, in protesting that his friends 'want me to end up like [Epictetus]'. It may be that Romans by this time were so corrupted by materialism that no one who lived as simply and frugally as Epictetus

could be considered a success at anything, philosophy included; by this time they had the example of Seneca before them – both fabulously rich and the first philosopher of his day. If more were known about this Italicus (and it is possible that he and the whole anecdote are an invention), all might be made clear, but as it stands the passage is obscure.

9. *It was no small advantage . . . after all*: In Greek myth, Menoeceus sacrificed his life to save his native Thebes.

10. *the father of Admetus*: Pheres, by name, who in Euripides' play *Alcestis* refuses to die in his son's place despite his advanced age.

11. *I bless Lesbios . . . nothing*: Lesbios is otherwise unknown.

12. *On Cynicism*: Cynicism was a school of philosophy founded in the fourth century BC by Diogenes of Sinope. Like the Stoics, Cynics taught that the key to happiness was living in agreement with nature. To a unique degree, however, Cynics emphasized the need for training (Greek *askêsis*), both mental and physical, to achieve this end – thus the stories about Diogenes walking barefoot in the snow, embracing marble statues naked in winter and so on. From Diogenes' point of view, the fewer artifacts and less technology he needed for survival, the more his life was in 'agreement' with nature. For this reason, too, his only shelter, supposedly, was an empty wine vat (or 'tub'). Although he is said to have imitated animals in systematically ridding himself of inessentials, he believed that it was not enough in man's case to reduce one's possessions to the minimum; human beings also had to live virtuously. Indeed, one point of shedding inessentials was to prove decisively that virtue alone, without the need of material goods, was enough to secure human happiness. Thus the negative side of Cynicism, its primitivism, was subordinate to this positive aspect, the belief it shared with the Stoics that virtue was man's end and a necessary and sufficient condition for his happiness.

Stoics called Cynicism 'a shortcut to virtue' (Diogenes Laertius, *The Lives of the Philosophers* VII 121). Implicit in this description is not only the Cynics' ethical absolutism but also their rejection of physics and logic (ibid. VI 103). Cynicism enjoyed a revival in the first century AD owing in part to the fact that their message resonated in a society (Rome) that regretted the loss of the virtues and values that originally made her great, in favour of materialism, hedonism and duplicity. What the Romans could not accept or imitate was the shameless side of Cynicism: the 'dog' side (Cynic means 'dog-like'), that is, their sometimes outrageous lack of dignity (cf. §80 below). Epictetus does his part here to rescue Cynicism for his Roman audience by replacing *anaideia*, a byword of early Cynicism meaning 'shamelessness' or 'brazenness', with its opposite, *aidos*, 'dignity', calling it the Cynic's proper 'protection'. And whereas the Stoic sage was a remote abstraction, the Cynic, the embodiment of virtue, was a very public figure, a man of the streets – devoted to showing others by his example that happiness was compatible with a life lived at the limits of purity and privation. The Cynic was avowedly extreme; but by demonstrating in tangible terms that such contempt for wealth, luxury and fame as he evinced was feasible, he also showed that loss of these things was nothing to fear: he was a living incitement to *ataraxia*: 'serenity', 'peace of mind'. As Seneca writes, Diogenes proved that nature imposes nothing that is impossible to bear (*Letters* 90. 14). Thus, the Cynic was for the Romans an inspiration as much as a realistic model for imitation. It is noteworthy that Epictetus in this Discourse has nothing good to say about the Cynics of his own day and spends more time discouraging rather than recruiting for the Cynic vocation. This may be just a test of the seriousness of one's commitment to the cause. But overall the Discourse is less a protreptic, that is, an exhortation to Cynic philosophy, than a doctrinal study of Cynicism, and an extended encomium of Diogenes, the ethical model cited most often in the *Discourses*, Socrates only excepted.

13. *he is also a spy*: The Cynic is compared to a 'spy' in several ancient sources. As a spy abandons the safety of his own camp and risks solitary incursion into enemy territory, relying on darkness and his own wits to survive, so the Cynic eschews the support of a family and the security of four walls and a roof in favour of a solitary and itinerant lifestyle among an enemy of his own creation, the *homme moyen sensuel*, whom he aims to shock and ridicule with his brashness and his outrageous theatrics. By calling him a 'spy' Epictetus also implies that the Cynic ideally plies his trade in the service of others, not for selfish or personal reasons. He 'spies out' the conditions of life that most men fear – poverty, austerity, exile, social ignominy – and reports – just by the example of his freedom, his good spirits and his wit – that far from being things to fear, and worth compromising one's integrity in order to avoid, these conditions comprise life nearer to, and therefore more like, the life nature meant for us to lead.

14. *He needs to be like Diogenes . . . Philip*: On this incident cf. I 24,

3–10 (above), and Diogenes Laertius, *The Lives of the Philosophers* VI 43.

15. *look at Myron or Ophellius ... which they are not*: Myron and Ophellius were contemporary athletes or gladiators – and presumably came to a bad end like Croesus. Reference to the plight of 'the rich of today' may allude to the practice of the first emperors of charging prominent citizens with treason (*maiestas*), with the covert goal of appropriating their assets for themselves. These paradoxical unfortunates may overlap with the statesmen who drew unwelcome attention to themselves by holding more than one consulship.

16. *Sardanapalus*: The last king of Babylon, and proverbial for luxury.

17. *He pulled many a hair ... my chest*: The quotes relating to Agamemnon are from the *Iliad* 10. 15, 91, and 94–5.

18. *You are rich in gold and bronze*: Epictetus quotes *Iliad* 18. 289.

19. *identify the Cynic ... leaves bare*: A Cynic characteristically wore his signature rough mantle (the *tribon*) with one shoulder exposed; this helps, for instance, to identify Diogenes in Raphael's painting *The School of Athens*. Sarcastic reference to 'large jaws' evokes the popular reputation of the Cynic as a parasitic glutton, a malicious parody of his true nature for which the writers of comedy were no doubt responsible.

20. *Take me to the proconsul at once*: The proconsul functioned as a judge in the provinces of the Roman Empire.

21. *the Great King*: The common designation for the king of the Persian empire, proverbially the most fortunate person on earth.

22. *the sceptre and the kingdom*: The Cynic's signature staff is featured as a royal sceptre, in line with the paradoxical presentation of the Cynic as the true king; cf. §34 above. At the same time he is 'minister' to Zeus, who sent him to rule among men; cf. §69 below.

23. *Friendship ... indefinitely*: As the Cynic was lampooned in ancient comedy as a parasite, so Epictetus represents parasitism as antithetical to the Cynic ideal of independence.

24. *who has the people ... concerns*: Homer, *Iliad* 2. 25

25. *his children will not be Cynics straight out of the womb*: I.e. they are not yet ready to survive on the Cynic's meagre regimen; they still have various material needs.

26. *Crates had a wife*: Crates' wife was named Hipparchia. Crates made adoption of his philosophy a condition of their marriage,

and out of love for him she complied: Diogenes Laertius, *The Lives of the Philosophers* VI 96.

27. *Epaminondas ... Priam ... Danaus, or Aeolus*: Epaminondas was a fourth-century BC Theban general who scored several notable victories over Sparta. Priam, Danaus and Aeolus are figures from the Greek epic cycle, which is why they are contrasted here with Homer, their chronicler. Like Priam, Danaus and Aeolus were mythical kings credited with epic-sized families; Homer, according to tradition, lacked both home and family.

28. *dogs who beg ... gate*: Iliad 22. 69; the word 'Cynic' comes from the Greek word for dog.

29. *A man charged ... concerns*: Homer, *Iliad* 2. 24–5; cf. §72 above. Diogenes' ability to give the next line of Homer's text and finish Alexander's thought instantaneously shows, in fact, that he was not 'sleeping the night away' but even when sleeping was actually half-awake – as Homer said a leader of men ought to be.

30. *what sleep he gets ... lay down*: I.e. his reason does not desert him even when asleep; so that, unlike most people, he is not prey to indecent dreams. Cf. I 18, 23 on the dangers posed by sleep, madness and intoxication.

31. *make Argus seem blind by comparison*: Argus was a mythical creature with many eyes.

32. *No, go inside ... in particular*: Homer, *Iliad* 6. 490 sq., partly paraphrased.

33. *The one where I described Pan and the Nymphs*: Evidently a reference to *ekphrasis*, description of a work of art, and a staple of epideictic oratory, which flourished when other types of oratory dried up after the establishment of the Principate, paralleling the history of rhetoric in Greece following Alexander the Great.

34. *Dio*: Possibly Dio Chrysostom, a contemporary of Epictetus whose writings represent some of the most successful blends in Greek literature of rhetoric and philosophy.

35. *Since this man is constant ... does the constant man have?*: A typically Socratic move to define a particular virtue, in this case, constancy.

36. *Lysias or Isocrates*: Leading rhetoricians in classical Athens.

37. *I often wondered by what sort of arguments*: The opening words of the *Memorabilia*, Xenophon's account of Socrates' life and teaching.

38. 'Anytus and Meletus ... cannot harm me': Socrates is quoted from Plato's Apology 30c; G. Vlastos (Socrates: Ironist and Moral Philosopher, Cambridge University Press, 1991, p. 219) rightly calls this Epictetus' 'favourite text'; cf. I 29, 18; II 2, 15, etc.

39. I've always been the sort ... my own affairs: The quote is from Plato's Crito 46b; Socrates is the speaker.

40. 'I know something and I teach it': I.e. Socrates was unlike the Sophists in declining to teach and take money, one proof of his contempt for his personal affairs. It also reflects his 'irony', i.e. his denial of any knowledge, hence having anything to teach.

41. 'It would not suit me ... callow youth': Plato, Apology 17c.

42. As the sun ... need of help: On the sun in Stoic physics, cf. I 19, 11.

43. Rufus: Musonius Rufus, Epictetus' teacher.

44. the epideictic style ... as a fourth subject: The epideictic, or display, style of rhetoric, is one of the three genres of oratory recognized by Aristotle in his Rhetoric, along with forensic and deliberative, though he limits its application to praise or denigration, as this was how it was actually applied in his day, when it was still a new form of rhetoric; a surviving example from around Aristotle's day is Isocrates' Helen. The protreptic style was developed as a means to encourage devotion to philosophy; Aristotle himself composed an influential early example, as did Stoics including Cleanthes. The elenctic style is not classified separately by Aristotle, although he does discuss refutational arguments (Rhetoric 1396^{b}25). The didactic style was presumably adapted for teaching; we know no more of it per se. By implying that the protreptic style should not be classified alongside the others, Epictetus presumably means that it is out of place in a philosophical curriculum.

BOOK IV

1. 'By the grace of Caesar, we are free': I.e. the form of the expression makes it self-contradictory. 'Free' in this context means politically autonomous and exempt from Roman taxation.

2. Thrasonides, who fought more campaigns, perhaps, than you: Thrasonides is the soldier-protagonist of the Misoumenos, a play by the fourth-century BC Greek comic playwright Menander; his pet slave was Geta. 'Campaigns' here puns on a secondary meaning of the word, to refer to love affairs, a usage derived from the language of Roman elegy.

3. *the five per cent tax*: In Rome the five per cent tax was levied on holders of high public office, the assumption being that the slave aspires to be free so that he will qualify to hold such office.

4. *a ring on my finger . . . blissful and complete*: Wearing a gold ring was the sign and privilege of the Roman equestrian (or 'upper-middle') class.

5. *he joins the army . . . third tour of duty*: Cf. II 14, 17: By a law of Julius Caesar, service in at least three campaigns was required for eligibility to become a municipal senator.

6. *the inability to apply common preconceptions to particulars*: On this topic, cf. esp. II 17.

7. *Caesar's friend*: On the semi-official status of being 'Caesar's friend', see F. Millar, *The Emperor in the Roman World* (Duckworth, 1977), pp. 110–22.

8. *buying, selling and other such mundane transactions*: I.e. buying and selling slaves, which has been declared irrelevant to the question of what true freedom consists in.

9. *twelve bodyguards*: Literally, 'twelve fasces,' a bundle of rods bound together around an axe with the blade projecting, carried before Roman magistrates as an emblem of their authority, by lictors, a magistrate's usual escort.

10. *a slave on holiday at the Saturnalia*: At Saturnalia restrictions were relaxed and slaves were treated as equals. Thus 'a slave on holiday at the Saturnalia' means someone enjoying mock, provisional freedom; cf. I 25, 8.

11. *we even honour them as gods . . . false as well*: The argument runs: whatever can confer the most benefit is a god. But this man (i.e. the emperor) has the power to confer the most benefit. Therefore the emperor is a god. The second (minor) premise is erroneous, resulting in a false conclusion. The emperors were honoured as deities after their death; the cult of Augustus Caesar was prominent in Epictetus' hometown of Nicopolis.

12. *How is a fortress demolished?*: The 'fortress' (Greek: *acropolis*) is a metaphor for the mind or, in Stoic parlance, for the 'ruling principle' (*hêgemonikon*). The use of 'fortress' to represent the mind (or soul) goes back to Plato (*Republic* 560b, *Timaeus* 70a); it is also used by Marcus Aurelius in this connection (*Meditations* 48).

13. *quaestor*: A Roman official in charge of overseeing provincial finances.

14. *a slave presenting your emancipator*: A slave had to present his emancipator before a judge as part of the rite of manumission.

15. *Which explains his behaviour ... captive*: An allusion to a famous incident in the life of Diogenes the Cynic, illustrative of how freedom is not a physical condition but a virtue of character and a state of mind. In his old age, sailing to Aegina, he was taken by pirates and carried to Crete, where he was put on the slave market. When the auctioneer asked him what he could do, he said, 'I can govern men; so sell me to someone who needs a master.'

16. *I continue to value ... healthy at all*: Epictetus alludes to his lameness.

17. *Diogenes*: Diogenes the Cynic (again) as in §114 above; he is presented here as a citizen of the world; the entire world is his 'country'.

18. *the Persian king ... Archidamus, king of the Spartans*: Personages representing the acme of power from the Greek and barbarian worlds, respectively, together suggestive of Diogenes' 'cosmopolitan' outlook.

19. *the law*: The universal or divine law.

20. *Socrates ... obey it*: The events in Socrates' life rehearsed in this section are taken from the account given in Plato's *Apology*.

21. *In his own words ... injustice*: A paraphrase of Plato, *Crito* 47d; the 'element' is the soul.

22. *resisted the Athenians' call ... vote*: The motion to execute the generals who commanded at the Battle of Arginusae in 406 BC, an episode in the Peloponnesian War.

23. *as Plato says*: *Phaedo* 64a, 67d-e.

24. *the Palatine*: The hill in Rome where the emperors had their palaces.

25. *Cassius and Masurius*: Noted jurists active in the first half of the first century AD.

26. *the same man ... prison walls*: Cf. Plato, *Phaedo* 60d, where Socrates is reported to have composed a hymn to Apollo while awaiting execution in jail.

27. *A soldier in civilian dress ... chains*: This probably refers to methods employed during the emperor Domitian's reign of terror in the early 90s AD, when Epictetus was still in Rome.

FRAGMENTS

1. *the universe*: 'The universe' is equivalent to God in the Stoics' pantheistic scheme; the general idea is paralleled at I 14, 1–5.

2. *Lycurgus the Spartan*: Lycurgus was the semi-legendary author of the Spartan constitution.

3. *the four basic elements ... above downwards*: The Greek word translated here as 'fire' is *aithêr*, recognized as a fifth element by Aristotle and other ancient writers. But Epictetus only mentions four elements, and in Stoic physics *aithêr* was identified with fire. The sequence of change – earth to water to air to fire – was supposed to correspond to the order of the elements in the physical universe, one positioned above the other – fire, on top, being the substance of the sun and other stars. Thus Epictetus speaks of change 'up' and 'down', or (in the latter case) 'from above downwards'.

4. *Attic Nights*: The *Attic Nights* of Aulus Gellius (c.130–80 AD) is an anthology of learning that, fortunately for us, includes the following passage featuring Epictetus. Besides developing one of his best-known themes, it incidentally tells us that there were originally at least five (not four) books of Discourses.

5. *our wise man ... any fear*: The 'wise man' is the Stoic sage who, by definition, believes that only vice is to be feared because it alone is bad (as virtue alone is good); second-order evils such as natural disasters are indifferent for him.

6. *Favorinus*: A Greek writer and orator of the second century AD.

7. *Against the Pagans*: Arnobius (died c.330 AD) was a Church Father who argues in his sole surviving work, *Against the Pagans*, that Christianity is consistent with the best of Greek philosophy.

8. *Archelaus*: King of Macedon c.413–399 BC.

9. *Polus performed Oedipus ... wanderer*: Polus was a fourth-century BC Athenian actor; the reference in all probability is to the lead roles in Sophocles' *Oedipus the King* and *Oedipus at Colonus*.

10. *Odysseus ... robe*: Odysseus goes disguised in rags in the central books of the *Odyssey*.

11. *it's demeaning ... one's living*: The implication being that only the rich are of independent means.

12. *those gloomy philosophers*: A wry reference to the Stoics themselves.

13. *Women in Rome ... without good reason*: I.e. it is hypocritical to try to enlist philosophers in defence of the most egregious vice (like adultery) when they actually advise against the least unconsidered act. Epictetus is in general right that Plato in his *Republic* eliminates traditional marriage, at least for the ruling class.

14. *Once, when he was preparing for lunch ... Aricia*: The same anecdote, in a slightly different form, appears at I 1, 28–30; the town of Aricia, where Agrippinus had an estate, lay on his way to exile.

15. *as Xenophon says*: Xenophon, *Memorabilia* I 4, 7.

16. *The Meditations*: A work grounded in Stoicism and much indebted to Epictetus in particular, by the philosopher who also happened to be emperor of Rome (ruled 161–80 AD).

ENCHIRIDION

1. *Restrict yourself ... detachment*: To exercise choice and (its opposite) refusal with 'detachment' means with an awareness that success in either case is not ours to guarantee.

2. *It is equally naive ... something different*: I.e. because vice, like virtue, depends on the free choice of the agent (the slave), not on the will of his master.

3. *Diogenes, Heraclitus*: Diogenes is Diogenes the Cynic, whom Epictetus often cites with approval. Heraclitus was a Greek philosopher of the fifth century BC for whom Stoics had a special regard; cf. Marcus Aurelius, *Meditations* VIII 3: 'Alexander and Caesar and Pompey, what are they compared with Diogenes and Heraclitus and Socrates?'

4. *But the assignment of roles belongs to another*: Cf. I 25, 13.

5. *If you hear a raven croak inauspiciously*: An allusion to the ancient belief in bird augury, a form of divination.

6. *Make use of divination ... should be used*: One version of Socrates' views on divination is recorded in Xenophon's *Memorabilia*, I 1, 6 sq.

7. *Just as the propositions ... conjunctive ones*: I.e. the disjunctive proposition 'Either it is day *or* it is night' is always true at any one time, whereas the conjunctive proposition 'Both it is day *and* it is night' is false at any moment.

8. *As you are careful ... at the same time*: E.g. by 'strutting' or otherwise walking in an inappropriate manner, or engaging in undignified thoughts or daydreams.

9. *Don't embrace marble statues*: Outdoors, naked, in cold weather: a bizarre and showy kind of austerity practised by Diogenes and other Cynics.

10. *And I will follow ... God's ways*: The quotation is from an unknown play by Euripides.